RAPID WEIHT HYPNOSIS FOR WOMEN + INTERMITTENT FASTING BIBLE FOR WOMEN OVER 50 + KETO DIET FOR BEGINNERS

3 in 1 - The Simplified Guide to Lose Weight Safely & Stop Emotional Eating

By

Karen Loss

RAPID WEIGHT LOSS HYPNOSIS

Extreme Weight-Loss Hypnosis for Woman! How to Fat Burning & Calorie Blast, Lose Weight with Meditation & Affirmations, Mini Habits, Self-Hypnosis. Stop Emotional Eating!

By

Karen Loss

TABLE OF CONTENTS

COPYRIGHTS _____ 7

CHAPTER 1: INTRODUCTION _____ 10

CHAPTER 2: ROOT CAUSES OF FOOD
ADDICTION _____ 14

CHAPTER 3: TYPES OF OVEREATING ____ 19

> OBSESSIVE OVEREATING _____ 19

> COMPULSIVE OVEREATING _____ 21

CHAPTER 4: WHY DO WE OVERHEAT? __ 23

CHAPTER 4: WHY WEIGHT LOSS IS
TEMPORARY? _____ 29

CHAPTER 6: WOMEN ARE DIFFERENT FROM
MEN _____ 33

> DIFFERENT BODIES _____ 33

> DIFFERENT MINDS _____ 34

> HEALTH RISKS FOR OBESE WOMEN
_____ 36

CHAPTER 7: SELF-HYPNOSIS _____ 39

CHAPTER 8: CONDITIONS FOR HYPNOSIS
TO WORK OUT _____ 44

1. MOTIVATION _____ 44

2. OPTIMISM _____ 45

3. DEFENDING _____ 45

4. CONCENTRATION_____ 46

5. ACCEPTABILITY _____ 46

6. IMAGINATION _____ 47

CHAPTER 9: CAN YOU BE HYPNOTIZED OR NOT? _____ 50

CHAPTER 10: HOW TO PERFORM SELF-HYPNOSIS? _____ 55

CHAPTER 11: OVERCOMING NEGATIVE HABITS _____ 75

CHAPTER 12: THE CRITICAL COMPONENT OF SELF-HYPNOSIS _____ 85

CHAPTER 13: COGNITIVE BEHAVIORAL THERAPY _____ 90

> **NATURAL THINNESS** _____ 95

> **MINDFULNESS** _____ 99

> **PROPER PLANNING** _____ 102

CHAPTER 14: LEVERAGING COGNITIVE BEHAVIORAL THERAPY _____ 105

> **STEP 1: RECOGNIZE BRAIN HUNGER** _____ 108

> **STEP 2: BREAK OBSESSIVE FOOD THINKING** _____ 110

> **STEP 3: NAME AND ADDRESS YOUR ACTUAL NEEDS.** _____ 111

> **STEP 4: MEASURE YOUR PROGRESS AND EXPERIENCE SUCCESS** ____ 112

CHAPTER 15: HOW TO START MINDFUL EATING _____ 120

> **RECOGNIZING PHYSICAL HUNGER** _____ 121

> **STEP 1: IDENTIFY STARVATION FOR THE SITUATION** _____ 121

4

➢ **STEP 2: BREAK THE OBSESSION _ 122**

➢ **STEP 3: NAME AND ADDRESS YOUR ACTUAL NEEDS _____ 123**

➢ **STEP 4: MEASURE PROGRESS ____ 124**

➢ **TAKE TIME TO PREPARE A HEALTHY MEAL _____ 124**

➢ **SITTING IN BEAUTY _____ 126**

➢ **EATING EXPERIENCE_____ 126**

➢ **ENJOY YOUR MEAL _____ 128**

➢ **SMALL BITES_____ 128**

➢ **FORK DOWN _____ 129**

➢ **CHEW SLOWLY AND THOROUGHLY _____ 129**

➢ **BREATHING_____ 130**

➢ **EXPERIENCE FULLNESS_____ 130**

CHAPTER 16: TOOLS FOR THIN COGNITIVE BEHAVIOR _____ 133

➢ **TOOLS FOR RECOGNIZING BRAIN HUNGER _____ 133**

➢ **MINDFULNESS AIDS _____ 135**

➢ **TOOLS FOR INTERRUPTING OBSESSIVE DIETARY THOUGHTS 136**

• **EDMR- EYE MOVEMENT DESENSITIZATION AND REPROCESSING _____ 137**

• **EFT- EMOTIONAL FREEDOM TECHNIQUE _____ 138**

- **NLP-NEURO-LINGUISTIC PROGRAMMING** _____ 140

  ➢ **TOOLS FOR IDENTIFYING ACTUAL NEEDS AND RESPONDING TO WHAT NEEDS ATTENTION**_____ 141

CHAPTER 17: SLEEP LEARNING SYSTEM 147

CHAPTER 18: WEIGHT LOSS AFFIRMATIONS_____ 152

CHAPTER 19: MEDITATION FOR WEIGHT LOSS _____ 159

CHAPTER 20: FORBIDDEN FOODS _____ 165

CONCLUSION _____ 168

COPYRIGHTS _____ 169

COPYRIGHTS

©Copyright by Karen Loss 2020
All rights reserved

This book: "**RAPID WEIGHT LOSS HYPNOSIS:** Extreme Weight-Loss Hypnosis for Woman! How to Fat Burning & Calorie Blast, Lose Weight with Meditation & Affirmations, Mini Habits, Self-Hypnosis. Stop Emotional Eating!**"**

Written by Karen Loss

resulting from the misuse or use of the procedures, procedures, or instructions contained therein is the total, and absolute obligation of the user addressed.

The author is not obliged, directly or indirectly, to assume civil or civil liability for any restoration, damage, or loss resulting from the data collected here. The respective authors retain all copyrights not kept by the publisher.

The information contained herein is solely and universally available for information purposes. The data is presented without a warranty or promise of any kind.

The trademarks used are without approval, and the patent is issued without the trademark owner's permission or protection.

The logos and labels in this book are the property of the owners themselves and are not associated with this text.

There is no denying that obesity and the associated health problems are one of the biggest challenges faced not only by western countries but also in many other developing countries. The Journal of Health Economics provides more than $ 200 billion annually in the United States for medical obesity research costs. According to SAD (Standard American Diet), processed foods and beverages high in fat, sodium, and sugar that are spread to other countries increase heart disease, diabetes, and other life-threatening problems. The food industry has been treating overweight people for decades (more than $ 2 billion in the U.S. alone in 2015) - most people have tried various diets and other programs that either fail or work temporarily and have made them even more discouraged.

You will find tons of help books that give you diet plans, but they are useless. If you question this, when trying to meet the diet's requirements, let alone allow all of the ingredients, you will lose weight with only the effort required to follow the diet. But here is the most critical statistic that anyone who wants to lose weight should know. Most people who lose weight successfully go on a diet and gain even more weight in the first year! These statistics include people who have participated in The Biggest Loser or whose stomachs have been stapled. This is the most suppressed statistic in the food industry: only 3 in 100 people who reach their goal manage to maintain this weight loss beyond the first year.

A post-mortem with the rest of the 97 people who struggled to keep their weight down showed that they were much hungry after trying their regular diet again than they were before the weight loss program. They have been busy eating since the end of their diet, and some are crazy about food. From the perspective of human evolution, eating is the phenomenon of the last second. Historically telling, the 1920s was a mere failure to promote less eating, but as a society, the cycle of dietary habits that triggered famine brain mechanisms began until the late 1960s.

A weight-loss diet, by definition, requires a reduction in food intake below what the body needs to maintain its current form. There is no real food shortage, but all the built-in mechanisms that ensure our survival record fat loss. This reduction triggers a neural circuit that uses an army of hormones that cause the order of overeating. This mechanism is simply called the famine brain.

Overeating works as the brain's primary reward system for dieting. Unfortunately, researchers have found that weight loss of all kinds uses our neurochemical weapons. If you have too much fat, your body won't know. It only "knows" if you risk losing fat. In a brave attempt to regain homeostasis, our system lowers the hormone levels that signal satiety (leptin and insulin) and pumps the fasting hormone 'ghrelin' into the bloodstream. This hormone results in heightened craving for food leading to extra calorie intake and eventually more weight gain.

Scientists are not yet aware of how the brain and physical starvation system interact to support or override each other. What we know is that many regular diets lead to a mind obsessed with food. Therefore, the root of the problem lies in the brain where this cycle continues.

The way we can save us from this cycle is to optimize brain activity. This optimization and control are what you will learn in this book. Thankfully, we can change our brain patterns to behave differently. In this book, we will study self-hypnosis, cognitive behavioral therapy, sleep learning system, and meditation to control our brain and overcome food cravings. To simply put, we will optimize the brain activity.

It also covers seemingly ordinary but very influential tricks to get rid of excess fat. We will also learn a few practical habits employing the techniques mentioned above. We will investigate the location of the problem and how it affects us so that we can suggest targeted actions.

Until now, you have been listening to multiple reasons for weight gain. Some may say that overeating causes weight gain; some may believe that it is because of hormonal issues. Some may say that the lazy routine is the cause of obesity. We cannot deny them. All of them are correct. But if you dig deeper, you'll find causes of most problems in your head, including overeating and other causes that are mentioned.

How does a food addict's brain differ from a naturally lean female brain? This section describes the main characteristics of the differences in the mind, especially in food addicts.

We are crazy about food. -We usually force us to eat. -We need more food to be full. -We often suffer from hunger. -We respond more strongly to food references. -Emotional imbalance causes brain hunger in us.

Functional magnetic resonance imaging (fMRI) uses the magnetic properties of blood to determine which area of the brain is most active when a subject experience a particular event. Neuroscientists can measure brain activity when food addicts are exposed to food labels, eat delicious foods, or eat certain foods. "It's like training," explains Dr. Ashley Gerhardt. "When you train a particular muscle, blood flows into that area. The brain seems to be working the same way, and you can track which area of the brain receives the most blood."

fMRI consistently shows that the convergence zone for sensory information is the prefrontal cortex, related to reward stimuli, particularly primary reinforcement factors such as food. To elucidate the neurobiological mechanisms by which weight, mood, and age affect the appetite response, Dr. Gerhardt presented healthy, average weight, obese adolescent and adult women with color photographs of foods with different fat content and caloric density while undergoing fMRI (high reward vs. low reward). She shows that food-addicted women responded to highly rewarded foods in the same way drug addicts respond to drugs.

Dr. Bart Hoebel, originally from Princeton University, he was one of the first to study a mouse for sugar addiction. He showed that every drop of sweet they swallowed increased the levels of dopamine. Similar to human addicts, Hoebel's rat sugar developed a hypersensitive dopamine receptor that was hyperresponsive to a variety of drugs, and its changes were long-lasting. Even after a month of self-discipline, the taste of sugar stimulates the rat to become addicted.

In a similar study, in Birmingham at the University of Alabama, Dr. Mary Boggiano figured out that a junk food attack in rats elicits the same pleasing receptors in the brain that drug addicts are stimulated when they ingest drugs. Dr. Boggiano's oleo-conjugated rats have long-term changes in endogenous opioids in the brain and become abnormally responsive to delicious food.

And if this cream puff tastes as good as sex, it's no coincidence. The dopamine reward system is the way we feel good and is associated with obsessive gambling, substance abuse, and sex. Food satisfaction results from some of the same neural signals and pathways that regulate orgasm. As a result, hundreds of neuroscientists have begun to record that obesity, eating disorders, and even healthy appetite resemble addiction. "Repeating dopamine over and over is what substance abuse does," says Dr. Hoebel. "This makes you wonder if food may have addictive properties.

Food gives you a discreet physiological response in the same way that drug consumption gives you a huge response," says psychiatrist Walter H. Kaye, director of the Eating Disorders Program at the University of California, San Diego. The drug takes over the food reward. "Drugs are addictive because they open the way for appetite.

Like other drug therapies, food therapy is an attempt to achieve the dopamine levels required by all addicts. In a 1954 study identifying amusement centers, two McGill University researchers, Dr. James Olds and Dr. Peter Milner, documented the effects of dopamine. In this study, rats were able to push the bar to electrically stimulate the amusement center or push the bar for food. Dr. Olds and Dr. Milner said electrical stimulation of rats to an amusement center is more rewarding than eating. The experience was so satisfying that the hungry rat ignored the food for pleasure the electrical impulse from the entertainment facility gave her. Some rats stimulated the brain more than 2,000 times an hour for 24 consecutive hours. Most mice died on an empty stomach.

Heroin and cocaine addicts also happen to forget about eating and lose a lot of weight while taking the drug. This fact explains why you get dopamine fixes from other sources. The first stage of love, all the activities that we find so enjoyable, we don't eat much and forget to eat! Poisoning is high dopamine, not food. If this mechanism fails, we end up eating too much food, obsessed with repairing dopamine.

So, that's how you overeat. You do not eat because you like it, but you eat because you are compelled to eat. Now we will look into types of overeating.

Based on the reason, the habit of overeating can be divided into two types:

- Obsessive overeating
- Compulsive overeating

OBSESSIVE OVEREATING

Dr. Gearhardt, a scholarship recipient at the Yale University Rudd Center for Food Policy and Obesity Center, conducted a neurobiological study and documented similarities in how the brain responds to drugs and delicious foods. Like drug addicts, food addicts struggle with increasing desires, encourage them to eat in response to food alerts, and may feel out of control when eating delicious food. Just as one drink sends an alcoholic beverage to a bend, some biscuits can also cause seizures.

"The results of this study back the theory that increasing expectations for food may partially cause forced diets," said Gearhardt. Depending on the expected food intake, participants with higher levels of food obsession showed more significant activity in the parts of the brain supposed to create the motivation and urge to eat, but with suppression of inhibiting mechanism during impulses. Responsible for consumption, which showed less activity in the area of responsibility.

Gene Jack Wang, MD, director of medicine at the Brookhaven National Laboratory in Upton, NY, and Dr. Nora Volkow, director of the 'National Institute on Drug Abuse,' said this was just a perspective on human imaging studies and grilled chicken. The smell of hamburgers and pizza releases dopamine into the brain. This food stimulus significantly increased dopamine levels in the minds of gluttons, but not in non-gluttons. The amount released correlates with the intensity of one's desire for food for a long time, the subjective impression "I seek for it."

"This is how our brain controls our desires," said Dr. Wang, many food addicts feel weak in their ability to control when and how much they eat. The entertainment center contains the striatum, a part of the limbic system that contributes to motivation, and the neurotransmitter dopamine, which controls the quest for pleasure and produces pleasure. "Now we're not just talking about balancing the energy level," he says. "We are discussing human psychology," said Wang.

COMPULSIVE OVEREATING

The ventral striatum of the brain is best known for its role in motor pathway planning and coordination. Still, it is also involved in a variety of other cognitive processes, including executive functions such as working memory. In humans, the striatum is activated by reward-related stimuli, but also by an aversive, novel, unexpected, or intense triggers and the symptoms associated with such events. When you see the brain like a train, the striatum on the ventral side is the accelerator.

When food enters the human body, it stimulates the amusement center, which increases the flow of dopamine. When overeating becomes standard behavior, three things happen:

1) The reward system is kidnapped,

2) Neuroplastic changes occur,

3) Serotonin and GABA (inhibitor) neurotransmitters involved in the "brake system" are reduced.

 Food addiction confuses entertainment centers. It is more like when brakes of a train break down, and runaway trains eventually jump off the tracks. All are accelerators, no brakes. Forced or compulsive overeating is like this.

Eating is one of our biological needs and is ensured by the joy we feel when we eat. But as soon as we got hooked on food, like long-term alcoholics became able to drink everyone under the table, and as drug addicts needed more and more medicine, we develop greater tolerance to food. All forms of addiction require increasingly addictive substances to reach dopamine levels. Chronically strong drinkers have few signs of addiction, with high blood alcohol levels, which are either impossible or fatal to non-drinkers. Tolerance facilitates the consumption of overconsumption of alcohol, which leads to long term physical addiction. Similarly, the addict's brain needs more food to produce the amounts of dopamine that are associated with normal high-grade foods.

Men who rely on web pornography during the study are one of the most moving examples of forgiveness. As soon as a man completely relies on this form of dopamine fixation, he reports that he is unable to be agitated or satisfied during intercourse with a real woman. They take months to go without an X-rated website and endure severe withdrawal symptoms before they can regain the joy of interacting with a real woman.

In 2001, along with his colleagues Dr. Volkow, including Dr. Wang, a Ph.D., obtained brain scans of overweight and normal-weight volunteers to study the enumeration of dopamine receptors. Dr. Wang noticed that overweight people had lesser dopamine receptors-the the more obese they were, the fewer these important receptors they had (the brains of addicts). He says the brains of overweight people and drug addicts are strikingly similar: "Both have fewer dopamine receptors than normal subjects."

All addicts are looking for a solution, but if we become more resistant to our drugs, in our case, eating food, a small amount of non-delicious food, reduces the sensation of joy and leads to underproduction of dopamine. Something stagnates in the process of the generation of dopamine in the brain. Genetic damage is called polymorphism. If one of the genes required for the dopamine process is a polymorphed, it will appear in those certain people with prominent symptoms.

Again, dopamine is a neurotransmitter produced by our brain when we enjoy eating. When you enjoy a delicious salad, pot, or slice of pizza, do it because your brain produces a healthy amount of dopamine. So, overeating is forcing us to fix dopamine.

The misconception that fat women have more fun while eating than thin women is flawed. The fMRI again shows that a healthy brain produces much more dopamine than the brain of a food poisoner. Food addiction has the same adverse effects as any other addiction. Addicts developed greater tolerance for the drugs of choice. Low dopamine levels mean less experience with pleasure. Therefore, most addicts consume a significant amount of food when they want to achieve the expected amount of pleasure. This fact is one of the obvious and measurable differences between a naturally lean female brain and an obese female brain.

This phenomenon explains why we act absurdly when we don't reach the food levels that cause the production of dopamine enough to experience pleasure.

Food poisoners suffer overwhelming hunger in the presence of food. Overeating obsessively and compulsively, when not hungry, are more susceptible to smells and a strong desire to eat, even after a full meal. Researchers call this phenomenon "external food hypersensitivity." British Medical Research Centre presents a study in which brain scans have shown how this food susceptibility affects people's diets.

Researchers Andrew Calder, Luca Passamonti, Ph.D., and James Rowe, Ph.D., sought to find out why some people tend to overeat. In the Journal of neuroscience (January 2011), brain scans of the human were presented to show three sets of images of participants (delicious food, boring food, and irrelevant photos of other subjects). Their response was then recorded.

"People who appear to be more attracted to food have different connections in their brains, " said obesity expert Marc Andre Cornier, MD, an endocrinologist at the University of Colorado, who has nothing to do with this study.

Dr. Gearhardt von Yale discovered that: "Addictive people respond physiologically, psychologically, and behaviorally to triggers, such as advertising. Very tasty foods are always available and highly marketed today. In the food environment, it is especially important that food-related symptoms can cause pathological reactions." Like drug addicts, food addicts have increased appetite and appetite in response to flood warnings. You may feel that you are out of control when you eat delicious food, and you lose your strength while eating, and the feeling that you can't help yourself becomes dominant. This is all in stark contrast to naturally lean women who do not even know that this kind of fighting is possible.

Emotional imbalance causes hunger. Take a positive person, whose strongest allergies are everything that influences his optimism, and who eats whenever his energy level is low. The stress is relieved by eating. Also, for uncomfortable feelings, difficult situations, and difficult people,

In the case of a tie mate picture, one can imagine himself in two situations where he is likely to overeat: between meals and at the dining table. With his eyes closed, he imagines a movie screen on the wall. He is on the screen himself, in every situation he finds when he is reading, chatting with others, watching TV, or having trouble calorie counting.

Instead of reaching for popcorn, potato chips, or peanuts as before, he is now simply focusing on the conversation, the television screen, or the printed page, perhaps except for a glass of water, and I congratulate you on being unfamiliar with anything at the table.

The second scene that catches your eye is the dining table. Do you tend to grab this second loaf? Instead, put your hand on your forehead and remember, "Protect my body." Looking at a cake, a loaf, a potato, or a cake raises the idea, "This is for someone. I'm good enough". With the fork down, take a deep breath and be proud to help one-person flow through the body.

Then, imagine a very simple and effective exercise method that simply puts your hand on the edge of the table and pushes it. Better yet, stand up from the chair and leave the table at this point.

Here's another image I'd recommend to a self-hypnotist. If you introduce yourself to the screen of this fictional movie, you will find yourself slim. Give yourself the ideal line that you want to see to others. Cut the abdomen and waistline to the and he repeated the steps of the deployment process. It was

"Yes," I replied, "It's a simple one to two. Do you want to do that?"

Again, he refused: "Oh, not me!"

This issue has not been raised again for several months. It must be mentioned that Mr. Happiness was a fat man and was instructed to lose weight for a heart attack. But what the battle: these potatoes, these rich desserts, and these knives! Then one day, he said to me, "I have done something I recently thought you might be interested in. When I go to bed at night, I count, one, two, three, and I say: I don't eat anything, I just drink grapefruit juice, but I still feel well filled. Patient in the letter: "I only count three.")

He then confessed to me that for the last few months, he had done this. He lost weight and felt comfortable doing it. Still, he didn't want me to hypnotize him.

This is, of course, the beauty of self-hypnosis. He didn't have to be hypnotized: he was able to hypnotize himself to accomplish what he wanted. We can do the same. All we need to do is to believe in what we are suggesting to ourselves and feel the power.

You have it-practically everything I know about the practice of self-hypnosis. As you learned in this book, the technique of defining it and using it for self-therapy is very simple, as the condition may define or understand itself.

This triple sided weapon-self-imaging-post-hypnotic suggestion provides the fastest cure that brings me to mind and body changes. There is even clinical evidence that better results can be achieved without the support of others. A few years ago, John Clifford-Luck experimented at Stanford University with both self-hypnosis and hetero hypnosis (Hypnotic state induced by another person).

In summary, he summarized his results: "... self-hypnosis without prior hypnosis is as effective as hetero hypnosis. So, it's clear that tradition is wrong. You can obviously be hypnotized without prior training-traditional hypnosis. While early self-hypnosis tends to help later hypnosis.

Therefore, I recommend studying the self-hypnosis procedure and practicing it until you feel comfortable and competent to bring you a relaxed state. Then, use self-therapy for a reasonable amount of time to determine if you are getting the desired results. Only if you get a negative result from such a fair process, you would want to discontinue the technique by yourself or contact an expert? The choice is all yours.

Obviously, "reasonable time" and "fair trial" are not always voluntary and will vary from individual to individual depending on variables such as susceptibility to hypnosis, exercise therapy, level of participation in developmental status, and depth of the problem, or difficulty to deal with the situation.

After setting these variables, I present the following rules of thumb. Even if you faithfully participate in the exercises several times a day for three weeks and give each performance full focus and commitment, there is no indication that you are. If you're not moving toward your goals, you're probably doing something wrong, or your symptoms are rooted in an emotional cause and need professional help to resolve them.

If so, I recommend that you review all aspects of your self-hypnosis to find places where you may not be on the right track. If you still cannot find the answer, seek outside help. If you're a hypnotherapist or feel a more soulful way, you can be a deeper cure expert.

Everything is based on the only principle we can choose. We can choose to be the master of our lives. I'm not talking about the creation of superhumans, but within the bounds of certain reasonable and practical limits, we can get control. I'm sure of that. Perhaps now is the time to take responsibility for a place in your life that can be achieved.

You can assume that each time you exercise, you can trigger your hypnosis faster and more skillfully. Besides, you can add suggestions for appropriate post-hypnotic implants.

"I find my skills in self-hypnosis increasing every day."

Therefore, the progress made by repeating the exercise itself is reinforced by the positive implants intended to reach the unconscious. Performance increases as your skill increases, and confidence increases as your performance increases. One moves the other until you feel more inner strength than you ever felt. You can make it happen. This does not mean that self-hypnosis is a panacea. There is no magic there. It speeds up the results that can be achieved by the more awkward methods of mental and emotional treatment.

The article in this book was clear to gain self-control through self-hypnosis. Before ending, the second important application of hypnosis, the "discovery" practiced in the therapeutic environment, that is, exploring the subconscious to find something hidden in the maze of one's memory. Let me touch on that. It is most useful to reveal important early experiences in our lives through hypnosis. For example, hypnosis highlighted the key memories that led to the successful treatment of Fred. Psychological tests are usually done under the supervision of a second psychotherapist or hypnotherapist. Still, during this time, it is not possible to stop the experiments to unravel the memory of self-hypnosis. Such information can prove valuable in your own self-treatment.

This discovery aspect of hypnosis is increasingly being used to solve puzzles of very practical nature. For example, a person involved in a car crash can hypnotize important details that have been forgotten. Notable is the kidnapping of 26 children on a bus in Chowchilla, California, in 1976. Under hypnosis, the bus driver remembered the kidnapper's license number. This fascinating aspect of hypnosis, the discovery of memory, deserves another opportunity for more extensive research.

At the moment, it's very simple, easy to learn, and powerful, and I'm happy to provide this technique that makes you feel good. It's a good idea to focus on yourself and personalize your controls. Emphasize emotions and feelings with self-hypnosis. Therapists of all beliefs agree with their importance for mental and physical health. So, in a self-hypnosis exercise, imagine a quiet place where you feel peaceful, cherishing your body and mind as kindly as you loved ones, and drawing your spiritual paintings like you. Imagine drawing; want to be-can be. For this reason, it's a good idea to change the wording and images after learning the technique to make it your own.

That is the end of my advice. I can guide you along the way, but you need to do it alone with mental tools and confidence. This is the goal of the analysis. To build the strength of the ego that allows individuals to function productively and happily.

CHAPTER 13: COGNITIVE BEHAVIORAL THERAPY

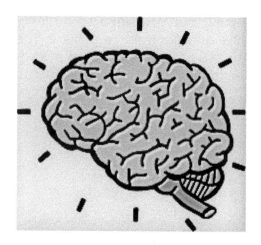

This new form of rehabilitation is known as Cognitive Behavioral Therapy (CBT). It is a widely used treatment used by psychologists around the world to treat obsessive-compulsive disorder, depression, addiction, and a variety of other issues. There is a step by step directions to how to use CBT to bring the brain back into a lean female brain.

There are four basic steps.

1 Learn to distinguish brain hunger (as opposed to physical hunger).

2 Suspending the fancy of two meals.

3 Name and respond to your actual needs.

4 Experience success and measure progress.

Unlike hunger in the brain, physical feelings of hunger have specific objective signs. You will be greeted with a variety of foods to end your stomach humming, low blood sugar, and physical hunger. Brain starvation usually requires very specific foods, and its only physical manifestation, salivation, is usually caused by external events. Step one is the motivation and courage to show two types of hunger. "I have no signs of physical hunger, but I'm hungry for food, I'm hungry."

Step two breaks the fancy of food. To us food is like a polite car salesman who is a friend and only he wants us to buy a car. Learn how to use various cognitive behavioral therapy techniques to redirect firmly fixed thought patterns. We have to recognize what it is and the hallucination of joy for our current wiring. Through mindful practices, you will learn to prove your desire and old belief that eating makes you feel better. In contrast to willpower, this step observes the desire gently but is not forced to react to it.

Step three demonstrates the actual need. Are we tired, stressed, disappointed, angry, or frustrated? We need to take breaks, run, and express disappointment. In other words, you need to meet and address your emotional needs, not your food.

In this step, we continuously recognize success, evaluate progress, and move forward. The human spirit is what we must progress to continue our long journey. The final step in restoring the brain from a food poisoner's brain to a healthy relationship with food depends not only on the level of food addiction but also on the joy you can experience as you progress. The less food addiction, and the more joy we can experience when recognizing progress, the shorter will be the rewiring process. Similarly, the inability to experience acute addiction and the joy of progress slows the rewiring process.

The book does not prescribe diet, but it does show that high flavored and high sugars and salts are addictive. Stopping food addiction means stopping the consumption of these types of foods. The step-by-step program in this book returns your brain to a healthy relationship with food. It does not overwhelm your craving for food. Success does not depend on willpower. Learn how not to allow food to be important in your life and how to regain a healthy perspective.

Cognitive-behavioral therapy was first developed when UCLA psychiatrist Jeffrey M. Schwartz developed it for patients with OCD. CBT is based on the reality that our thoughts provoke emotions, which determine our behavior. To understand the mechanism of CBT, Dr. Schwartz undertook the investigation. Dr. Schwarz's treatment was an obsessive-compulsive hand-wash disorder. Dr. Schwartz first presented a CAT scan of normal brain activity in patients with OCD. Then he showed them photos of his dirty hands. OCD patients are immediately frightened when measured by a brain CAT scan. After observing the CAT scan before and after, and the brain's response to a dirty handheld photograph, the patient was able to change the automated response gradually.

Using a mindful approach, a revolutionary voluntary approach, gradually rewired the brains of OCD patients to see dirty photos on their hands without anxiety. Encouraged by the success of CBT in treating obsessive-compulsive disorder, other medical and psychological experts have begun investigating the use of CBT across obsessive-compulsive disorder. Below is a summary of how CBT was used beyond the initial OCD patients.

Dr. Michael Melzenich, a neurophysiologist at Johns Hopkins, and Dr. Polar Talal, a neuroscientist at the University of Cambridge, work together with children with dyslexia to improve reading accuracy when trained to do the same. It is dramatically improved but distinguishes different sounds. The success of these studies has created "Fast for Word", an organization that has supported more than one million dyslexics in over 40 countries.

Dr. Edward Taub, a behavioral neuroscientist at Columbia University, has extended the CBT protocol to develop obsessive-compulsive exercise therapy. This has led to significant advances in helping thousands of patients recover from stroke-related nerve damage.

Another UCLA neuroscientist, Dr. John Piacentini, has documented the efficacy of CBT in Tourette's syndrome. Dr. Piacentini's CBT protocol includes tic recognition training. It teaches Tourette patients how to monitor themselves for early signs of imminent tics. Training with competing reactions teaches patients how to engage in spontaneous behavior designed to be physically incompatible with the next tic, interrupting cycles and reducing tics.

Dr. John D. Teesdale, a researcher at Oxford and Cambridge, created a unique CBT protocol for clinically depressed patients based on a multilevel theory of mind called Interacting Cognitive Subsystems (ICS). The ICS model explains that the mind has several modes of receiving and processing new information, cognitively and emotionally. This theory links a person's susceptibility to depression with trust in only one of the available modes and falsely blocks all other options. Prevention of recurrence of depression is based on the individual's ability to easily move between the many modes available, away from the black and white thought modes.

Initially, it was difficult to get the scientific elite to believe that people could alter the workings of the brain by focusing their attention in another way. This process did not include not only self-initiated neuroplasticity but also effective drugs that change the mind and comprehensive psychoanalytic counseling. With so much success, CBT is internationally favored as a practical tool for overcoming psychological and physical conditions that overcome long-term disability. This positive and practical remedy is popular with both therapists and patients. It is to restore the natural neural network that changes our attitude towards our impulses in this case about food.

Yes, our addicts had flaws in their brain wiring that caused overwhelming cravings and forced us into slavery when we were not physically hungry. However, what CBT offers is the ability to use the activity in an existing healthy circuit using mental focus. George Guilder, the author of Microcosm and Telecosm, nominates the doctor Schwartz's CBT "Bold rescue of the Free Will Concept."

In this chapter, we will first look for how the brain of a thin woman works, and then we will compare it to the will powered thin woman. Then we will finally explore how the use of cognitive-behavioral theory while practicing mindfulness can help to lose weight without going through emotional suppression and stress.

NATURAL THINNESS
I would like to make an important distinction between naturally lean women, and will powered lean women, with willpower, self-denial, and strict routines. What I have found is that there are striking differences between women of both types. A thin woman has a healthy relationship with food, in contrast to the fat woman, who is trying to lose fat by forced calorie counting, excessive exercise, and life focused on her profession, to stay thin at all costs. I know her strategy very well and have seen people continue using the same fanatic methods to reach the thinness for many periods.

Small dishes, strict nutrition, counting all calories, drinking a lot of water, and all the tools used by lean women with a strong will are useful and can be used as useful starting points. However, this book is not intended to increase your diving board. Check out at the supermarket, and you'll find many of them in most women's magazines. We're presenting a way to go beyond crutches because if you throw them away before a meaningful cure, your injury will recover. Weight loss is temporary and will be avoided if it is based on the use of aids. The thinness of nature is not a function of willpower. Willpower is limited and exhausted by many of our external demands and our emotional challenges. And a functional crutch should be thrown away when its purpose is achieved.

The central nervous system (including the brain and spinal cord) is formed of two basic types of cells, neurons and glia. Neurons are messengers of information. They are structures that exchange chemicals that emit electrical impulses that send signals not only between different regions of the brain but also between the brain and the rest of the nervous system. Everything we think and feel begins with the brain, correlates with the neural activity that affects other parts of our body, and is reflected in nerve cells in the spinal cord. As we humans learn new skills, the wiring of our brain becomes more complex and interrelated.

As a person who has been witnessing people overeating for years and years, I know there are quite a few neural circuits that support these behaviors. One way to think of the neural network of overeating is that it is part of an organic program that sends electrical and chemical signals whenever emotional, situational, or social stress causes hunger. What we have learned in our program is that we can equally restore the neural networks that recognize hunger in the brain and, in some practice, empower them. programming. Therefore, our goal is to restore a neural network of naturally lean women.

Changes are biological and can be measured at the brain level and CAT scan and MRI. It is to restore the behavior of the naturally lean women, including the ability to experience satisfaction in a luxurious feast. It's not a coping tool that calls your friends or, in our case, runs to the fridge each time you face a stressful challenge. It's also not emotional. It doesn't survive the longing for another. Many of us experienced an early stage of love that resisted the fascinating things in your life. This is exactly the process that is happening in the brains of lean women with a strong will, overwhelmed by power-the need for overeating overpower the desire to stay lean. Many of us can maintain this inhibitory mechanism, but only if we have enough emotional energy to overwhelm our insatiable appetite.

I have lived in the Will powered thin woman administration. And, like most women, I'm sure they'll resort to overeating as soon as they don't get a small plate or their lover is gone. In this book, we will restore the neural network of a naturally lean woman by rewiring the brain and selecting behaviors that lead to a healthy relationship with food. This is not an act of will or intellectual structure. It's a sensation triggered by organic brain structures, and the naturally lean female neural network does not equate overeating with pleasure.

The goal is to move from a conceptual brain understanding of the sacred. If at the moment, we recognize the joy of eating and have the ability to recognize it without the overwhelming urge to enjoy it. At the biological level, naturally, lean women have different structure of the body. It is organic and natural, and through negotiations about inner conflicts and what to eat, it leads to the confidence and brain signals without the stress experienced by an unmotivated lean woman. The wiring of naturally thin exhibits wisdom and, at the same time, allows you to accept the potential pleasure of eating and consciously choose to lose or delay that pleasure until you are gradually hungry.

Be clear about women who eat like a naturally thin woman and women who eat like will powered thin woman. There are physiological differences between the brains of both types of women, those who are naturally thin, and those who are working hard to lose weight. Thinning at the expense of high stress and will is a recipe we've all tried and has failed many times. There are healthy and workable ways to lose weight all at once. One of these ways is practicing the mindfulness through which cognitive behavioral modification is administered in everyday lifestyle, leading to normal weight maintenance without stress and anxiety.

MINDFULNESS

The most important skills needed to administer cognitive behavioral therapy is the ability to be mindful.

Modern women usually do not currently exist in the present. Usually, she looks at past events and predicts the future. Mindfulness sometimes means accepting and maintaining a curiosity about our thoughts, feelings, physical sensations, and perceptions of the environment. It may sound useless. But learning to experience the present moment in a way that abolishes judgment and self-criticism has an incredibly good impact on our biology, happiness, and ability to maintain equality of events that normally lead to overeating. This gives you a broader perspective and gives you additional options and clarity when making decisions.

It's not just about paying attention to teachers 'lectures and friends' conversations. It's a "meta-consciousness," and it notices where your attention is directed. So, if you're paying attention during a lecture, you know you're paying attention. While driving, paying attention not only to focus on the road, but also to the movement of the hand that holds the steering wheel, the movement of the neck when checking traffic conditions, and the grunts under the road. Mindfulness is the ability to pay attention intentionally.

Mindfulness also requires acceptance. That means not believing that there are "right" or "wrong" ways of thinking and feelings at a particular moment, and paying attention to your thoughts and feelings without judging them. When practicing mindfulness, our thinking is in harmony with what we feel in the present moment, rather than warming the past or imagining the future.

At any time, focus on the myriad aspects of your current experience. For example, suppose you had dinner, and your child immediately said, "I hate chicken!" You pay attention to your body's reactions, the anger, and frustration that develops. When I notice the racing pulse, the idea of "I worked hard on this dinner after a long day..." comes to mind. Not only do you realize you are experiencing anger, but you accept anger and accept something without judgment. The next paragraph describes how Jon Kabat-Zinn, one of the leading mindfulness teachers, described his progress.

"When I started practicing mindfulness, I thought at every moment to see how amazing everything was. One of the books I read was dishwashing, water, soap. When I tried it, the inner monologue said, "Oh, the water was very warm, this soap has a very nice scent and is very relaxing." A delusion is felt that was strange, strange, and light. Getting mindful attention means knowing and accepting what it is. Perceive the sensation without assigning a positive or negative value. You only notice that there is water in your hand or the scent of soap. Do not notice and judge.

This is not a creepy story. Because this is where the left side of the brain penetrates. It's about being aware of our thinking and responding to challenges in a balanced way."

Bringing this kind of mindful consciousness to hunger should be relatively emotional, so it's a relatively easy way to start practicing. And as it learns new skills to pay attention to the small cases of hunger in the brain, it helps combat the overwhelming desire to overeat when it occurs. By witnessing, we begin to weaken excessive eating habits and eliminate subconscious reactions. I also arrest negative soliloquy that comes to my mind.

Most people find it helpful to know that mindfulness practices produce very high returns. A simple analogy is physical muscle development. When heavier, it modifies the body's tissues in two ways:

• Increase in basic strength.

• Increase in basic flexibility.

When investing in mindfulness practice, try formal procedures (such as meditation) that alter the organization of consciousness in two ways.

• Making the baseline clearer.

• Increasing basic rewards.

The purpose of strength training is not to achieve a temporary state of strength and flexibility that exists when you exercise and then disappears throughout the day. The goal is to increase your strength and flexibility gradually. In other words, the purpose is to acquire the permanent properties of your body.

Similarly, the goal of mindfulness practice is not to achieve the temporary state of clarity and serenity that exists when you meditate and then disappear all day. The goal of mindfulness practice is to elicit the desire for overeating but gradually improve the clarity and develop equality for observing overeating without forcing a response. It is not to develop an intellectual understanding of excessive feeding activity, but to cultivate a calm, reliable balance and confidence to respond to excessive food triggers that are conscious and impulsive and respond without fear and force.

The sooner we can experience equality, the sooner we can start using the Falls of Mindfulness Practice.

PROPER PLANNING
The better this program helps you to recover your healthy brain at a time, and once you are ready to return to a healthy weight, the more likely you are to succeed.

You need to spend time on activities that promote you and improve your quality of life. Scientists are recording the power of positive thinking. By utilizing the force of the positive posture, the time required to restore the NATURALLY THIN WOMAN'S neural network can be greatly reduced.

Resilience and tenacity are important during this transition home. Self-sympathy also contributes to success.

One of the last tips I suggest is a serious commitment to stress-free your brain. Most of today's stress comes from our thoughts, not from the outside world. In other words, you can manage your stress by changing your mind. Investing in a healthy reseller for what really costs you will improve the overall quality of your work and life. Remember, that is a process. Through strategies such as meditation and frequent mindful moments, you can achieve the equality needed for a successful, NATURALLY THIN WOMAN program. And don't forget to get acquainted with what works for you. What worked for me may not work the same for you. This is what our topic was designed to overcome bumps on the road. This is not a single program. It is a program aimed at adjusting to your health and the meaning of nature to you, not to other societies.

CHAPTER 14: LEVERAGING COGNITIVE BEHAVIORAL THERAPY

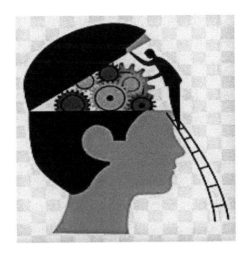

The question after I learned about CBT was simple. These types of treatments can be used to rewire the brains obsessed with the food. But do you mostly adopt the behavior of lean women naturally? The answer was yes!

Needless to say, if we can eliminate food obsession, obsessive eating, and pointless overeating, we can free ourselves from the diet tyranny. Rewiring the brain to have a healthy relationship with food has nothing to do with obsessive or modest self-discipline. It's not even a dreadful watch that allows so many women to lose weight but feel stressed. Instead, we naturally regain a thin behavior as a normal dietary response.

Because the brain can change (neuroplasticity), the process of consciously repeating mindfulness changes the brain's neural circuits at the physical level. A measure for achieving the behavior of naturally lean women is that food does not create an internal struggle that appears to require willpower. We have already mentioned the various behaviors characteristic of naturally lean women. Let's take a closer look at one of these major actions, especially eating on an empty stomach.

To understand what is physical hunger, let's first look at what is happening in the body:

When our bodies burn food in our stomachs, and our blood sugar and insulin levels begin to fall, the cells that line our stomachs produce a hormone called ghrelin. Ghrelin communicates with the hypothalamus, deep in the brain. The hypothalamus regulates basic physical functions such as hunger, thirst, sleep, and libido. As soon as the hypothalamus receives a message from ghrelin that it needs to eat something to keep moving, it triggers the release of our appetite-stimulating neuropeptide.

My God! I'm starting to get hungry.

The specific signs of physical hunger are:

Your blood sugar level is low, and you may feel nauseous. The taste of the tongue awakens completely, and you welcome any kind of food. You do not want a specific meal.

The problem is how your brain reacts when you look at food. Overeating leads to a desire to eat, often in response to visual cues, when you are not physically hungry. This is known as "external food hypersensitivity," and also known as EFS. Food addicts also respond to "situational starvation." Let's see what hunger means:

Social. We hope to connect us with others and want to eat to share shared experiences. We also tend to dine in social situations to avoid inappropriate feelings or because the party is uncommitted.

Sensual. Eat because there is food at the restaurant, see ads for a specific meal, or pass by a fragrant bakery. The desire to eat reacts because it is closely linked to a particular activity (watching TV, going to a movie, attending a sporting event, etc.).

Thought. Eating as a result of negative self-talk or as an excuse for a meal. The irony is that if you scold yourself for lack of willpower, it can be triggered.

Physiological. Eating in response to physical ailments such as headaches and other pain.

Emotional. Eating in response to stress, boredom, fatigue, tension, anger, fear, and loneliness. Instead of effectively dealing with the underlying emotions, eating suppresses emotions and shifts the focus to what seems initially to be a joy. Unfortunately, we indulge in a reminder after eating.

You can learn how to keep an eye on the fear of starvation in context. The Thin Cognitive Behavioral Protocol (see TCB) consists of four basic steps.

Step 1: Recognize brain hunger.

Step 2: Break obsessive food thinking.

Step 3: Name and address your actual needs.

Step 4: Measure your progress and experience success. The goal is to perform these steps for 21-42 consecutive days until the rewiring is deeply rooted. The first three steps are important, especially at the beginning of the process.

STEP 1: RECOGNIZE BRAIN HUNGER

When it comes to overeating, there are many situations and emotional imbalances that cause obsessive feeding fantasies and the need for forced feeding. Craving for food has a real physiological effect on our bodies. Water begins to come out of our mouth. It's exciting to expect the fun of eating. This can be measured as an increase in brain activity. Your heart rate will increase, and your anxiety level will increase. I want to experience this fun. The brain releases neurochemicals, lowering blood sugar levels in anticipation of the next sugar. This is why we feel unstable and moody when we have brain hunger.

An important first step is the ability to recognize brain hunger. This is not achieved by superficial, occasional observations. Rather, we consciously recognize that "hunger," which feels very compelling, is not physical, but an obsession. Useful help is to check for signs of physical hunger when taking a deep breath. The other is to ask yourself when you were full or when you were feeling full at the end. This process allows us to be proactive in: This is hunger, and this desire is an obsession. "The goal of Step 1 is to figure out if the need arising is a misfire in the brain." The brain has a biochemical imbalance. Wired to experience an imbalance. This desire is a misfire in the brain."

It does not resist the urge to overeat. We are already using a lot of willpower to stick to our diet. Instead, it recognizes and names the hunger for what it is, without rattling our brains or causing additional fear. Learning to calmly and unambiguously name the hunger of the brain enhances our ability to observe it without devoting it to something to eat. The willingness to accept that hunger is not physical is a huge step forward. Acknowledgments stop the forced and automatic reaction to hunger in some situations. It changes impulses. However, recognizing situational hunger without performing steps 2 and 3 does not eliminate hunger.

Trying to call hunger "situational" or "emotional" scares us, but we continue to invest in tools that improve our ability to perform Step 1, especially in the practice of mindfulness.

STEP 2: BREAK OBSESSIVE FOOD THINKING

The ability to interfere with the idea of obsessive eating was examined by Dr. Suzanne Segerstrom of the University of Kentucky. She assumed the theory she called "pausing and planning." Dr. Segerstrom documents that what we experience as an internal conflict is the ability to pause or slow down and weigh the effects of "I want to experience this joy" and "I do not want to." This personal ability determines the ability to perform this interrupt step.

If you can stop the automated reaction to eating, there is usually emotional conflict. Let's see what gets activated in our brain when we experience the struggle of "I want to" and "I don't want to." As explained earlier in the previous chapter, there are many chemical changes in our brain that we overeat. A chronic diet rewired our brain and experienced a hungry brain without food shortages. Biologically, you have the opportunity to enjoy food even if you are not hungry. Finally, we have formed strong bonds between some foods that meet some of our emotional needs-comfort, excitement, relaxation, love, to name a few. The brain has deep structures called the caudate nucleus. Scientists around the world are studying this structure and believe that the caudate may not function properly in people with obsessive-compulsive behavior. Think of the caudate as a processing center for body movements, physical emotions, learning, and planning. The Caudate core, together with its sister structure Putamen, functions like an automatic transmission in a car. These guarantee a smooth transition from one behavior to another.

During a normal day, we make lots of fast, smooth, easy, thoughtless, and quick behavior changes. It is the caudate and putamen that make this possible. The problem with obsessive-compulsive people is that the smooth transition of thoughts and actions is disturbed by disturbances of the caudal nucleus. As a result of this dysfunction, the front part of the brain becomes overactive and consumes excess energy. It looks like your car is stuck in a ditch. You spin the wheel, but you can't get out of the trench until you manually shift gears to get traction. If a brute force bin feels "I'm hungry," and it doesn't go away, it's the same as spinning our tires. It is necessary to carefully investigate what triggers situational hunger by switching from automation to manual mode and unknowingly accepting "I'm hungry." If you succumb to brain hunger, you will feel temporary relief. The technical term for this is the "suction effect." But in a very short time, the urge increases and sometimes walks its own life, becoming a full-fledged binge!

STEP 3: NAME AND ADDRESS YOUR ACTUAL NEEDS

The most difficult task is following this step. Our brain is always running programs like computers. We are aware of some of them. Some of them are completely unconscious. Many of these programs are so deep-rooted that they have an involuntary response as well as a knee-like response when hit with a rubber mallet. The important point to be aware of is that due to the current wiring, various unconscious programs lead to overeating.

By naming and addressing needs, we stop overeating and instead direct energy to what is currently disguised as hungry. Part of the hunger reaction is due to situational triggers and another part of the chronic suppression of our basic emotional needs. If naming is difficult, you may need self-advocacy coaching or help with history to help control the root cause. Are you stressed about work, money problems, difficulties with loved ones? Do you just want to fit unconsciously in a social situation where everyone else is eating? By naming hidden needs, we can approach our processes so that our emotions are not kidnapped and address our real needs rather than overeating.

As a result, repeating steps 1 to 3 alters the biochemistry of the brain, causing atrophy of the neural network that causes contextual hunger.

STEP 4: MEASURE YOUR PROGRESS AND EXPERIENCE SUCCESS

Neuroplasticity is the ability to change our own brain, occurs when we quietly observe the hunger of our brain and are not afraid. This does not happen overnight. Like strength training, it requires repetition, which leads to healthy structure and creates habits. This strengthens the connections between neural networks (brain cells) and increases the likelihood that they will fire together in the future. Neural networks, the cells that carry information in the brain, essentially reinforce the affinity between neurons by reorganizing their electrochemical relationships. The neuroscientist mantra is "the cells that fire together wires up."

Upon success, dopamine will be given. If we are happy with our progress, this shows that the naturally lean female neural network is self-healing and rewiring. The more involved in the behavior of naturally lean women, the more likely it is that some satisfaction will be created. Keep in mind that when you reach your goal, dopamine is also created. If we fail, it means that the behavior of a naturally lean woman has not been captured.

In the field of the computer industry, the importance of progress is often documented. Among the well-known publication Computer-Human Interface Percentage Progress Indicators, Dr. Brad A. Myers of the University of Toronto says that he prefers progress indicators when waiting for a task to complete. Software development teams whose goals are shared in the short term and whose progress is visible are 90% more likely to complete their projects successfully than teams whose progress is tracked loosely and not shared. In her book Rules of Play, Katie Salen (Ph.D.) from New School for Design and Eric Zimmerman (MIT) from MIT, unless participants have a meaningful tool to measure progress, we have concluded that consistent engagement is unlikely.

Naturally, I am satisfied with achieving my goals, even if they are mini-goals. This advancement increases satisfaction and increases the likelihood of continuing the rewiring process. "When we completed a complex task, we found that the brain released a large number of endorphins."

Tracking progress plays an important role in rewiring because it affects the ability to find, complete, and comply with the Thin Cognitive Behavior (TCB) protocol. There is no motivation without progress. What has proven to be effective is certain persecution in a way that is important to you.

An image on the front of the refrigerator that shows weekly progress as a number and / or image and / or graph.

Measuring and experiencing the progress during the reroute will make the reroute much more likely. If you're not motivated, you'll never finish rewiring, because nothing prevents you from reaching your next goal, your next improvement. If you don't recognize your progress, you are more likely to give up. Without motivation, there is no progress. It won't end without progress!

"It's often said that motivation doesn't last. Well, neither does bathing, and so we recommend it every day."

Jig Ziggler, Motivational Writer, Speaker.

Step 4 evaluates the effectiveness of the TCB process. Here we measure whether or not the repetition is rewarded. If you suffer from brain hunger, compare this present situational hunger event with its last occurrence. Ask yourself:

Since you have identified hunger as a situation, can you identify the root cause of the misfire? Can you effectively deal with the underlying trigger? That is, how easy and difficult were steps 1 to 3 this time? Are they effortless, natural, fluent, and free of trauma?

The psychological view of progress inevitably shapes and inspires our efforts. In this step, "Experience Success," you will evaluate your progress. It's important to track progress so that everyone can complete the rewiring process. Without indicators, progress cannot be measured. Without measuring progress, the chances of success are low. I am preparing for failure.

The following scale shows my commitment to the rewiring process. This type of scale is important for tracking your progress. In human psychology, we are most likely to give up if we do not experience progress. How a mental process progresses is emotionally different when compared to stagnation. Progress contributes to endurance and builds confidence.

Use the table below if it helps. If it doesn't help, create it yourself.

Difficulty = Emotional experience.

10 = Willingness with white knuckles, stratospheric fear, the tremendous concentration required.

9 = Intense concentration required, extreme fear.

8 = High fear level, difficult concentration still required.

7 = Challenge to fear, Concentration still needed.

6 = Fear level is still increasing, and caution is still needed.

5 = Fear level is still above normal but manageable.

4 = Some fear. However, I'm sure the steps are complete.

3 = Fear is low.

 2 = recognition of fear.

1 = Zero fight.

DON'T BE AFRAID

Due to several issues and the complexity of status triggers, the "measuring progress" in this step is probably not evenly evaluated for each trigger. For example, progress may be easier to understand when you need a break than when you feel an inappropriate feeling.

After using the TCB protocol, I found that my "morning hunger" was caused by my inability to recognize physical limitations. Within a week of the start of the protocol, this type of need for food quickly recognized the need for a break, as the intensity of the "requires a snack" dropped significantly. I was able to change gears, go for a walk, and get back to work without a snack. When I measured my progress in the morning snack area, it went from 9 (requires effort) to 2 (awareness of anxiety).

On the other hand, dealing with loved ones, especially those with a long history of conflict, is like spinning a wheel in the mud, and I have measured zero progress. I was just frustrated and ran in the fridge. I kept trying to use the TCB protocol but couldn't go through step 1 (I know I'm was physically hungry). After realizing that I was stuck, I finally admitted that I needed help in this area.

One of my friends suggested listening positively. It's a communication skill developed by Carl Rogers. This process requires that one person speak and reflect on what they hear before the second person speaks. This exchange is repeated until both people feel what they hear. After using the active hearing process, it took a month before the effort was significantly reduced. It was gradual but eventually reached a low number. I haven't solved all the differences with this person, but now I can interact with them without overeating.

Note that the first type of situation (which requires a break) starvation was to meet personal needs. However, the second type (competition) involves interacting with others. The second type required additional resources (in the form of communication tools) before being comfortable.

For this reason, it is important to distinguish between significant progress and challenges. Little or no progress, this usually means an area where external assistance is needed. Return to an automatic analogy: In most cases, a manual switch will help you get out of the mud. However, if the mud is deep and slippery, you may need a tow truck.

You certainly already know: Naturally lean women have several properties that lead to a healthy relationship with food:

1. They only eat when they are physically hungry.

2. They take time to prepare a healthy meal.

3. They focus on their eating experience and, if possible, eat them silently.

4. If possible, they eat in a nice place.

5. They enjoy the food.

6. They only take a small bite.

7. They often put the dishes down.

8. They slowly and completely chew the food.

9. They breathe consciously before chewing the food.

10. If food loses its taste, they stop eating immediately.

What is the basis of most of these habits? Eat wholeheartedly. I was always intrigued when Naturally Thin Women used this phrase. But what is mindful eating? I wanted to know what they did when they ate carefully. Use four TCB steps to restore these 10 NATURALLY THIN WOMEN'S properties. Let's check them out:

1: Recognize old patterns step

2: interrupt the old pattern step

3: Perform NTW operation steps mindfully and with complete attention

4: Measure progress and experience success

Now we will go through all these properties of naturally thin women in a detailed manner:

RECOGNIZING PHYSICAL HUNGER

STEP 1: IDENTIFY STARVATION FOR THE SITUATION

Five types of triggers instigate current overeating programming. All of them are explained below:

Social Incentives: They eat to avoid feelings of inadequacy or to share a common experience, hoping that it connects them to the others. There is scientific evidence that we eat quite a lot when we eat in a social environment.

Sensual Trigger: Eat for Opportunity, Eat Donuts at Work, Advertise Food for Food on TV, or Pass by the Bakery. I didn't feel the need to nourish my body, but I had the opportunity to experience joy and suddenly felt hungry. In these cases, the desire to eat is an opportunity to experience the learned reaction, a pleasure to external triggers. We weren't hungry until we saw the visual food.

The motivation for thought: Eating as a result of internal dialogue that condemns oneself. We offend ourselves, and ironically, succumbing to overeating usually reprimands us for lack of willpower.

Physiological trigger: Eating in response to a physical effect (e.g., headache or other pain).

Emotional triggers: Eating in response to boredom, stress, fatigue, tension, depression, anger, fear, and loneliness. These triggers are as simple as a lack of cognition in the body (I need a physical break) or as complex as suppressed emotions (I'm a member of a toxic family).

STEP 2: BREAK THE OBSESSION
My brain is crazy about food. I'm hungry and wired to make me feel obsessive about responding to food. This is my current wiring that uses food depending on different situational triggers.

STEP 3: NAME AND ADDRESS YOUR ACTUAL NEEDS

Depending on the situation, you have the option of how to respond effectively to the trigger.

Social Trigger: To fulfill the desire to connect with others, I can try a few small bites and rave about the food. Even better, you can start an exciting conversation about something other than food.

TCB Answer: This is not a pang of physical hunger. This is my desire to adapt to society.

Sensual Trigger: Recognizing my usual reaction to the visual appeal of food. I admit I wasn't hungry before I saw the food. We must admit that this is not physical hunger; it is an automated response to the unexpected.

TCB Answer: This is not a pang of physical hunger. This is my Pavlov's response to a highly charged stimulus. I want to enjoy the pleasure that food presents. If I eat this sweet, I will feel better.

Motivation: Recognizing the usual reaction to negative thoughts, pain, and discomfort. Ending emotional stress is a normal human reaction. I have alternative and meaningful ways to deal with feelings of inadequacy.

TCB Answer: This is not a pang of physical hunger. Eating is a way for me to calm down and how I weaken my painful thoughts. I have the tools or can get the help I need to deal with the painful dialogue inside.

Physiological triggers: There are more effective tools (medication as needed) to deal with physical complaints.

TCB Answer: This is not a pang of physical hunger. This is a learned response to physical illness.

Emotional triggers: You can identify what triggers your emotional hunger and choose to act effectively.

TCB Answer: This is not physical hunger. That is my standard coping mechanism and current wiring.

STEP 4: MEASURE PROGRESS
What about after performing steps 1-3? The scales in the Step 4-Measures of Progress and Experience of Success section help you measure progress as you adopt individual characteristics. The more you practice, the easier it will be.

Is possible for you to respond to each signal in an appropriate manner? If the answer is no, what is your stress level? Need to reduce stress first? What are the wise decisions to meet your actual needs?

TAKE TIME TO PREPARE A HEALTHY MEAL
Home cooking has many advantages because it's a form of mindfulness. You personally choose high quality and nutritious ingredients. Keep in

mind that grocery stores are based on cheap fats and cheap carbohydrates, not your nutritional value. You are controlling where your calories come from: they come from trans fats, additional sugars, well! They ensure that there are no flavor enhancers like MSG or other brain-disrupting substances. As mentioned earlier, the net effect of these addictive substances is that you eat more. Creating a healthy diet is expressing your love for yourself and your family. It's a creative achievement. Save money with this exciting vacation-like activity in Tahiti, Paris, and the Galapagos Islands. You can spend as much time as you want. You can come up with several tricks and shortcuts to save time in the kitchen. It is honest and to recover your cooking skills. It only takes a few hours to revive the master chef inside. While to go somewhere to pick up food. Clarify the facts, go there, park, get food, eat there, or take it home. According to the Center for Disease Control (CDC), cases of more than 76,000,000 people who suffered from food poisoning annually due to bacteria, viruses, and parasites that lead to food contamination.

Think about it; you have to eat carefully. The only area that affects 95% of this possibility is the quality of the food you eat. If you don't know who cooks or exactly what ingredients they use, are they cheap trans-fat oils, lots of extra sodium, extra sugar? How can you manage yourself?

SITTING IN BEAUTY

Establish a simple and beautiful environment, especially if you eat alone. Even if you're hungry, it can take a few minutes to reach an attractive setting. If you don't have the time, are in a hurry, and want to eat directly from the fridge, this is a big sign that you're usually absorbed in foods that are perceived as high levels of anxiety. This may feel irresistible while restoring a naturally lean female neural network. This heals the "hungry brain," so it is important to calm before eating. There are several ways to reduce high levels of anxiety. Deep breathing, meditation, journaling, active jogging, and anything else that seems personally effective in reaching a place of peace. Remember to measure your progress. Can you set up the table without fear? If not, could you be wise to identify the cause of anxiety and address it?

EATING EXPERIENCE

In a culture that emphasizes multitasking, eating is a secondary activity. We do not combine food with the nutrition of our bodies. Eating is what we do without attention while doing more meaningful work.

Have you automatically turned off your car radio while looking for a new address? I instinctively know that removing a voice stimulus increases your ability to focus on finding its address. Silence also allows us to pay attention only to food and to be fully present for a dining experience. Watching TV, interacting with computers, talking on the phone, reading books, and doing other activities is not a supplement to a careful diet. Mindful meals require indiscriminate attention, so it's a great way to overeat.

If you have resistance to silent hoods, rewiring can help you recognize that you ate for the first time when you had another activity. It is a custom that has been cultivated for many years. You rarely eat the main focus.

When you sit quietly and eat, you can hear inner conversations such as how to enjoy the meal and subtle messages from the body when you are satisfied. If turning off competing stimuli creates fear, inhale, and note the cause of the anxiety.

If you are dining with your family, invite them to participate in the careful process of eating. Trying to turn off as many distractions as you can during your meal is better than overeating during multitasking. Discuss your senses and taste of food. Slow food does not have to be extreme. Nevertheless, it is a good idea to remind the family that eating is not a race. Encourage the family to chew on every slice of food, examining the taste, texture, and odor in detail. Ask them about their feelings, thank them for collecting brownie points, and thank them for their blessings and share their meals with their families.

Remember to measure your progress: how do you feel in silence after a meal? Can you eliminate all distractions and eat quietly without fear? Is practicing this property easier to eat silently?

ENJOY YOUR MEAL
Of course, the thin women have an internal dialogue of appreciation and appreciation and joy: "This is delicious. And it saturates. Shoveling food not only misses every bite of taste, but the entertainment center is in place. You'll need more food to meet gourmet merchants because you're not inspired by it.

We acknowledge that this resistance to internal dialogue is the current practice of not attending for the pleasure of eating. Usually, our conversation feeds on something other than our body, so it's more relevant to issues, concerns, and current to-do lists.

If you pay 100% attention to eating and enjoy eating carefully, you will find that the restoration of NATURALLY THIN WOMEN'S wiring is approaching.

Remember to measure your progress. How do you feel after allowing an internal dialogue about the pleasure of eating? Do you enjoy this conversation without fear? If the answer is no, what are the obstacles to achieving this trait?

SMALL BITES
If you overeat food, you will burn more calories and experience the same amount of pleasure. We must recognize that we have made significant

efforts in the past. The wise action is to eat some meals with a small spoon like a wheel while we learn to take smaller bites. However, once you measure progress in this area, it is essential to make the scoop larger. The reason is that if you take a small bite just because the spoon is low, the neural network won't be restored, and you are entirely dependent on the tool.

Don't forget to check for your progress. How does it feel like after eating the whole meal with just a few bites? How was your fear? Did you experience the fun with such a small morsel? Did you have to hit the kitchen and get a more oversized spoon? Or did you just start eating with your fingers?

FORK DOWN
Whatever your fork or tableware is placed in a bite, you are encouraged to eat wholeheartedly. We are ready to enjoy every bite, every bite, every subtlety, every spice, every texture. Eating is foreplay, not a race. It's a sensual experience. Arashi defeats the purpose.

Remember to measure your progress: how do you feel after eating a complete meal and placing a fork in a bite? What is your fear level? Would you like to enjoy the delicacy of food?

CHEW SLOWLY AND THOROUGHLY
For many obsessive eaters, diet represents a solution for drug users. The faster you can move

the shovel, the quicker you can get up. Unfortunately, this behavior leads to total calorie burn and shortens the sensation of pleasure. We try to raise our dopamine levels as soon as possible! We've been doing this for a long time, so biting slowly and slowly can be anxious.

The digestion begins with the first bite, causes the release of saliva, disinfects food, and smooths the way to the stomach. As we bit, the brain releases neurotransmitters that tell the hypothalamus that we are full. Wholly and slowly chewing will remove even the slightest aroma and increase your enjoyment.

Remember to measure your progress. How do you feel after biting slowly? What was your fear? Can you enjoy the slowdown without fear?

BREATHING
After swallowing, breathing three times will reconnect with the body. If you prefer, it is a kind of palate wash. Readjust for the next bite sensual experience. This is also an opportunity to help us determine if we are full.

Remember to measure your progress. Do you breathe three times during one bite with one meal? Did you notice that your anxiety is growing? Did you enjoy your meal?

EXPERIENCE FULLNESS
If you eat it carefully, you'll be full if you lose the taste! By contrast, they are looking for salt,

ketchup, mayo, mustard, sugar, or barbecue sauces as overeaters. It's something you can regain a comfortable experience and "enjoy" your food. Additives are an attempt to nullify the intelligence that tells you that you have enough.

I've certainly heard the advice to wait 20 minutes for your brain to catch up with your ecstasy. But when we eat at piranha speed, we consume a lot of food. We don't know how to wait. Until then, everything was invisible. Besides, our brain isn't too slow! By paying attention to when food loses its initial appeal, we can instantly know when it is full.

Note that the beginning of this process feels strange. After all, we are used to consuming everything on the plate. For many of us, throwing away food is very difficult because our conditioning to eat everything on the plate is rooted. A useful tool is to visualize excess food as fat in your favorite body parts. Your taste will tell him that he is good enough, and all overconsumption turns into fat.

Also, understand that we are accustomed to stomach congestion and no food consumption. Initially, this is done mechanically, but if you repeat this a few times, you get the actual saturation. Besides, regaining confidence in the palate signal feels free, as you no longer need to experience the severity of a clogged sensation after a meal. The energy satisfaction after eating, rather than lethargy or immobility, regains your sense of freedom.

Remember to measure your progress. Can you say "it was great" and "I'm full" without having to stuff myself? Can you recognize the abundance?

In this chapter, we will discuss useful tools for thin cognitive behavior. We will do it for each step, so first let's review what these steps are:

1. Recognizing brain hunger
2. Interrupting obsessive food thoughts
3. Naming and addressing the real need

TOOLS FOR RECOGNIZING BRAIN HUNGER
Detecting brain hunger is the key to the rewiring process. We try to restore this ability when our anxiety level is in the stratosphere, or when we feel the pressure to participate in social ceremonies, or when we do not have access to masquerades where hunger exacerbates the problem. Mindfulness practices give us equality

to physically recognize the body, more easily accept emotions, and protect ourselves from the unhealthy response to social pressures. If we're careful, instead of cutting off the overwhelming wiring depicted as desire (due to uncomfortable social circumstances, peer pressure, or inadequate emotions) and spending powerlessly, you can engage in alternative practices.

Meditation is most commonly referred to as a means of achieving mindfulness and thereby recognizing brain hunger. If the idea of meditation is actively provoking you (and this is understandable for today's modern-day women), try some form of active meditation (such as swimming).

Here are other helpful tips for achieving mindfulness without meditation:

For example, decide whether to return to mindfulness several times during a busy day, move slowly in your life, or be overly aware of your surroundings. An example of how you can become over conscious is to recognize something new every day as you walk through the park you want to walk.

The decisive factor is to be careful, and it just doesn't happen. By developing a Mindful Trigger as described in this chapter, you can remind yourself to lead a conscious life. Remember, we have to be aware of the hunger of the brain, and we need to be aware of physical hunger. The success of repeating TCB steps accelerates and strengthens rewiring! These neural networks are restored when a food panic occurs and can calmly observe what is called brain hunger, and identify emotional needs that need to be addressed. This is an experience where you don't have to worry about it, and you don't overeat.

MINDFULNESS AIDS
Following are some tips that will be helpful to obtain mindfulness:

- **Laugh in Public**-Laughing not only makes you feel better, but it also creates a positive energy exchange when you interact with someone. Name the mood-Running the same activity in different moods will produce different results. Note how mood affects biology? Reconnect with Your Body-Be aware of your body position and how it affects you. Is your body nervous or open and fluid?

- **Return to yourself before being with someone**-Breathe and return to yourself before interacting directly with someone by phone or email. When the phone rings, you need to be careful again. The caller makes you fresh, present, and available.

- **Something old or new-**become aware of something new when you are walking down a frequent path. There can be multiple things you can pay attention to, such as computer keystrokes, birds' chirping, the gentle roar of an airplane above you, or Your footsteps or many more.

- **Pamper the child inside**-it may be as easy as lying in the grass. It may seem silly at first, but don't let others decide your life. Feel the leaves, the breeze, and the sun on your skin. It always brings me back to that moment and gives me a mysterious, childlike feeling that lasts all day.

- **Decide to go slow-**it is the nature that connects us again with the eternity of the moment. At each moment of this consciousness, we return to the title of the world phenomenon of Eckertall, "Power of Now." Torre wakes up his readers for a self-centered life as the creator of suffering and encourages them to live a painless life by living fully in the present. This book is highly recommended for anyone interested in learning the behavior of naturally lean women through the power of mindfulness.

TOOLS FOR INTERRUPTING OBSESSIVE DIETARY THOUGHTS

If you eat too much, you need to develop equality that raises the question of starvation. Step 1 of the Thin Cognitive Behavior protocol is to identify hunger in the brain. If you admit that your hunger is not physical, then step 2 of the protocol is to stop thinking about compulsive diets. Without disturbing the pattern, the obsession with brain hunger becomes stronger when it manifests itself in physiological symptoms. We compared the ability to break obsessive patterns with the mechanism of shifting gears. This is called the caudate of the brain, and if it appears to be stuck, it must be moved manually.

We believe, to some extent, overeating makes us happy and feels good. It's the opposite; they feel embarrassed after most women overeat. By interrupting the pattern, we stop the growth of food thinking strength and begin moving brain hunger out of the compulsion spectrum. Two techniques that we consider to be accessible and effective to prevent obsession with food Eye Movement Desensitization and Reprocessing (EMDR) and emotional freedom techniques (EFT). Both techniques are equally effective in stopping food obsession before a compulsive diet.

- **EDMR- EYE MOVEMENT DESENSITIZATION AND REPROCESSING**
The EMDR explains that our eye movements are inextricably linked to brain processes. Remembering how delicious this la-carte cake was, your eyes will automatically look up to the left. Given how good it tastes, we look down and look down on the right side. The image below shows how your eyes move to the left when you remember the food, and to the right when you fancy food. The eyes move up, sideways, or down, depending on whether you are fantasizing, listening, or remembering.

The importance of EMDR to our toolbox is that if you're daydreaming about food (looking down from the bottom to the right), you can quickly interrupt your pattern in all directions until your desires stop. EMDR is a simple, light, and effective tool that requires focused eye movements within 30 seconds to keep the brain from sticking to food. This interruption mechanism allows us to stop the typical abduction that occurs when the attraction of food imagination attracts us.

- **EFT- EMOTIONAL FREEDOM TECHNIQUE**
  Emotional Freedom Technique (EFT) is another tool that is useful when a pattern break. The acupuncture points used in EFT are listed below and were identified as the end of the meridian in the body centuries before China. When pressure is applied to these points, we shift the energy in our bodies. The EFT process quickly opens these acupoints until the emotional energy changes.

First, ask yourself on a scale of 1-10. One is none; ten is overwhelming how strongly you experience emotional hunger. Let's say you are ten years old. Repeat the following setup statement three times while tapping the left-hand karate intersection. I'm overwhelmingly emotionally hungry, but I accept myself deeply and completely. EFT only works if you believe the setup instructions. If you say the statement out loud and you feel it is not true, you need to modify the statement to fit your beliefs. For example, you can change the setup statement as follows: I'm overwhelmingly emotionally hungry, but I think practicing can change the auto attendant. Focus on your feelings and accept them sincerely. Complete the knock sequence, take a deep breath, and ask yourself.

Has your emotional hunger subsided? If you're still feeling emotional hunger, go back and update your writing to your current level of obsession. For example, if it changes from overwhelming to moderate, change the statement to Repeat the beating process until emotional hunger is gone. EFT alone does not restore the neural network, but it helps to escape the obsessive-compulsive illusion that fuels overeating. EFT does not restore the NATURALLY THIN WOMEN'S neural network, but staying within the metaphor keeps the car away from the hills, which are more likely to prevent damage.

Following are the acupressure points which work for interruption of food obsession:

1. The inner side of eyebrow near the nose
2. Karate chop
3. Side of eye
4. Collar bone
5. Under the nose
6. On the chin
7. Crown of the head
8. Under the eye – on the cheekbone

- **NLP-NEURO-LINGUISTIC PROGRAMMING**

Anchors are the mental connection between stimulation and reaction. When the stimulus occurs, the reaction from the subconscious mind is automatically invoked. The brain has several anchors. For example, if you experience certain emotions while listening to a song, listening to the same song again will automatically revert those emotions. The advertising industry often uses anchors by creating incentives in food commercials that trigger contextual starvation reactions.

You can develop your anchor by consistently linking selected stimuli to specific emotions. Pressure points are usually set as anchors somewhere on the body. Anchors are compressed when they experience an unwanted sensation. Let's say you want to return to your peace of mind each time you press your left middle finger. Each time you experience peace of mind, you make an anchor by pressing your left middle finger until it becomes an anchor. When the anchor is firmly fixed, and you return to the tornado, press your left middle finger to return to your eyes. A possible scenario would be: You have a very stressful working day. There is no evidence of physical hunger, but it is currently wired to produce stress hormones in difficult, demanding, or hyperbaric situations. Your stress reaction is the feeling of overwhelming emotional hunger that takes you directly to the machine. If you hold your left middle finger at this point, you can feel peace of mind. Inner peace and overeating are mutually exclusive.

So resting and regaining balance can handle anything that needs attention. Anchoring is an effective tool to stop the unconscious and automatic hyperphagic response to many of the triggers that currently govern our behavior.

Many products try to serve the same purpose. They can serve as a springboard for greater progress. However, these products should be used as tools or auxiliary wheels. When these tools are used beyond their intended purpose, NATURALLY THIN WOMEN'S neural network restoration is not supported. If you need a product to get started, you can use it. Keep in mind that auxiliary wheels need to come off at some point so that everyone can learn how to ride a bike.

TOOLS FOR IDENTIFYING ACTUAL NEEDS AND RESPONDING TO WHAT NEEDS ATTENTION

Step 3 consists of two parts. Part 1 is the ability to identify needs that manifest as hunger in the brain. There are many causes for non-physical hunger: social situations (social hunger) that you think you need to eat to adapt, or if you feel socially uncomfortable and believe that overeating makes you feel good. If this can also be caused by an emotional imbalance (emotional hunger), we can't name it, deal with it, or develop it to calm ourselves. As your mindfulness develops, you will have more time to succumb to brain hunger as you better understand the causes of your brain cravings and take on the personal need for self-advocacy. Until the day overeating is history.

Part 2 of Step 3 is a feature that addresses all the needs of hunger. Once you have identified what needs your attention, you can develop skills that meet your needs rather than curb your needs. If we eat or eat too much, we continue the cycle of shame. By having the courage to name and address the underlying needs, we are strengthening a healthy neural network. So, most of it starts with emotions. Following are ways to recognize some of the emotions:

• **Blues**

Low energy with no signs of physical hunger. In most cases, your dopamine levels are low. Moderately intense physical routine and / or meditation can increase dopamine levels to a considerable limit. In chapter 19 of this book, meditation practice with a helpful suggestion is explained.

• **Boring**

Remember that boredom is a form of self-rejection. It's important to work on one of your dream projects, the diary, the vision board, reconnect, and re-invest in one of your life's challenges. If you don't know what your interest is, promise to discover it from now on. There are thousands of resources and workbooks to help you with this search. Shift your energy towards this discovery process. This will take your attention and interest away from thoughts of food.

- **Disappointed**

Express your disappointment clearly and loudly! Call friends, diary, scream! You do not need to stuff yourself with negative thoughts. You should share your insecurities and disappointments with the relevant people. Otherwise, they will lead to emotional imbalance and eventually to overeating.

- **Tired**

If you overeat due to chronic sleep deprivation, investing in sleep hygiene best helps your ability to rewire your brain. Meditation is the number one recommendation for improving sleep quality as it calms the monkey. Start the "shutdown cycle" one hour before going to bed. Soothing music, low testosterone levels movies, soothing baths, sensual pajamas, dim light, no computer time, fewer excitement books, in short, a loss that increases the excitement.

- **Loneliness**

If you are feeling lonely, you may call a friend. Go outside, meet someone. Do something good to someone, even strangers. Go to the hospice or children's crisis management center to help. The urge for food will subside, as the actual problem is mitigated.

- **Anger**

If the problem is chronic, seek treatment from a specialist with anger expertise. If you are occasionally angry, make a loud voice, hit your bag, or walk while expressing anger. You may try to calm yourself by doing meditation or sleeping for some time.

- **Stress Accumulated**

Work out or perform intense exercise. -Scaling down to get the point of view, you have two options: indulge in worst-case thoughts (and increase stress and anxiety) or have the option to let go of your black and white thoughts. Observe meditation for the relief of stress.

- **Lost Control**

Face your worst fear of what loss of control means to you in a general sense. -Are you likely to concentrate on the worst scenario, the black and white way of thinking? -Do you need control?

-What are you afraid of failing if you have no control?

If you don't know what you are doing, do a breathing exercise, reconnect to your body, and continue to ask quietly. What do I feel? What is my energy level? "Important changes are exercise, meditation, using your favorite music, keeping a diary of your emotions, or taking a cold shower. It's something you can do immediately rather than unknowingly eat, and that's not a problem as long as you know it helps you pay attention to your real needs. Be prepared to repeat as many times as you need. If, for some reason, you're limited and can't perform an alternate activity, imagine doing it carefully and in stages.

Reprogramming the subconscious mind during sleep is a very effective method that can be used to make positive changes in our lives and reveal goals. There are various tools you can use to get some sleep time.

As we grow older, it makes sense that our lives get busier. Many people recognize that the mind is as important as the rest of us, and that programming it well is also important.

How can we change, how we see things, our feelings for a particular idea, and how we carry ourselves? It is only natural that our subconsciousness is a powerful force in us because we all have a subconscious mind that remembers everything and preserves our beliefs and feelings. It acquires a specific pattern at a very young age and consequently forms most of the habits that we do most of the time unconsciously.

Many people may want to change some part of their lives, but they don't necessarily want to use their work or effort, but others don't know where to start. The truth is that you have to reprogram your subconscious to see the change. One way to do this is to reprogram the subconscious during sleep. Since we live a hustle life, it's much more effective to do this when we're asleep than when we're awake, because it's easy to be distracting.

Few people know that the subconscious never sleeps or stops. It always works, paying attention to and taking in everything that is happening, even when we are asleep. You can reprogram virtually anything by yourself. Some things you can improve with sleep include improving self-confidence, improving relationships, learning to love yourself, and promoting a business career.

Overall, reprogramming the subconscious requires replacing old restrictive beliefs and bad habits with new positive beliefs. Our subconscious is programmed between 1 and 7 years.

This means that many of us have retained our unhelpful negative beliefs and bad habits since we were young. In these times, our beliefs depend heavily on our parents, the way we set up our homes, and the people around us. As we grow older, we discover more and more to become better people and reach our goals. It's harder to move forward if we still have past threads to solve now because we have different ages, different mindsets, different lifestyles.

Now that we know how important it is to reprogram the subconscious, an effective way to do this during sleep is to speak to yourself using assertions. Before going to bed at night, you need to be positive and strong about what you are working on and what you want to do to change your life.

Confirmation is more powerful when expressed in the present as if they were already true. Do not use future assertions as if they happened or should have happened. For example, if your goal is to build muscle and your body has recently become non-muscle, this is "I'm healthy and strong, I have big muscles throughout my body, and It's a strong and positive affirmation like "I like the feel," as strong an affirmation of the nation. If you listen to yourself with a positive and strong assertion before going to bed each night, you are more likely to dream of how to reach your goals. This is one of the ways our subconscious mind speaks to us.

The University of San Diego has proven that reprogramming the subconscious mind during sleep is more effective than hypnosis. Many recruits use this technique to assist in training. A very powerful technique is to say yes at bedtime. My eyes begin to close, and I feel sleepy. Immediately before going to sleep, you are in a theta mental state, where suggestions and confirmations easily occur unknowingly. Imagine what you could do with it every night before bed!

149

The second way to reprogram the subconscious mind during sleep is to hear a positive stimulating voice. You can use the pre-recorded audio that you have verified, or you can create your own audio. Share your affirmation with your recording device and play it automatically overnight. In addition to affirmations, you can record and tell the specific scene you want and hear it during your sleep. You can do this while sleeping or before bed, as your subconscious mind is awake and recording everything.

The subconscious mind is always functional, so listening to audio while sleeping is the same as listening to it while you are awake. Many think that they can't remember or hear, but the subconscious has already learned and heard, whether or not they are conscious. The next day you feel more vibrant, positive, and open, and suddenly you are full of ideas. This is evidence that the subconscious has absorbed audio information during rest.

The subconscious mind controls about 90-95% of our actions. This proves to us that our subconscious mind is ours today and plays a major role in the way we present ourselves to the world. The sooner you realize that the mind is as important as our body, the more you can rule your life and prevent it from controlling you.

In this chapter, we will learn about weight loss affirmations. Weight loss affirmations are a great way to stimulate your journey to weight loss. You can use these positive weight loss affirmations to program your mind with positive habits.

We all know that weight loss is not easy. The use of these weight loss affirmations can help people facing stubborn internal resistance when trying to lose weight.

These are the affirmations that you can suggest yourself while practicing self-hypnosis, cognitive-behavioral theory, or Sleep learning system. In the first two methods, these affirmations can directly be suggested, and in the third method, you can record these and listen to them while sleeping.

You must be careful while choosing theses affirmations. It is suggested that you should select the affirmations that you believe yourself and do not raise an objection when they are suggested to you. The failure happens because if you do not believe yourself, then it will not work for you. Moreover, it is suggested that you use a few affirmations that you think are effective for you. Do not try to suggest all at once. It may retard the effectiveness of the methods. There are also chances that the brain may become confused in case of any two opposite affirmations. So, better select your affirmations very carefully.

Now we will list the affirmations for excessive weight loss:

• Weight loss makes sense to me.

• I want to reach the goal of weight loss.

• I lose weight every day.

• I love to exercise regularly.

• I eat foods that contribute to my health and well-being.

• I only eat when I am hungry.

• I can see myself clearly with my ideal weight.

• I love the taste of healthy food.

• I can control how much I want to eat.

- I like training. I feel better.

- Through exercise, I will be stronger and stronger every day.

- I can reach the ideal weight and maintain it.

- I love and care for my body.

- I deserve a slim, healthy, and attractive body.

- I always have a healthier eating habit.

- I lose weight every day.

- It looks good and feels good.

- I can do what it takes to be healthy.

- I am happy to redefine success.

- I decided to train.

- I want to eat food that looks and feels good.

- I am responsible for my health.

- I love my body.

- I put up with building a better body for myself.

- When I wake up, I have a great time doing exercise every morning to achieve my desired weight loss.

- I am working on a weight loss program by changing my diet from unhealthy to healthy.

- I am happy with everything I do to lose weight.

- I get thinner and healthier every day.

• I am developing an attractive body.

• I develop a lifestyle with life health.

• I can create a body that I will like and enjoy.

These were general affirmations that you can use in a normal condition. You can move to more specific affirmations later, when you feel that now it is time to modify my practice. Some of these affirmations are given below that will help you cope up with weight gain with a more specific approach.

• Discovering my unique diet and exercise system for weight loss is exciting.

• I accept and enjoy my sexuality. You can feel it sensually.

• I am a beautiful person.

• I am a lovable person. I deserve love. It is safe for me to lose weight.

• I am a weight loss success story.

• I am happy to lose 20 pounds.

• I am ready to develop new ideas about myself and my body.

• I choose to trust the ability to make positive changes in my life.

• I congratulate myself on choosing the right food.

• I drink eight glasses of water daily.

• I eat fruits and vegetables every day, mainly chicken and fish.

• I enjoy walking 3-4 times a week and have at least three toning exercised a week.

• I free the need to criticize my body.

• I have a strong weight in the world due to my low weight.

• I learn and use mental, emotional, and spiritual skills for success. Ready to change!

• I love and appreciate my body.

• I will take care of my body in optimal health.

• I'm happy that I have the ideal weight.

• It feels good to move your body. The practice is fun!

• It feels great to have lost more than £ 10 in 4 weeks and can't wait to meet my girlfriend.

• It's easy to follow a healthy diet plan.

• My lifestyle changes my body.

• My metabolism is excellent.

• My stomach is flat.

• Take a deep breath to relax and deal with stress.

• My efforts are worth reaching the ideal weight.

You can make your own affirmation to that suit your routine and efforts. These affirmations in a normal routine or combined with methods that we discussed in this e-book can help reduce the weight quickly without affecting the emotional health.

CHAPTER 19: MEDITATION FOR WEIGHT LOSS

Meditation is a daily exercise, where you clear your mind and return to a place of calm thought and emotion. Some people only practice 5 minutes a day, but most meditation specialists recommend working up to 20 minutes a day.

Meditation is not difficult. If you're just getting started, immediately wake up and spend 5 minutes to cleanse your mind before a busy day. Close your eyes and concentrate without trying to change your breathing pattern. Just focus on your breathing. If your mind wanders and it's probably the first-just put it back into your breath without judgment.

Libshtein recommends practice 10 minutes a day (5 minutes in the morning, 5 minutes in the evening) but finds that "time is not as important as just doing it regularly." Developing new habits can be difficult. So, if you start with 5 minutes a day, that's fine. If you find it most comfortable for you, feel free to sit and lie down.

"Meditation is an effective way to help people lose weight," Libshtein says. What made meditation so powerful in this regard? "Agreeing to the changes we want to apply to our behavior reconciles consciousness and unconsciousness," he explains. These changes include controlling cravings for unhealthy foods and changing diets. It is important to include the subconscious. The reason is that the harmful and weight gaining behaviors, such as emotional eating, are fixed. Meditation can help to recognize it and nullify it in some exercises, and even replace it with a slimming habit.

But meditation will soon pay off. "Meditation can directly reduce stress hormone levels," explains Libshtein. Stress hormones such as cortisol signal our bodies to store calories as fat. If large amounts of cortisol are pumped through your system, it will be difficult to lose even if you make a healthy decision. That seems difficult. We are all stressed, and it seems impossible to shake. However, a study by Carnegie Mellon University found that 25 minutes of meditation for three consecutive days was required to significantly reduce stress.

According to Yi-Yuan Tang, the chair of the neuroscience funded by the president and a professor of psychology at the Texas Institute of Technology. Research shows that self-control may also increase with daily practice. Researchers have found that the parts of the brain most affected by meditation help control ourselves. So, by meditating for a few minutes a day, you can easily pass this second cookie and avoid ice if you feel unwell.

How can meditation help you when dieting and exercising go wrong?

"Stress is often the main cause of excessive weight gain or inability to lose weight effectively," explains Libstein. So, if you're on a diet or exercise and you're constantly stressed, you may not be solving your weight problems. Again, stress releases hormones that store additional fat; that's exactly the thing we don't want! It can also trigger a stress cycle. You cannot lose weight because you are under stress, and you feel stress because you cannot lose weight. It's an easy pattern to get stuck, but you can break it-and meditation can help.

To successfully manage or relieve stress, you first need to understand what causes most of your stress in life. Some stressors are easy to identify, while others are subtle. "I recommend using WellBe to understand, monitor, and address stress," says Libshtein. The WellBe is a bracelet that acts as a physical activity tracker but is the first of its kind to focus on emotional well-being instead.

If you want to add meditation to your weight loss weapon, it's important not to stress it. Meditation is designed to help relieve stress and does not cause stress. For this reason, we asked Libhstein for three easy ways to incorporate calm habits into our daily lives without feeling this is an additional obligation or task. Of course, practicing meditation and spending a few minutes each day will give you the best results.

You can create a mantra to focus on your goals. A mantra is a word or phrase that focuses on your practice and repeats to bring you back to the center when you are wandering. As Libshtein explains, "Mantras can give you something to focus on during meditation." Many find it useful in practice, but especially what you appeal to. If you choose, it is not necessary. If it feels natural or useless, you don't have to force yourself to use it. If you choose either, Libshtein recommends repeating as you inhale and exhale. Common choices are "I am loved," "I am peaceful," and "Om." If the mantra doesn't feel right to you, Libshtein tells you to focus on your breathing.

"Try to use four counts for inhalation and eight counts for exhalation," Libshtein suggests. But meditation is to reduce stress. If these counts feel tense or unnatural, you can deviate from them. Try increasing the number each time you meditate. "Don't worry if you need time to perform up to eight counts," says Libshtein. "We only know that stretching your breath can calm you down considerably."

There are many records, podcasts, websites, and phone apps that connect you to an expert who can guide you in meditation exercises until you feel alone. The Libshtein website, Mentors Channel, is just one example of such a service.

Look for guided meditations that focus on it, especially if you want to use meditation for weight loss. Video or audio recording professionals will ask you to imagine various things: how they look and feel after losing weight, the moving person who has already lost weight, and what they can think and feel? What they are likely to do to succeed in losing weight and losing weight, and how these habits can be integrated into their daily lives.

Meditation is just one of the entire weight loss toolkits. Diet and exercise are also important parts of the equation, and combining all three to create a long-lasting lifestyle always yields the best results. The key to meditation, such as eating and exercising, is dedication. You need to stick to practice to witness the permanent changes. "Research shows that meditation alters the structure of the brain after long practice, for example immediately after 21 days," says Libshtein. That's why the Mentors Channel offers a 21-day program. This program allows you to see permanent changes.

Preparing for success will make it easier for you to begin your meditation routine. Creating a calm meditation room, including meditation equipment, can facilitate your practice.

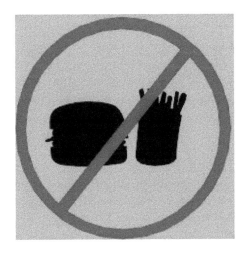

One of the main mistakes in weight loss strategies is to avoid or minimize the entire food category (fat, carbohydrates, sugar, etc.). Finally, what we understand is that classifying foods as forbidden, instigates the brain to an obsession with more of such foods. We now understand that withdrawing all categories of food to establish healthy eating behavior is counterproductive. The reason is simple. As long as we believe these foods are "banned," they retain high emotional values for us, as well as the power of illegal love arouses to crave such foods even more.

Marking these foods as banned is harmful as it creates an effect called the Polar bear effect, and the person cannot resist always thinking about the forbidden food items. Humans crave something prohibited, for it is a part of human nature. Researchers call this the "forbidden fruit hypothesis." At the moment we experience the exhaustion of our ego, we encounter these uncontrollable "forbidden fruit hypothesis" when there are difficult days when we need to feel at ease and comfort like a moth of light. This feeling explains the frenzy and frustration when we eat these foods after the suppression mechanism is exhausted.

Cognitive studies have shown that exposure to food triggers and prevention of reactions is a very effective technique for rewiring the brain. If you learn to not force yourself to eat, you must reintroduce "Forbidden Foods" and eliminate the illusion of food.

When we can trust that we can eat with all our hearts, eating what we want is paramount. Then miracles will occur! We choose to eat nutritious, cheerful foods, and when we eat "forbidden foods," we do not overeat them anymore. Therefore, the solution is to use the TCB protocol to control mindful eating. If you have the evidence that your mindfulness connections are well-developed and you can be convinced that you can eat those foods in a normal limit. Even if they are initially mechanistic, until these fascinating powers disappear, it is important to include prohibited foods in your menu.

A person banned having nachos and ice cream at home while he had a pointless meal. But after a particularly rewarding day in the office, he usually stopped by a supermarket and, as you might imagine, bought a bag of nacho chips and some ice cream tubs. Then he overdosed these forbidden foods. The moment the attack ended, he hit himself. The next day, he gave his friend the rest of the ice cream and nacho chips. This act is a performance that has been repeated over and over again in his life.

After understanding the effects of ego depletion concerning the forbidden fruit hypothesis, his story of oppression, and finally biting makes sense. Next, his goal was to plan a meal with Nachos as the main event. He made a nacho supreme, ordered a nacho platter at a restaurant, and devised my own nachos recipe with healthy toppings. A week after the Nacho Festival, the bag of tortilla chips was able to stand in the kitchen without fear or difficulty. The forbidden food technique is out of date and must be discarded now. You have now mysterious power up your sleeves.

Whenever we see a naturally thin woman claiming that she can eat whatever she wants, we think that how is that even possible. The answer is, although they do not ban food for them, but they do not overeat them. Their mind produces enough dopamine with minor amounts of such foods. So, to conclude, we need to know that there is no need for banning food categories anymore. Let not your dopamine level exhaust over such small things. Change your wiring and eat all you want, while staying in control.

Food for all!

CONCLUSION

This book is a blend of all the effective techniques to help people who are suffering from excessive weight gain. It presents a different dimension of how the key to weight loss lies in your brain. It covers the techniques of self-hypnosis, Cognitive behavioral therapy (CBT), Sleep Learning, and Meditation. All of these techniques involve the active involvement of the brain and change in the wiring pattern of the brain to raise a satisfactory level of the brain to stop the urges of overeating. The book contains a detailed account of all the activities, processes, and requirements to make all these techniques work out for you in a healthy manner.

This book serves multiple purposes. It not only guides about weight loss techniques but also the root causes of the other emotional problems that promote overeating. This book serves as a complete guide to a fatless, healthy, happy, and satisfactory lifestyle.

INTERMITTENT FASTING BIBLE FOR WOMEN OVER 50

The Weight Loss Solution to Increase Longevity & Energy, Slow Aging with Self-Cleansing Program, Autophagy and Metabolic Reset, Enjoying Dietary Habits

By

Karen Loss

172

TABLE OF CONTENTS

COPYRIGHTS.. 177

CHAPTER 1: INTRODUCTION................. 179

> INTERMITTENT FASTING IS BASED ON YEARS OF RESEARCH.......... 181

> FASTING AND REPAIR GENES ... 182

> SOME FACTS ABOUT FASTING ... 183

> WHAT IS INTERMITTENT FASTING 185

CHAPTER 2: TYPES OF FASTING............ 192

> SPIRITUAL FASTING 192

> MEDICAL FASTING 194

> FASTING SCIENCE...................... 194

> FIVE INTERMITTENT FASTING VARIANTS 195

> SO, WHAT ARE THE STEPS?....... 203

CHAPTER 3: BENEFITS OF FASTING 207

> PHYSIOLOGICAL BENEFITS....... 209

> PHYSICAL BENEFITS 215

> FASTING GUIDELINES............... 217

> CAN FASTING MAKE YOU SMARTER? 220

CHAPTER 4: REASON FOR STARTING 224

> BAND HISTORY 231

> INTERMITTENT FASTING AND DIET 232

CHAPTER 5: THE CHALLENGE OF INTERMITTENT FASTING........................ 235

➤ **HAVE FUN**..................................... 236

➤ **JUNK FOOD** 237

➤ **MENTAL FRAMEWORK** 237

➤ **LEVEL 1 BREATHE NATURALLY** .. 238

➤ **LEVEL 2 CONTROLLED BREATHING** 239

➤ **LEVEL 3 VISUALIZE DISTRACTIONS** 240

CHAPTER 6: INTERMITTENT FASTING: MY JOURNEY.. 243

➤ **GET ON THE SCALES** 244

➤ **BODY FAT** 245

➤ **BLOOD TEST** 245

➤ **FASTING AND MOOD** 246

➤ **FASTING AND THE HEART** 248

➤ **INSULIN - THE FAT-PRODUCING HORMONE** 249

➤ **FASTING AND CANCER** 251

CHAPTER 7: WHEN WILL YOU START?... 254

➤ **FLEXIBILITY: THE KEY TO SUCCESS** 260

➤ **HOW YOUR ANATOMY CHANGES?** 261

➤ **FEMALE SPEED: MIMI'S EXPERIENCE**.............................. 263

➢ **12 WAYS TO MAKE A FAST DIET EFFECTIVE**................................. **265**

➢ **FASTING AND FUSSING**............. **271**

➢ **CHOOSE THE RIGHT MEAL**......... **272**

➢ **INGREDIENTS FOR HEALTHY FAST FOOD**.. **272**

➢ **FASTING FUTURE: WHERE TO GO FROM HERE?** **273**

CHAPTER 8: FAST DAY COOKING TIPS .. 277

➢ **TIPS FOR A FAST DAY COOKING 277**

➢ **TASTE AND INTERMITTENT FASTING** **280**

➢ **FOOD TO RETHINK** **283**

➢ **HOW TO CHOOSE ZERO-DAY?**.... **284**

➢ **DAILY SWITCHING**..................... **287**

➢ **DAILY STRATEGY** **288**

➢ **WHAT TO EAT?** **289**

➢ **DO YOU HAVE A HEADACHE?**..... **295**

➢ **HOWEVER, DO I SLEEP HUNGRY?** **296**

CHAPTER 9: SHOULD YOU FAST?........... **300**

➢ **LISTEN TO YOUR BODY** **300**

➢ **FASTING AND DIABETES** **301**

➢ **GET DOCTOR APPROVAL**........... **301**

➢ **MANAGE CHRONIC ILLNESSES .. 302**

➢ **PREPARE FOR FASTING**............. **303**

➢ **STARTING YOGA** **303**

➢ **MAKE FASTING EASY**................ **304**

CONCLUSION 307

COPYRIGHTS..310

with the written permission of the publisher and all liberties authorized.

The information provided here is correct and reliable, as any lack of attention or other means resulting from the misuse or use of the procedures or instructions contained therein is the total and absolute obligation of the user addressed.

The author is not obliged, directly or indirectly, to assume civil liability for any restoration, damage, or loss resulting from the data collected here. The respective authors retain all copyrights not kept by the publisher.

The information contained herein is solely and universally available for information purposes. The data is presented without a warranty or promise of any kind.

The trademarks used are without approval, and the patent is issued without the trademark owner's permission or protection.

The logos and labels in this book are the property of the owners themselves and are not associated with this text.

CHAPTER 1: INTRODUCTION

Eating habits have disappeared in recent decades, but the usual medical advice for a healthy lifestyle remains the same: eat low-fat foods, get more exercise than skipping meals. Over the same period, obesity skyrocketed worldwide. So, is there another evidence-based approach that depends on science, not opinion? When we first read the supposed benefits of intermittent fasting, we were as skeptical as others. Fasting appeared intense and challenging. We knew that diets were usually doomed to failure, although both were described. But we did thorough research and tested it ourselves, so we are convinced of its tremendous potential. One of the doctors interviewed for this book said, "Do nothing to your body that is as strong as fasting."

Fasting: old ideas, modern methods. Fasting is not new. Your body is designed to fast, as you will learn in the next chapter.

It was developed at a time when there was a shortage of food. We have been the product of festivals and famines for thousands of years. The reason we respond so well to intermittent fasting is that it mimics the environment in which modern humans train much more closely than three meals a day. Of course, fasting is a product of faith for many. Lent, Yom Kippur, and Ramadan are just a few of the most common examples. Greek Orthodox Christians are advised to fast 180 days a year (according to Saint Nicholas of Zicha, an overabundance makes a dark and anxious man, but a fast makes him happy and brave), Buddhist monks fast every month on the moon. But many of us seem to be eating most of the time. We are rarely hungry. But we are not satisfied. Our weight, our body, and our health. Intermittent fasting can bring us back into contact with humans. It is not only for weight loss but also for long-term health and well-being. Scientists are just beginning to discover and demonstrate the power of a tool. This book is the result of his cutting-edge research and his impact on current thinking on weight loss, disease resistance, and longevity.

But it is also the result of our personal experience. Here, we study intermittent fasting from two complementary angles, because the laboratory and the lifestyle are relevant. First, using physical and medical training to test his potential, Michael explained the science behind intermittent fasting and the 5: 2 diets, and caught the world's eye last summer. The context and history of the fast made it possible to understand the process.

INTERMITTENT FASTING IS BASED ON YEARS OF RESEARCH

Animal fasting research dates back 80 years. Research on human fasting goes back at least six years. More and more clinical studies are underway for research.

In an early 1945 study, mice were fasted for four days, one day, three days, or two days. Researchers have found that fasted mice live longer. They also found that fasted mice were not physically stunted, unlike calorie-depleted mice. Since then, at least in rodents, the value of fasting has been confirmed in numerous studies. But why is fasting useful? What is the mechanism?

Valter has access to his supply of transgenic mice called dwarf or Laron mice. These mice, although small, hold records of the extended lifespan of mammals. In other words, they have lived surprisingly long. The average mouse has a modest lifespan, probably two years. Laron mice last twice as long, and many have a calorie restriction for more than four years. In humans, this equates to almost 170 years. What makes the Laron mouse attractive is the fact that it not only has a long lifespan, but it also keeps most of its life very long through opting the intermittent fastings. They just seem less prone to diabetes and cancer, which is a natural cause when they die. Valter told me that autopsy often fails to find the cause of death. They just seem dead.

FASTING AND REPAIR GENES

Not only does it reduce the circulating levels of IGF-1, but it also activates many repair genes during fasting. The reason for this is not fully understood, but the evolutionary argument goes that way. As long as we have enough to eat, our body is primarily interested in growing, having sex and reproducing. Nature has no long-term plans for us. It does not invest in our age. If it is produced, it is disposable. So, what happens if you decide to fast? Well, the body's first reaction is shocking. A signal is sent to your brain to remind you that you are hungry and to encourage you to go out and get something to eat. But you resist. The body determines that you are now in starvation because you are not eating as often you usually would. In the past, this was very normal.

In a famine situation, there is no point in spending energy on growth and sex. Instead, the wisest thing your body can do is spend its precious energy storage on repairs and keep you rational until the good times come back. As a result, not only you are taking your foot off the gas, but your body is being pulled into the cell's equivalent of the garage. There, all the small genetic mechanics are ordered to start some of the urgent maintenance tasks that have been postponed. For example, calorie restriction involves the activation of a process called autophagy. Autophagy means "eating yourself," a process in which the body breaks down and recycles old and tired cells. As with a car, it is essential to remove damaged or aged parts to maintain proper functioning.

There are blather believes that people with a BMI above 25 will benefit from fasting only if they plan to fast more than a day. The research supports the argument that, although, the prolonged fasting is an unnecessary intervention, however, if done right, it can be mighty in your favor. If it is done wrong, the extended fasting for a few days may cause a drop in blood pressure and a relatively deep metabolic reprogramming. Some people become faint. It is uncommon.

SOME FACTS ABOUT FASTING

2. HUNGER MODE

Studies that demonstrated the adverse effects of fasting were done in the 1950s. In this study, they took several young men and asked them to live on about half their regular calories. They tracked for six months, apparently losing weight dramatically. There was a severe problem when her body fat dropped to 5%. Well, it is radically fast for a long time. There was no excellent structure in this attempt, and weight loss was completed too early. It has led to adverse health problems. Intermittent fasting is not like that.

3. MEDICAL DISCOVERY OFTEN BEGINS WITH SELF-EXPERIMENT

Until you try it, you are not sure how fasting can help. Everyone is different, everyone is unique, and it is essential to monitor it. What works for others cannot work for you. If your fasts do not work, try another one.

4. INTERMITTENT FASTING HELPS REDUCE FAT, NOT MUSCLE

Fasting speeds up your metabolism, resets your digestive system, and activates your metabolism.

Fasting promotes longevity - studies have shown how the lives of people in certain cultures have improved as a result of their diet.

Fasting improves hunger - it takes 12 to 24 hours to feel the real need. You will notice this when you are fasting.

Fasting improves your brain function - because it increases the production of a protein called the Brain-Derived Neurotrophic Factor (BDNF).

Fasting improves your immune system - because it reduces free radical damage, regulates inflammation in the body, and stops cancer cells from forming. When you are sick, your instinct is to focus on resting rather than eating.

Fasting helps to clean the skin and prevent acne. It is because the temporarily undigested body can concentrate its regenerative energy on other systems.

HOW SHOULD IT BE?

Let us dive into the "heart of the problem" by providing you with some idea of why and how intermittent fasting should be considered. Intermittent fasting allows you to structure and work towards your aspirations; for example, weight loss, we find that fewer calories consumed are correlated with weight loss. During the period of your fast, the calorie intake is significantly reduced because of the time window for eating has also decreased. The phenomenon encourages better adaptability to insulin secretion of the growth hormone, two essential components for losing weight and muscle profit. This practice will not only help you lose weight but also maintain your weight, which is the path to your goal. During the process, you will notice how everything comes into perspective. You will realize that not only your weight loss goal is achieved, but your other goals as well, by seeing how your daily tasks and behaviors become simpler. The process eliminates the need for food preparations (what, when, and where to eat). Which could inevitably save you more of your reduced diet?! Now you have time to focus on other activities instead of contemplating at three or more meals a day; the 16/8 method only requires preparing two meals. This method now allows you to enjoy larger portions of your time. You are causing the stomach and taste buds to fill up while consuming simultaneously fewer calories.

WHAT IS INTERMITTENT FASTING?

Fasting means to abstain from food, and sometimes even drinks, for a certain period. Intermittent fasting, however, is a different phenomenon, but one that is drawn from the concept of fasting. It is an eating pattern that involves alternating between regular intervals of eating and fasting. Hence the name intermittent. The period of fasting can vary based on your preferences, and it can be as short as skipping a meal to extended as going without food for several days. During this fasting period, you are allowed to consume drinks such as coffee, tea, water, and other beverages, although alcoholic drinks are frowned upon. The fasting is then followed by a period of eating, where you can eat any type of food you prefer. Intermittent fasting and fasting, in general, should not be confused with starvation, which is the involuntary absence of food. With fasting, the food is present and readily available, but you just choose not to consume it for one reason or another.

Fasting is not a new concept, but one that is as old as time itself. Human beings have been fasting for thousands of years due to a myriad of reasons. Sometimes, fasting was done out of necessity due to a lack of food. Other times, it was due to religious reasons, with many, if not all, religions observing some form of fast. Intermittent fasting (IF) is now one of the most amazing health and lifestyle in the world. People use it to lose weight, improve their lifestyle, and simplify their routine. Many studies have shown that it can have a significant effect on your physical and mental health and can help you live longer. In a fashionable world full of diets, it is essential to start by understanding that intermittent fasting is not a diet, but nutritional protocol, a set of different protocols. Intermittent fasting is a diet regimen that repeats a period of fasting and eating. It also specifies when to eat rather than what foods you can (or cannot) eat. If you are looking for a way to improve your health, lose body fat and become leaner, fitter, more dynamic and able to eat a range of foods without fear of becoming fat again, intermittent fasting (IF) could be something that will catapult your results to a new level. The IF approach is not rocket science. Food came from unprocessed sources; obesity and weight gain were probably the exceptions rather than the norm.

Whether for religious or spiritual reasons, fasting is still practiced in many spirits. However, the intermittent fasting, we are going to talk about concerns about health and body composition, not religion. It has gained a lot of traction and media attention in recent years and been addressed with a series of emerging books. In the meanwhile, taking advantage of the benefits of intermittent fasting, I tend to find many of these books somewhat misleading, the authors more interested in making quick money by jumping on the IF train than trying to help people take control and balance in their nutrition and physical goals. There have been a series of high-profile celebrities like Hugh Jackman, Liv Tyler, Beyonce, and Ben Affleck, who recount their success with IF. Still, there are millions of "normal" people around the world who have also seen impressive results and finally found a diet plan that fits their lifestyle and heals their bulging size. This book will explore the concepts behind intermittent fasting for faster fat loss, muscle gain, improved energy levels, calorie control, and more. Unlike most diet books, I will provide you with a system to calculate your daily calorie intake, weight loss can be difficult, but intermittent fasting can help! This dietary pattern involving a fasting-eating cycle has received attention not only because it has been identified as what you eat but when you eat.

All in all, fasting for religious reasons, despite the religion, is done to achieve various spiritual gains: from blessings to forgiveness and a closer spiritual relationship with the deity. To Lose weight while traditional fasting becoming a popular objective. When you fast, your body is deprived of the energy produced from the food you eat. For survival, it is forced to tap on the reserves, mainly the stored fat. The burning of the fat results in gradual weight loss, which can see you lose a few or several extra pounds depending on the period of fasting. Aside from promoting the burning of the stored fat, fasting can also help to boost your metabolism, which even much helps with weight loss.

Studies conducted on the effects of fasting, particularly periodic fasting such as intermittent fasting, have shown that other than for health and medical reasons, fasting can also be done for therapeutic reasons. This concept is as old as the ancient civilizations. The Greek physician, Hippocrates, is famous for his medical views, which included fasting to unlock the natural healing of the body. This concept is based on the instinct of the human body or even animals to refuse food when they are sick, with the appetite for food science of fasting. For most wild animals, celebrations and famines are the norms. Our distant ancestors often did not eat 4 or 5 meals a day. Instead, they kill, lie down in the canyon, lie down, and spend a long time without eating anything. Our bodies and genes were forged in a rare environment, interrupted by occasional large-scale bangs.

Today, of course, things are very different. I always like fasting, the voluntary refusal to eat, is not considered unhealthy and is considered somewhat eccentric. Most of us expect to eat at least three meals a day, and in between, we will eat quite a few snacks. In addition to meals and snacks, here's a milky cappuccino, a weird cookie there, or maybe a smoothie because it is "healthy." There were once parents who told their children not to eat between meals. These times are behind us. A recent study in the United States, comparing the eating habits of 28,000 children and 36,000 adults over the past thirty years, found that the time between, what the researchers shyly called, "eating options decreased by an hour on average in other words, in the past few decades, the amount of time we spent "not eating" has decreased significantly.

In the 1970s, people like my mother spent about four and a half hours without eating, and children like me spent about four hours between the meals should take. It is now reduced to three and a half hours for adults and three hours for children, and this does not include all the drinks and snacks. The idea that eating small amounts and frequent eating is a "good thing" was partially promoted by the creators of snacks and trendy diet books, but was also endorsed by medical institutions. They claim that eating many small meals is better because it makes us less hungry and less likely to consume high-fat junk. I can accept the argument, and some studies suggest that eating small meals regularly can have health benefits unless you eat more. Unfortunately, that is precisely what is happening in the real world.

In the above study, snacks are about 180 units of more calories a day compared to 30 years ago, not only in the form of dairy products and carbonated drinks but also in the form of the regular diet. I found out an increment of an average of 120 calories per day. In other words, snacking does not seem to mean that you are eating less with meals. Eating all day is quite common and expected, and it is almost shocking to say that it is worth resisting. When I started to fast, I discovered something unexpected about myself, my attitude towards food, and my beliefs. I have found that I eat a lot when I do not need it. Later, I worry if I'm hungry or just because the food is there, so I'm going to do it. When I am hungry, it gradually hardens, and I stick my face in a tub of ice. Instead, I found that hunger is gone, and when you are starving, you are no longer afraid of it. When I was fasting, I felt distracted and unable to concentrate. What I discovered is that it sharpens my senses and my brain. I wonder if I pass out all the time. The body was becoming incredibly flexible and active.

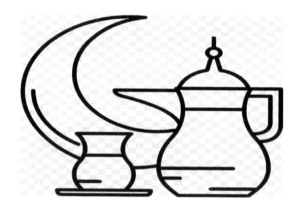

SPIRITUAL FASTING

Fasting was and is an integral part of different religions and spiritual practices around the world. When fasting is used for religious purposes, it is often described as a cleansing or cleansing process, but the basic concept has always been the same: avoid eating for a fixed period.

Unlike medical fasting, which is used to treat illness, spiritual fasting is considered an essential catalyst for the well-being of the whole body, and a variety of religions share the belief that fasting has the power to heal. In Buddhism, fasting is a means of exercising restraint on human desires. A reluctance which, according to Buddhist monks, is part of the puzzle to reach Nirvana. Many Buddhists fast daily, eat in the morning, but abstain for the rest of the day until it is time to eat the next morning. Besides, Buddhists often start fasting with water for days or weeks.

MAHA-SHIVARATRI

Hinduism is believed to deny the physical needs of the body through fasting to increase spirituality. Although fasting is an integral part of the Hindu religion and is practiced frequently, one of the most popular Fasting is during Maha-Shivaratri or the "Great Night of Shiva." During Maha-Shivaratri, the followers fast, participate in ritual baths, visit a temple where they pray, and practice the virtues of honesty, forgiveness, and self-discipline.

There are many reasons for fasting in Judaism, including asking for God's mercy, marking important life events, thanking God or praying to get out of grief; however, if you fast, it is common to keep the fasts private.

LENT

In Christianity, fasting is a way to cleanse the soul, the body is pure, and it can establish a connection with God. One of the most popular times for Christians to fast is during Lent, which is 40 days from Ash Wednesday to Easter. Once upon a time, those who observed the lent gave up eating and drinking. Nowadays, Christians can still do without food and drink, but often they choose to do without specific things. This practice is said to be a 40-day commendation that Jesus Christ spent in the desert and was forced to fast.

RAMADAN

Ramadan is probably the most famous fasting and an essential part of the Islamic religion and the ninth month of the Islamic calendar. During Ramadan, Muslims not only stop eating and drinking from dawn until dusk, but also avoid smoking, sexual relationships, and other activities that can be considered guilty. It is believed that periods of fasting and the light dehydration resulting from the lack of body fluids can cleanse the soul from harmful impurities, transform the mind into spirituality and keep it away from worldly desires.

Ramadan is one of the five pillars of Islam.

MEDICAL FASTING

Hippocrates, who was called the "father of medicine," fasted as early as the 5th century BC as a medical therapy for some of his sick patients. One of the famous quotes from Hippocrates says, *"If you are sick, you eat your disease."* He believed that fasting allows the body to focus on healing and that forcing food into a sick state could harm your health because instead of giving energy for recovery, whatever was available energy, your body would consume indigestion. On the other hand, if sick patients abstain from eating, the digestive processes are interrupted, and the body would give priority to natural healing.

FASTING SCIENCE

Intermittent fasting has been accused of being a temporary epidemic, as have other nutritional concepts that take precedence over the health and diet communities. Still, the science behind the benefits of fasting is already growing. There are several theories as to why intermittent fasting works well, but the most frequently studied and most proven advantage is stress.

The word stress has been unpopular many times, but up to some emphasis, is right for your health. For example, exercise is technically physical stress (mostly the muscle and cardiovascular system). Still, this stress ultimately strengthens your body as long as you have adequate recovery times in your daily life.

According to Dr. Mark Mattson, Principal Investigator and Director of the Institute for Neuroscience, National Institute for Aging, Professor of Neuroscience, Johns Hopkins University School of Medicine, intermittent fasting is a movement. Refusing food to the body for a defined period puts a small amount of stress on the cells. Over time, cells adapt to this stress by learning to manage it well. Your body's ability to cope with stress increases your ability to resist illness.

FIVE INTERMITTENT FASTING VARIANTS

WARRIOR DIET 18-20 HOURS FAST / 4-6 HOURS

This variant is for this reason. It is very intense if you fast in the first 18 to 20 hours of the day or take a particularly recommended meal in combination with your workout. Then consume most of the food within 4-6 hours and then repeat the relining or fasting period. It may be more convenient to place a feeding window at the end of the day. You can adapt it to your schedule at any time.

FAST FOR 36 HOURS EVERY OTHER DAY / 12 HOURS

Feed with this strategy. You eat every other day. It may seem extreme, but the faster, the more experienced, the less worrying you can go about this task. On regular days we only eat 12 hours, for example from 9 a.m. to 9 p.m. Then quickly overnight and quickly 24 hours the next day. Eat the next day again from 9 a.m. to 9 p.m. and fast for a total of 36 hours. In general, everyone can eat faster, which is what they like on days without fasting. However, choosing the right diet leads to better results.

EAT STOP EAT 24 HOURS QUICKLY, 1-2 TIMES A WEEK

This method fasts the entire 24 hours once a week or twice as needed. Then follow a smart diet for the rest of the week. This method is very adjustable. The 24-hour Lent can be any day of your choice.

SKIPPING MEAL

It is a somewhat random approach to fasting. It is a more natural, prehistoric form of fasting. It is believed that our ancestors were not as interested and attached to food as they are today. Nutrition and exercise are random and eat raw healthy food. This method allows you to skip meals 1-2 times a week at random. It is very flexible and no worries.

5: 2 fasting, 5: 2 diet (also known as the 5/2 diet) is a fasting diet plan that limits caloric intake for two days and then eats a regular diet for five days. The general idea behind a 5: 2 diet is to reduce calories for two (non-continuous) days. However, you can eat very low-calorie (but very nutritious) foods two out of seven days a week and the regular diet for the other five days.

LEAN GAINS 16H FAST / 8H FEED - THIS IS THE FAST WE RECOMMEND IN OUR WORKSHOPS
This type of fasting feeds for 8 hours, then 16 hours, but there are additional rules that must be followed. Foods should be high in protein, and carbohydrate intake should be maintained by circulating carbohydrates, such as in an empty stomach or timing nutrition. Training should begin shortly before the end of the 16-hour fast. After exercise, eat the largest of a couple of meals. The fast start again in the evening before bedtime lasts 16 hours and repeats daily. (Be careful! This fast-recommended protocol is for people who are moderately active or above. If you have low sports activity or are new to sports, keep your protein intake low and your carbohydrate intake to a minimum level. Keep in mind, especially simple carbohydrates, which are intended to consume more natural foods and fiber if possible).

Carbohydrates are found in almost all organisms and play an essential role in the proper functioning of the immune system, fertilization, blood coagulation, and human development. Lack of carbohydrates can cause malfunctions in all of these systems. However, the deficiency is rare in the western world. Excessive intake of carbohydrates, incredibly refined carbohydrates such as sugar and corn syrup, can lead to obesity, type II diabetes, and cancer. Unhealthy carbohydrate foods include dried fruits, cereals, crackers, cakes, flours, jams, bread products, and potato products. Healthy carbohydrate foods are vegetables, legumes (beans), whole grains, fruits, nuts, and yogurts.

Fasting has physical and psychological benefits. One of the main advantages of fasting and one of the main reasons why many people fast at times is fat loss. Understanding the difference between a fed and a fasted state can help you know how it works.

The fed state is the state in which our bodies digest and ingest food. It starts with eating and takes 3-5 hours as your body digests and intakes this food. High insulin levels make it challenging to burn fed fat. After digestion and absorption, your body stops processing food. This relaxed mode lasts about 8-12 hours after your last meal, and you are hungry. In this state, your insulin level is so low that your body is more likely to burn fat. Because of these 12 hours, our body is in a quieter state than when burning fat. Fasting can lead you to this fat-burning condition. It is the number of people who start fasting, burning fat without changing their diet or exercising.

Further advantages have been demonstrated in both animal and animal experiments. Some of these benefits include, but are not limited to, low blood lipids, blood pressure, inflammation markers, oxidative stress, and cancer risk. It also increases cell turnover and repair, fat burning, beneficial growth hormone release, and metabolic rate, as well as the release of other harmful body aging hormones (IGF-1). Finally, the effects of appetite control, blood sugar control, cardiovascular function, chemotherapy, neurogenesis, and neuroplasticity were improved.

Training the mind is the most outstanding achievement of fasting. Psychologically retrain the brain and body's response to hunger. Through fasting, we find that need is not an emergency. Our bodies are trained on how to approach panic and how to curb the desire for immediate satisfaction. It is a great skill you need to master today in the time of the fast-paced modern world. You can see that feeling of hunger is just a feeling. If you are devoted to fasting all day long, you will soon realize that hunger is not upsetting. If you miss a meal, your body will die without switching off. Our prehistoric ancestors did not have fast-food restaurants in every corner. There is a difference between physiological and psychological hunger, and we often confuse the two. Understanding the difference between the two helps you understand the signals in your body. If you feel starving, a record that sensation, usually at the end of a fast, and use it as a reference when you think you are hungry. If you compare the two, you can see which one is hungry.

Eating is a privilege and responsibility that we often receive when we take it for granted. Fasting helps us reassess why we eat and what we incorporate into our bodies. It enables us to recognize that we have little or no food to eat, and we eat our meals every day as usual. Eating processed nutrients without food is also bad for our body, and we are forced to use the feeding window in a more limited and nutritious way. We are always surrounded by endless marketing campaigns targeting consumers. Food ads, especially junk food ads, send subliminal signals that usually fly under the radar when we are full. We store this information and pull it out when we feel hungry. As you fast, you become more aware of the urges, desires, and ways in which these messages need to be fulfilled. The more clearly you see the operation, the less likely you are to lie. Power and control are closely related to consciousness.

Before going into the details of creating a fasting plan, we must first decide why we want to fast. What is its goal? Your diet and exercise program will depend on the goals you are trying to achieve. Next, you need to identify the diet and exercise plan to include based on your goals. How many calories do you eat during your feeding period? How often and for how long do you exercise each week? These are the questions you need to answer before you start fasting. Knowing the answers to these questions will help you succeed in fasting. Pre-programming these items eliminate the additional stress and worry that can arise during planning. There are many websites with tools to calculate calorie intake based on your lifestyle and exercise plans that will help you reach your goals.

When you are ready to plan your diet and workout, the best place to start lifestyle changes is with the exam. It will help determine tolerance and abstinence on an empty stomach. If you are not familiar with fasting, you will notice slight discomfort when starting a fast. It is mainly after a while, as we usually do not refuse our body food. Your body signals to let you know that you are hungry. It is natural, and the stimuli for mood swings and changes in hormone levels are also natural, but when you learn, the meaning of that feeling in the body is the sense of fat loss that begins with others. It can be converted to many benefits. The test should be comfortable and straightforward. Try it for 14-16 hours without a meal. It allows you to feel a deliberate hunger to get used to this feeling. Controlling appetite is essential for weight loss and health. A quick test is also a great way to see if a form of long-term fasting is right for you. Monitor and record the response of your body to this deliberate hunger. You may not want to try to fast for long periods if your reaction is severe and you experience signs of depression, or if you have extreme mood swings or irritation. Try Fast Eat - Pick a day when you do not eat for 14-16 hours on weekdays and do not eat anything.

Here are some things to remember and relieve stress.
• You can have tea and coffee during the fasting period. If you cannot drink it without milk, you can just apply the color with splashes. No sugar is allowed, but artificial sweeteners are acceptable and preferably all-natural stevia.
• During this period, non-calorie soft drinks, chewing gum, and mint are also allowed.

• Drinking water will reduce your hunger. (Hunger is the feeling that the body is burning fat, releasing beneficial growth hormones and repairing cells while lowering the body's release of aging hormones).

• Watch for body signals. If you feel stressed or frustrated during the fast, relax.

• Homes always have healthy food options and are ready to fast. Having healthy food options ensures that there is no temptation to spoil at the end of the fasting period.

Once you have a better understanding of what you expect from a daily fast and you decide that this quick option is what you can take, you are ready to start the lean gains. Eating for 8 hours and then fasting for 16 hours is always "difficult," but "easy." If you can, give yourself time to relax and meditate. It helps you stay focused and remember your goals. I want to make sure your mind and body are in balance.

If you do the math, you can say to yourself, "Are you sure you want to skip breakfast?" The answer is yes, and no! Of course, this is a very controversial approach in today's society. We often hear that breakfast is the most important meal of the day, which is true. However, if you are fasting because you think breakfast is what you meant, you do not have to worry about it every time you eat. Your main concern is to eat healthy when you are fasting. If you have to eat breakfast early in the morning due to your busy schedule or medical reasons, you can schedule a fast this way. Eat your last meal 8 hours before bedtime (assuming you sleep 8 hours). It allows you to exercise and then eat the biggest meal of the day in the morning. It is not the usual planning approach; it has more challenges, but it sometimes works.

Another critical point to remember is that the 16/8 speed is for those who want to be skinny. Having previous fitness and health routine makes this easy. It also seems more comfortable and works better for men. Women can quickly correct this, if necessary, by eating more and reducing hunger. It is especially true if you are generally a busy person and misses the opportunity to eat. If you do not have the time, you may want to increase your meal window to eat healthier. Listen to body signals, especially when you are in the feeding zone. Now you know when to eat, how much to eat and when to eat. Exercises and plans are defined. You can use intermittent fasting to achieve your goals or use it as a permanent lifestyle change, but always pay attention to your body and know what works best for you. Now let us summarize instead of eating several times a day to eat.

SO, WHAT ARE THE STEPS?

1. DETERMINE THE START DATE
We strongly recommend starting on Monday. It makes more sense. After you have selected a day, you can thoroughly prepare for the start time with a few steps.

2. SELECT THE DISTRIBUTION OF FAST / MEAL DETERMINE WHEN TO EAT AND FAST
16/8 is recommended for beginners. You have to get used to it a lot, and it is not too difficult the

first time. Select a window and decide when to stop eating the night before fasting. It will serve as a separate house. We recommend that you stick to it for the first week. After practicing FI for a few weeks, it is only natural to change windows and schedules. However, it is best to keep the same time during the first week. So, if you stop eating at 9 p.m. on Sunday, you won't eat at 1 p.m. on Monday. From 1 p.m. to 9 p.m., it will be a dining room window.

3. SPEND A FLIRT DAY
Spend one day on the day before the first fast. Eat a lot and eat whatever you like. It has two purposes. First, the more foods there are in the system, the easier it is to make fast-first. Secondly, if you eat the things you want the night before, that means you won't thirst for these foods for a week.

4. TEACH PEOPLE
I highly recommend talking to your loved ones about the new habits you are adopting. Explain why you do it and why you are hired-politely informed them that you do not eat at certain times and that you will like their support, please. Warn people to make up for your chances of getting food during a fast. One of the most difficult challenges you face is that of a friend, family, or colleague who provides you with food-inform your FI and avoids it.

5. BUY BRANCHED-CHAIN AMINO ACIDS (OPTIONAL)

Branched-chain amino acids (BCAA) are beneficial on an empty stomach. These are pure forms of protein and incredibly powerful for more prolonged fasting. Consuming 10 g of BCAAs can help reduce hunger without fasting. Do not exceed 10 g per serving, but two servings are sufficient during fasting. If you want to exercise, I recommend BCAA. If you are going to exercise, we recommend that you exercise 60 minutes before and during exercise at one of the following times:

6. TRAINING AND INTERMITTENT FASTING
You do not have to exercise to take advantage of intermittent fasting. However, when you select training, you'll see unprecedented levels of results. As explained earlier in this book, IF increases growth hormone and testosterone production and attacks adipocytes and stores. With the addition of an exercise routine (we recommend strength training), the results you see are incredible. Strength training combined with increased hormones can help you build muscle faster than expected. Lifting weights also increases the production of testosterone and growth hormone, so your body receives twice the dose of hormone production. Weight training is also very metabolic, so shred fat from your body and remember, as I said, you have more muscles, which means less fat.

I would also like to mention that strength training and exercise are probably the most effective way to protect your body from whatever the world throws at you. It has been proven to reduce stress, help with depression, increase energy levels, improve mental function, increase your happiness, improve your life, and help you live longer. Therefore, it is highly recommended to start training. If you do not have a good gym, strength exercises like pushups, squats, and lunges can help you on your journey. Finally, I would like to add one thing, if it can be speeded up, run it. I understand that planning does not mean everyone can do it, but one way to improve is to exercise and fast with a meal after exercise. Do not eat more than 2 hours after weight training, as your muscles will be disrupted, and this will negatively affect your goals.

Do you want to lose fat, build muscle, gain energy, and feel like a new person simply and sustainably? And do you need a diet-free approach that delivers results at significantly accelerated rates? Now let me introduce you to intermittent fasting - the most sustainable and most comfortable fitness trick to get you into the best shape of your life. Intermittent fasting has grown in popularity over the past year, as its benefits and consequences have become apparent. You were used by celebrities like Hugh Jackman, Beyonce, Benedict Cumber batch, and Ben Affleck. This book is short and deliberate. I want you to act, and you haven't sat and read books for hours. Knowledge is not power but potential power. Power comes from the implementation of experience. And that is precisely what intermittent fasting is. To precisely convey the knowledge, you need to perform actions and display results and to achieve excellent results. Now let us practice the simple habit of intermittent fasting to get the best shape of your life. Well, it is not a diet; it is a new approach to eating. Intermittent fasting is a cyclical process of eating along with the periods you are not eating. These short fasting periods cause various hormonal reactions in your body. These answers lead to incredible benefits and results.

BENEFITS

Here are some examples (do not diet or restrict foods that you can eat)

-Increase muscle mass quickly
-Increase in energy level
-Increased production of testosterone and growth hormone
-Improve cognitive function

Fasting is the most effective way to stay fit and well, as fasting is based on scientific knowledge, not "bro-science."
If you are in good shape and have failed, do not despair. The problem with most diets is that you place too many restrictions on what you can
eat. Intermittent fasting is the opposite-you do not have to make any changes to your diet to earn rewards.
So, what are you waiting for? Immerse yourself in the book now and learn everything you need to know about intermittent fasting. We will walk you through each step and provide a simple, easy-to-follow guide to get the results you have always wanted.

I think that the popularity of IF is increasing mainly due to the following two factors.
-An extensive list of significant benefits.
-Easy acceptance and maintenance.
It is essential because it has been shown that most diets and diet plans fail due to the two main obstacles. These obstacles are the complexity of managing nutrition and the time it takes to demonstrate results. How many times do you think "eating this food negatively affects my diet"? or "I eat XYZ in 2 weeks, but I cannot get the results I expected". Have you heard Intermittent fasting cleanly breaks through these barriers due to their simple and straightforward procedure and the speed with which they arise? The IF concept contradicts many of the longstanding beliefs of the fitness and health industries, but as this book describes in detail, something is popularized by everyone and their grandmother, and this does not mean it is true. Prevailing myths of fitness and nutrition Intermittent fasts underwent massive tests at the start of their emergence, as they violate everything that has been taught in the fitness industry for the past 50 years. At first glance, the concept of not eating deliberately is a fitness error. However, by exploring your ideas and using scientific data to challenge past assumptions, you will find shocking things.

PHYSIOLOGICAL BENEFITS
— Rapid Fat Loss
— Increase in Testosterone and HGH Production
— Lean Muscle Gain
— Increased Energy Levels

— Ability to Easily Control Hunger
— Higher Sex Drive
— Improvement to Hair and Skin
— Longevity of Life

LIFESTYLE BENEFITS
- Improvement of cognitive capacity
- Better sleep
- Win time and money
- Easy to follow
- Reduction of stress

Therefore, intermittent fasting has many benefits that make it the perfect way to lose fat, build muscle, and feel good. One of the main factors behind the ability of FI to burn fat quickly is that when the body is starved, the body attacks the fat to start providing energy. Another way for IFs to lose weight fast is to cut calories in the diet simply. By changing the time to eat and reducing the amount of time you can eat naturally, you will reduce the number of calories you eat, and this will start to shed unnecessary body fat. Fasting also increases the oxidation of fatty acids, which in turn speeds up the fat-burning process. It allows your body to burn fat at high levels during and after the fast. Many hormonal reactions also occur when the body is fasting. One of the primary responses is that growth hormone and testosterone begin to be secreted by the body is considerably increased amounts. How significant is the increase? In one study, another point that I want to explain is that fasting also reduces the production of the hormone ghrelin. It is a hormone that affects hunger and satiety. If you've ever suffered from hunger, ghrelin has been produced more. When it is sober, it becomes dull and effectively prevents the feeling of hunger when fasting. As I mentioned at the beginning of the book, fasting is not a diet but a diet. For me, this is one of the most important advantages. It is easy to follow, suitable for all lifestyles, and you can enjoy all of its significant benefits without disturbing your social life. Eating is beneficial and religiously very practical, but this is often difficult because many foods are prohibited. Have you ever been on a diet with your friends? It is stupid to find something on the menu. Remove intermittent fasting as it does not benefit from the food you eat, but from the physiological reactions that cause it. Following specific nutritional guidelines (discussed later) will, of course, speed up your results, but the critical point is that you do not have to eat the same meal more than once. Intermittent fasting style In the IF world, you can use different methods.

Each class has advantages and disadvantages, but both have the miracles described in the previous chapter. The effect of benefits will vary slightly between individual options. Therefore, choosing the style that best suits your lifestyle is paramount. All IF techniques revolve around the same basic concept. In other words, a large fasting window and a small dining room window. The most common fasting meals/hours are 16 divisions. Each day consists of 16 hours of fasting, followed by 8 hours of meals. It is the simplest to adopt, and it is recommended for beginners. If you sleep about half the time, hiring is very easy.

Division 18/6. Each day consists of an 18 hour fast followed by a 6-hour meal window. After 6 p.m., the fasting effect increased significantly, speeding up the results of the 4 p.m. window. It is recommended to do this after experiencing the 16/8 division. Division 20/4. Each day consists of 20 hours of fasting, followed by 4 hours of meals. I think it is a convenient window, but it is as fast as 20 hours a day, so it is tough to avoid this effect-24 hour quickly. It takes place twice a week. Once you have that, it is not for beginners to have experience with various fasting windows, so you can jump to it, but do not try it as a beginner. Beginners who try to fast for 24 hours often fail because they are not yet used to fasting.

Thirty-six hours quickly once every 8-10 days. Only well-trained intermittent accelerations. The 36-hour speed is a mental struggle to be overcome. The benefits are enormous but challenging to complete and to challenge to integrate into your lifestyle. Do not exceed 36 hours as your body burns all your fat reserves and starts attacking your muscles for energy. The final meal / fast time you choose does not significantly affect your goals, as each option offers the desired benefits. However, what matters is consistency in respecting the options you choose. If you like it, do not do it by accident. To get results and benefits, you must continuously adhere to fasting times. You do not have to stick to the same meals and fasts every day, but sticking to them is much more comfortable. It is a lifestyle, not a diet.

In this chapter, I would like to deepen this concept. First, let's see what defines a meal in the dictionary. "A selection of certain foods that have been developed or prescribed to improve a person's physical condition, such preference or limitation of the amount a person eats to lose weight that of a specific person or group food is consumed. "When I read these sentences, I only see the limit - it is about eating in my head. You set too many restrictions on what you can eat and how much you can eat, and everything is more confusing than it should be. Now I would like to point out that a diet can be beneficial, but I find it very specific for a purpose (such as achieving single-digit body fat percentage) or for medical reasons. For most people, the diet is not sufficient, but it does not give the desired results and has a massive failure rate. The plans are limited. Intermittent fasting is not limiting; it frees you from all the technical details of the project. When you start exercising when you do not have to stick to incredibly strict dietary rules, instead, you can eat what you want (with reason) and more (with reason again). Eating fast food every day makes sense as if you are eating ridiculous, and drugs, fitness routines, and supplements will not help you lose weight and lose weight. Fast food is harmful to health, harms hormones, the brain, and internal organs.

Intermittent fasting is different from the diet because the food rules do not bound it. Do you want to eat white carbohydrates? You are welcome! Do you want a pizza for tonight? You are welcome! Do not you want to change your current dining style? Well, it is the answer. If you are going to go one step further and see significantly accelerated results and more significant benefits, you can make specific nutritional choices. Accelerate results with food As I mentioned earlier, the primary use of IF is the hormonal response that occurs when your body is fasting. However, you can speed up your results by changing your current eating style and following certain principles. Following these guidelines and regulations will speed up your results when you eat foods such as:

- Increases the production of testosterone and growth hormone
- Helps burn fat
- Reduces insulin spikes
- Helps in muscle growth
- Improves cognitive function

So, if you are looking for accelerated results, here are the guidelines that I follow.

-Avoid processed and manufactured foods
-Avoid white carbohydrates
-Increase the amount of protein in your diet
-Increase the number of healthy fats in your diet (olive oil, avocado, etc.)
-Make sure 80% of the carbohydrates come from legumes and beans
-Make sure the remaining 20% of carbohydrates come from whole grains and whole wheat
-Eat green vegetables with each meal
-Use the following seasoning: garlic, pepper, cayenne pepper, chili flakes, black pepper, sea salt.

-Reduce fruit consumption and limit yourself to 1 fruit per day
-Drink only black coffee, herbal tea, and water
Again, you do not have to follow these guidelines, but if you follow them, your results and benefits will be accelerated. Now you've read all about IF and understand how powerful it is. We recommend that you read this chapter rather than fasting. Before you start practicing FI, I suggest some steps. The information here will help your neurotrophic factor (BDNF).

PHYSICAL BENEFITS

Fasting improves your immune system - because it reduces free radical damage, regulates inflammation in the body, and stops cancer cells from forming. When you are sick, your instinct is to focus on resting rather than eating. Fasting helps to clean the skin and prevent acne. This is because the temporarily undigested body can concentrate its regenerative energy on other systems.
Body reaction when stopping
The following happens to your body during a fast:

1. THE DECREASE IN BODY FAT
It leads to weight loss and helps reduce the risk of heart disease, stroke, cancer, diabetes, etc.

2. CHOLESTEROL DEPOSITS ARE DECOMPOSED
When you are hungry, remove waste quickly. Cholesterol usually includes cholesterol stored in the inner lining of blood vessels. Cholesterol

levels may increase in the first week after fasting when the body detoxifies, but they decrease.

3. FIBRINOLYSIS
Dangerous blood clots that accumulate in the body are easily broken down on an empty stomach. This process is called fibrinolysis.

4. ACCELERATION OF SELF-DECOMPOSITION
Every cell in the body contains its seed of destruction. When it needs itself, the section releases its self-destructing enzymes and self Destruction. That is self-decomposition. During fasting, this type of tissue is destroyed during the process of autolysis, affecting normal function.

5. INCREASED DIURESIS
Diuresis is the excretion from the kidney. During the fast, the body voluntarily and automatically eliminates salt and water without damaging the tissues of the body. This diuresis has enormous health benefits.

6. ACCELERATE PHAGOCYTOSIS
During the rapid defense of white blood cells, they destroy toxic bacteria and accelerate their ability to digest waste products. White blood cells of fasted people were very effective in killing toxic bacteria. Below are the four most popular fasting style guides. This list is not exhaustive and covers only the most popular, but it will undoubtedly give you an idea of your goals. Below you will find the four most popular fasting style guides. This list is not extensive and only covers the most

popular, but it will certainly give you some thoughts about your goals.

FASTING GUIDELINES

1. REGULARLY FAST (EAT STOP EAT)
This is usually a 24-hour speed that you will pace regularly. You can start this at any time of the day and do it once or twice a week. This type of fasting is sifted through by Brad Pyron, and it is recommended to fast for 24 hours every 3-5 days to lose weight.

2. LEAN GAINS
Use this method to fast for 16 hours at a time. For example, from 10 p.m. to 2 p.m. After that, three meals are taken in the remaining 8 hours. Martin Berkhan wrote lean gains, and the plan also includes details about the movement. So, if you want to fast and continue exercising, this could be your plan.

3. NATIONAL ASSEMBLY OF WARRIORS
This is just a step away from lean gains. This method only promotes one healthy meal a day (usually dinner). Research by State et al. Let's take a closer look at that. In this study, familiar weight participants used enough energy to maintain the weight of one meal or three meals a day for eight weeks. Despite the same calorie consumption, participants lost weight between one meal a day and three meals a day. Fat mass

was significantly reduced, and muscle mass tended to increase after eating one meal a day for eight weeks. However, during the 8-week study period, hunger increased steadily with just one meal a day, suggesting that appetite hormones were not adjusting.

4. FAST EVERY OTHER DAY
This is an intermittent fasting style. Food is consumed for 24 hours and is restricted the next day. Heilbronn etc. We conducted a detailed survey on this. The study was conducted on eight healthy-weight men and eight women who fasted every 21 days. Participants lost approximately $2.5 \pm 0.5\%$ of body weight, including $4 \pm 1\%$ of fat, over 21 days. The fasting blood sugar and ghrelin (appetite hormone) levels did not change before and after the procedure. Still, the fasting insulin level was low, indicating a high level of insulin sensitivity. Studies also showed that the metabolic machinery needed to generate energy from fat was sufficient at the start of the course.

FACTS ABOUT INTERMITTENT FASTING
Here are some facts about intermittent fasting you may not know, but you should know before you start. Most of the initial long-term studies on the benefits of fasting are done in rodents. They also gave us important insights into the molecular mechanisms underlying fasting.

FASTING AND BRAIN

As Woody Allen once said, the brain is my second favorite organ. Nothing else would work without them so that I could put it first. The human brain, about three pounds of a pinkish-grey exaggeration, is Tapioca's constant object, which is described as the most complex object in the known universe. It enables us to build, write poems, rule the planet, and understand ourselves. It is also a very efficient energy-saving machine that does all this intricate work and makes sure your body is working correctly while using the same amount of energy as a 25-watt bulb. The fact that our brains are usually very flexible and adaptable makes it even more tragic when they go wrong. I know that as I grow older, my memory becomes more error-prone. I've supplemented it with various memory tips I've learned over the years, but I'm still having trouble remembering names and dates. But much worse than that, is the fear that one day I may completely lose my head and probably develop some form of dementia. I want to keep my brain in the best possible condition and keep it as long as possible. Fortunately, fasting seems to provide the necessary protection.

It was Professor Mark Mattson who talked about the brain. Mark Mattson, professor of neuroscience at the National Institute for Aging, is one of the most respected scientists in his field, researching the aged brain. I find his work exciting - which suggests that fasting can help fight diseases like Alzheimer's, dementia, and memory loss. I could have taken a taxi to his office, but I wanted to go. I like to go for a walk. Not only does it burn calories, but it also improves mood and helps to keep your memory. Although the brain shrinks typically with age, a study found that in everyday pedestrians, the hippocampus, an area of the brain essential for memory, is enlarged. The mind of a seated person. Mark, who studies Alzheimer's disease, lost his father to dementia. He was not willing to work directly on this area of research, but when he started working on Alzheimer's disease, he told me that his father had not been diagnosed, so he provided insight.

Alzheimer's disease affects approximately 26 million people worldwide, and the problems increase with the aging of the population. The tragedy of Alzheimer's disease and other forms of dementia can delay, but cannot prevent, unavoidable deterioration after diagnosis, so a new approach is urgently needed. You can get worse and worse until you need years of ongoing care. After all, you may not even notice the faces of those you once loved.

CAN FASTING MAKE YOU SMARTER?

Marc took me to see mice, as Valter Longo did. Like Valter's mouse, Mark's mouse is genetically modified but modified to be more vulnerable to Alzheimer's disease. The rat I saw was in a maze and had to navigate to find food. Some mice do this relatively quickly. Others are confused and confused. This task and others are designed to reveal signs of memory impairment in mice. A struggling mouse quickly forgets which arm of the maze has already gone down.

Genetically modified mice with Alzheimer's disease develop dementia as soon as they take a regular diet. By the time they are one year old, they represent the average human age, and they usually have evident learning and memory problems. Animals continue to fast intermittently. Mark calls this "intermittent energy limitation" and is often up to 20 months without any signs of dementia 9. They do not start to get worse until the end of their lives. In humans, it is the same as the signs of Alzheimer's disease appearing at age 80 rather than age 50. I know which one I prefer. Worryingly, these mice descend much faster than a normal-fed mouse on a regular junk food diet. "We fed mice a diet high in fat and fructose," Mark said, and "this has a dramatic effect. We have a lot of problems accumulating a lot of amyloids and finding ways in the maze test." In other words, junk food makes these mice fat and stupid.

One of the most significant changes that occur in Mark's hungry mouse brain is the increased production of a protein called the neurotrophic factor from the brain. BDNF has been shown to stimulate stem cells into new neurons in the hippocampus. As mentioned earlier, this is a part of the brain that is essential for everyday learning and memory. But why does the hippocampus grow in response to hunger? Mark points out that it makes sense from an evolutionary perspective. After all, you have to be smarter and, on the ball, if you do not have a lot to eat. "When animals are in areas with limited food resources, it is essential to remember where the feed is, where it is at risk, predators, etc. I think people in the past have had a survival advantage."

It is not known precisely whether new brain cells will develop in response to a fast. To be sure, researchers need to intermittently fast and kill volunteers, remove the brain, and look for new signs of nerve growth. Many people rarely volunteer for such projects. But what they are doing is a study that uses volunteers immediately and then MRI to see if their hippocampal size changes over time. As mentioned earlier, these techniques are used in humans to show that regular exercise, such as walking increases the size of the hippocampus. Hopefully, similar studies show that intermittent fasting two days a week is good for learning and memory. On a purely anecdotal level, using a sample size of 1 seems to work. Before I started the fast diet, I did an ingenious memory test online. After two months of testing, performance improved.

Most major religions advocate fasting (except Sikhs, which allow it for medical reasons), but I have always found it to be a way to test yourself and your faith. I thought there was. I could see potential spiritual benefits, but I was deeply skeptical of physical benefits. I also had many sensitive friends who had tried to fast me over the years but did so because they were "resting the liver" or "removing the liver." I could not accept the explanation. Toxin for medically trained skeptics like me, none of the answers made sense. I remember a friend who told me that his urine turned black after a few weeks of fasting, proof that the poison had disappeared. I saw it as evidence that he was an ignorant hippie and that everything that happened in his body as a result of fasting was very harmful. As I wrote at the beginning, I was convinced that I would try to fast: my situation in the mid-'50s, hyperglycemia, a little overweight, and a combination of the new scientific findings.

What does not kill us makes us stronger!? Several researchers influenced me in various ways, but the one who stands out is Professor Mark Mattson of the National Institute for Aging in Baltimore. A few years ago, she wrote an article with Edward Scalabrese in New Scientist magazine, "When a little poison is good for you."

"Small poison is good for you" is a colorful way of explaining the theory of Hermes's: the idea that humans and other creatures can be enhanced when they are exposed to stress and toxins. Hermes is not just a variant that "if you join the army, you become a man." It is now the accepted biology explanation of how things work at the cellular level. For example, consider something as simple as exercising. When you run or pump iron, it damages your muscles and causes small wear & tears. If it is not thoroughly exceeded, your body will respond with repairs, strengthening your muscles.

Vegetables are another example. We all know that fruits and vegetables are full of antioxidants, so you should eat a lot.

The problem with this generally accepted explanation of how fruits and vegetables "work" is that they are probably wrong or at least incomplete. The level of antioxidants in fruits and vegetables is shallow and obviously cannot have the profound effects they have. Furthermore, attempts to extract antioxidants from plants and provide us in concentrated form as a health-promoting supplement were not convincing in long-term trials. Beta-carotene is suitable for you if taken in the way of carrots. When they took beta carotene from carrots and administered it as

225

a supplement for cancer patients, it seemed to make them worse. By looking at how vegetables work in our bodies through the lens of Hermes's, we see that the reasons for their benefits can be very different.

Consider this apparent paradox. Bitterness is often associated with poison in nature and should be avoided. Plants produce a wide variety of so-called phytochemicals, some of which act as natural pesticides to keep mammals like us from eating them. The fact that they taste bitter is a clear warning sign: stay away. So, there is an evolutionary reason why we should not love ourselves and avoid bitter-tasting foods. However, even as adults, many of us find it hard to love them because some of the vegetables that are particularly good for us, such as cabbage, cauliflower, broccoli, and other members of the family of crucifers, are so bitter.

The solution to this paradox is that these vegetables are bitter because they contain chemicals that can be toxic. The reason they do not harm us is that these chemicals are contained in low, non-toxic doses. Instead, they activate the stress response and activate the genes that protect and repair.

Valter has been studying fasting for many years and is a determined believer. He is far from research, following a low-protein, vegetable-rich diet that his grandparents cherish in southern Italy. Perhaps not coincidentally, her grandparents live in parts of Italy where people are highly concentrated in the long run. In addition to a reasonably strict diet, Valter skips lunch and loses weight. Beyond that, once every six months, he has an extended fast that lasts for several days. Tall, slim, energetic, and Italian, he is an inspiring poster designer for future fasts. The main reason he is so interested in fasting is that his and other studies have shown an exceptional array of measurable health benefits that you get from it. As he explained, many "repair genes" can be activated and bring long-term benefits, even without a short-term diet, he explained. "There is a lot of early evidence that temporary fasting can lead to permanent changes that can have a positive effect on aging and illness," he told me. "You take people; you fast them. After 24 hours, everything is revolutionary. And even if you take a cocktail of drugs, a potent drug, you will never get closer. The nice thing about fasting is that everything is fine."

"To maintain a metabolic burn, you need to eat a small meal 5 to 6 times a day."

Unless you have lived under a rock in the past 20 years, I'm sure you've heard of it. It spreads like wildfire and is one of those few pieces of advice that everyone accepts. This advice is prevalent and is nearly taken for granted.

However, this is a lie without scientific evidence. Yes, one of the best fitness and health tips is wrong. The logic behind this theory is that a small meal during the day will burn more fat. This is based on the idea that if you eat frequently, your metabolism will increase as your metabolism increases. Unfortunately, this has not been proven, but many studies have tried and failed. As always, in scientific research, some groups try to prove the theory, and others try to deny it. The teams that refute it have won thanks to this frequent theory of diet, and several articles have been published on the subject. The best known is the article entitled.

"We cannot lose weight by increasing the frequency of meals."

A team of Canadian researchers refuted the frequent eating pattern and said that the frequency, but the frequency, was not necessary.

I would point out here that you can lose weight with six small meals, but the reason for the weight loss is not the frequency or timing of the meals. Breakfast is the most important meal of the day. This sounds perfectly logical and has some inherent advantages, but not always, and there is plenty of evidence to deny this. I am not saying that breakfast is terrible or wrong or should be avoided. Just be aware that just being famous is not fair and that there are more effective strategies. The concept that breakfast is the most important meal of the day is that it helps you start the day, energizes you, and nourishes the day. You should keep in mind that most people make bad decisions at breakfast because these points are worth it for you. These decisions are the opposite of the expected benefits. In connection with this, the idea that eating food (especially carbohydrates) increases fat late in the evening - this is another common myth that science is debating. Subsequent feeding can lead to some of the following benefits: less fat, more testosterone, more sleep, and more muscles. There are advantages to not eating late at night, but there are indications that the benefits of eating later outweigh the benefits of eating early.

If the practitioner recommends skipping breakfast, we will go into more detail later.

Another essential requirement for fitness and nutrition is that you need to eat certain foods and follow specific diets to achieve your goals. It does not matter if your goal is to lose weight, build muscle, or live longer and healthier lives, every guru, dietitian, and personal trainer uses their favorite diet as the only way to reach that goal.

Some of the everyday meals that you could follow are:

-Low in carbohydrates, high in protein, free of fat

-High fat and high protein content without carbohydrates

-Slow carbohydrate diet

-a DASH diet

-Paleolithic

-Bike cycling

-Atkins

There are hundreds of different diets that you can follow. Each has its strengths and weaknesses, but often all are lacking in one area. Of course, each of these diets can help you reach your goals, but no matter how effective your diet is, religious practice can hurt your progress. If you focus on a diet, limit your choices, and make it very difficult to follow. This leads to diet failure. Intermittent fasts avoid this because it does not promote a particular diet but suggest changes in the frequency and window of the diet. Yes, there are certain guidelines that you should follow, but they are very loose, and in most cases, you can eat whatever type of food you like. Before and after before after. Instead, take "before" and "after" (or "progress") photos. You can later compare them side by side to see how your body has changed over time. Photos can be a motivating tool because you may not notice the small changes that occur every day when you look at them. Make sure that your current dissatisfaction with your body does not prevent you from taking "front" pictures. They would be happy if they were on the go.

ANTHROPOMETRY

Anthropometry is helpful. You can start building muscle, especially if you exercise or do strength training regularly. When your body begins to change, you may not notice a significant change in scale, but your body composition can change dramatically. Measurements help you track your progress by monitoring the inches lost from different areas of your body.

TAKE THE FOLLOWING MEASUREMENTS:

•**Bust:** attach the measuring tape to the nipple and measure the entire breast.
•**Chest:** measurement: Measure directly under the chest or chest muscles and around the back.
•**Hips:** Find the widest part of your hips and measure your entire circumference.
•**Knee:** Measure up to just above the knee while standing upright.
•**Forearm:** Measures the entire forearm under the elbow.
•**Thigh:** Measure the entire thigh while standing upright.

●**Upper arm:** Measures the entire upper arm from the elbow.

●**Waist:** Find the narrowest part of your waist (usually just under your chest) and measure your entire circumference.

BAND HISTORY

For correct measurement, a measuring tape without elasticity is required. Hold the tape straight around your body and parallel to the floor. When making measurements, wrap the tape as close to the skin as possible, but do not squeeze the tape measure into the skin or squeeze it hard enough to create an indentation. It is helpful for someone else to take your measurements for you and allow you to stand straight. If no one is doing it, measure in front of the mirror and make sure the tape is held straight and in the right place.

Create a list of readings in your notebook or mobile phone notepad. Take measurements every few weeks and write down the numbers in the same place each time. You can use the measures to record your progress over time.

There are ups and downs. Like everything in life, you experience intermittent fasting, mostly ups and downs at the beginning. Do not expect everything to go smoothly from the front or be wholly absorbed in it. You glide as you will sometimes eat outside your feeding window, and it is okay. If you know you'll do your best, but you know that it can take some time to get used to the transition, you are less likely to be overwhelmed if your plan isn't on track.

FAST IS YOUR FRIEND
The benefits of fasting cover every aspect of your health, both physically and mentally. If you do it responsibly and carefully, it can help you control your body and well-being. There are many options for intermittent fasting. You need to choose a method that works best for you and helps you reach your health goals. We sometimes combine and experiment with techniques until we find one that we can commit to fasting and a healthy lifestyle.

One of the most common reasons people fast sometimes is weight loss, but it barely scratches the surface. Intermittent fasting does more to your body than helping you to lose weight. It also stabilizes blood sugar levels, relieves chronic or widespread inflammation, and improves heart health. Studies also show that intermittent fasting contributes to brain health and helps reduce the risk of developing severe brain disorders such as Alzheimer's disease. Finally, some researchers have proposed that it can help prevent cancer and improve the effectiveness of chemotherapy for people suffering from the disease.

INTERMITTENT FASTING AND DIET
Studies show that people who follow a nutritional plan tolerate variations in food choices such as intermittent fasting, eat more than the people on a strict calorie-controlled diet, more likely to stick, and maintain weight loss. A rigid diet is also associated with symptoms of eating disorders

and a higher body mass index (a measure of body fat based on weight and height).

In the case of IF, even if you agree with the theory that the way to lose weight is to reduce calories and do more exercise, "you do not have to count calories, overeat, or avoid healthy fats," it is the good news.

CHAPTER 5: THE CHALLENGE OF INTERMITTENT FASTING

If you do this and have spent the first week, you will probably stick to the intermittent fasting lifestyle. The hardest part of fasting is the state of mind we bring to the table. You are not the only one. Millions of people come to the table with everything but lack nutrition.

They come to a family reunion at the table. They come for the pleasure of the taste and decoration of the food. They come from habit, but they do not recognize it. They come to fulfill their obligation to eat even when they are not hungry.

The most important thing when you get to the table is that you think you are going to come there to eat. Consider food to refuel and repair your body. It may be one of the most boring ways of looking at it, but that is precisely what you do. It is time to experience a food revolution and stop thinking about food as a source of pleasure and food as a source of life. Food is part of the life cycle, and food allows us to go out into the world to be more than we currently think about.

BE CAREFUL AND EAT
At the heart of intermittent fasting is a concept that most people only notice when eating when we understand our condition. When it is time to eat, we are usually in a hurry or busy doing other things. It is both a source of entertainment and a source of joy. None of this contributes to a healthy diet.
If you practice intermittent fasting, you need to change your view of the diet and practice a conscious diet.
Conscientious eating is not just about filling, but also about your food and your focus on the food processor. If you eat only twice a day, once in the morning and the afternoon, you should not eat for more than 20 to 30 minutes. Do it quietly and record the experience.

HAVE FUN
Fun is not sinful. There are many things you can do in life, but you should not think of all these things for joy. Driving to work every day, paying attention to your car and other drivers on the road, is a conscious experience. Pay attention to driving and routes to your destination. But just because you love racing cars on weekends does

not mean you have to drive fast on the road. Eating is eating. Enjoying means entertainment. Eating can be fun, but it is an exception and not standard.

The power of intermittent fasting is to distract the focus and habits of unnatural and unhealthy things. It removes your body's dependence on repeated food intake and deprives it of where it belongs, the resources it is stored on. It also controls the type of food and increases your dependence on a healthy appetite. The power of intermittent fasting is that it is a liberalizing promise that allows you to take control of your life.

JUNK FOOD

The exception to the grocery list is processed junk food. This term is used in this book without exaggeration. Junk food is undesirable for your health and changes your taste from healthy to its reciprocal.

Why choose a healthy diet and continue to avoid processed foods? You can eat s**t and lose weight during an intermittent fast. It is not a permanent solution. You will lose the excess fat, but your body will eventually break down. Be careful what you put in your mouth.

MENTAL FRAMEWORK

Once you have your first experience of intermittent fasting and become familiar with it, you should start clearing your mind. We do this with mindfulness through breathing exercises. Wait, what could you say? What does mind cleaning have to do with intermittent fasting? These are lifestyle changes. Eating how your body is supposed to eat is only part of the equation. For this reason, we then consider some mindfulness practices that I found useful in connection with fasting.

In the first phase, the exercise, you will be introduced to a series of breath and mindfulness exercises. There are four stages you will experience before you realize the effect that will amaze you.

Starting, Stage 1 is easy. Find a comfortable place. There are no other tasks to do with your eyes closed. All you must do is watch your body breathes. If you do this with your eyes closed, it looks like you are looking right above the bridge of your nose, in the middle of your forehead, between your eyes. It just looks like that. Identify this as your inner seat.

Watch your breathing as soon as you close your eyes. That is all you have to do. Remember to put on hold all other distractions. When sitting and observing breathing, count the time it takes to inhale until the breath reaches the end of the natural cycle and prepares for expiration.

Remember, you are controlling, not just watching. Whatever respiratory rhythm is part of you right now is what you are looking at. Do not inhale profoundly or change to exhale completely.

LEVEL 1 BREATHE NATURALLY

If you do this, you will know the number of seconds it takes to inhale. Then count the time it takes to exhale. The time it takes to exhale may be the same time it takes to inhale, but it does not matter at this time. All you need to do is to know the number. Do this for the first 10 minutes. As it progresses, expiration can be prolonged compared to inhalation, and breathing can be extended to 15-20 minutes. In the end, open your eyes and relax in the same position, allowing the rest of your life to enter the conscious observation slowly. Listen to each sound as it enters your consciousness. Then open your eyes and let the information overflow.

If you notice the surroundings, remember only what you need to remember. What you have seen is that when information is inundated, your mind can only pay attention to one thing.

Repeating this for a week each day will do two things. To slow down and remove all the stress you face, even if you do not know it. But this is only the first part. To understand nature, slowing down is a significant element of success.

LEVEL 2 CONTROLLED BREATHING

The second part is when you start to control your breathing so that it corresponds to the hours of inspiration and progress. By adjusting the times, you intentionally control your breathing. But do not skip this step right away. You must take it slow. You probably look like 99% of the people in the world, and your breathing techniques are wrong. If you learned to breathe at a young age, your diaphragm is muscular, and you can control your pace well.

As you practice this breathing technique, you will notice that, apart from the best breathing habits and the silence of your mind, your extremities start to tingle. It just means that your pulse oxygen rate is increasing. You send more oxygen to the rest of your body, and it wakes up. With this simple exercise, with little effort, you began to cleanse your body and oxidize most of the gaseous toxins present. Faster weekly water also cleans the colon and improves blood quality. As blood quality improves and breathing increases, enough oxygen flows, and cells are activated. Increasing vitamin C in the fruits, you are currently eating as an alternative to junk food also helps the immune system improve its performance.

LEVEL 3 VISUALIZE DISTRACTIONS

The third stage of meditation helps to end eating habits and pave the way for good health. The third step is pretty easy too. You just need to increase the time you spend on meditation.

The idea is to visualize your pastime, and the food is a pastime. When we reach this stage, we recognize that we are distracted but not distracted. You will find that your thoughts have their mind. These thoughts are beyond you and separate you from the random pieces of view. Do not worry - everyone has it. If you watch your breath, you will find that you can monitor everything that is going on around you. When I looked at the same thing, I started to understand not only what I was doing with my breath, but also what I was doing in my heart. You can see the ideas that have become more visible in the eyes of your mind without interacting with them. The advantage of this third step is that you become the master of the mind. Therefore, it can reduce stress in many situations. To enjoy the benefits, never stop daily meditation routines and weekly fasting.

Just as fasting and vegetarianism cleanse the body, mindfulness and breathing exercises cleanse the mind.

The mindfulness exercises you practice can remind you of an outstanding truth: past and future are not necessary, but moments are essential. Mindfulness is at this moment. When you try to do something in this world, the vital thing in the world is to be in this moment.

LEVEL 4 INSTANT FOCUSES

When you reach this stage, the idea is to control your breathing instantly, which is, what your heart is doing instantaneously, your current position. And, if possible, you have reached the height of simple meditation—no need to visualize anything. Your breath is the strongest in the world. Between your heart and your breath, there is very little you cannot heal. In Stage 4, it is time to move meditation to other parts of life. Pay attention to what you do everywhere.

Make sure you are at the moment, wherever you are, especially when you are eating. Be careful whether you are on the bus or an airplane. Being mindful does not mean being withdrawn. You are fully aware of what is happening around you. You do not participate, but you see.

There are ups and downs, like everything in life, you experience intermittent fasting, mostly ups and downs at the beginning. Do not expect everything to go smoothly from the start or be wholly absorbed in it.

241

CHAPTER 6: INTERMITTENT FASTING: MY JOURNEY

As you read, I first tried a 4-day fast under the supervision of Professor Valter Longo. Despite my improved blood biochemistry and his evident enthusiasm, I could not imagine extended fasting for the rest of my life. What's next? After Dr. Having met Christa Baladdy and had learned everything about ADF (Alternate Day Fasting), I decided to give it a try.

But after a while, I found it too physical, social, and psychological. I needed some patterns in my life, and it was messy because I couldn't determine if I could meet friends for dinner on a particular evening without a calendar and lengthy calculations. I also found that fasting every other day was a little too tricky. Many of Christa's volunteers somehow stick to it, but they are in a challenging situation and very motivated. It is an effective way to lose weight quickly and change your biochemistry a lot, but it wasn't for me. So, I decided to eat 600 calories, two days a week. It was a reasonable compromise and, above all, seemed workable. I tried to eat all the foods in one meal, as Christa did in the study, but long before lunch, skipping breakfast made me hungry and irritated. So, I divided my food into two parts: moderate breakfast, missing lunch, and light dinner. And I did it twice a week. It turned out to be very manageable.

After experimenting with different versions of fasting, we have found that the 5: 2 approach is the most effective and practical way to take advantage of fasting and still protect your nutrition plan in the long run. A 5: 2 fast diet is a realistic integration of current thinking about intermittent fasting and is the best way to guarantee success.

Before starting a diet, I decided to have it adequately tested to see how it affects my body. Below are the tests I did. Most of them are easy. With one exception, blood tests should be the tests that your doctor is happy to perform for you.

GET ON THE SCALES

The first and most obvious thing you want to do is to weigh yourself before embarking on this adventure. First of all, it is best to do this at the same time each day. As you know, the first thing in the morning is when it gets the brightest.

Ideally, you want to make sure that your body fat percentage drops. Therefore, you need a scale to measure your body fat percentage and body weight. Inexpensive machines are not incredibly reliable. They tend to underestimate their actual appearance and provide false relief. But what they're pretty good at is measuring change. So, if your existing number is close to 33%, you may be informed at the beginning that your body fat percentage is 30%. But if their numbers decrease, they should be able to tell you that.

BODY FAT

Body fat is measured as a percentage of total weight. Machines that can be purchased through a system called impedance. The device measures the current when even a small amount of current flows through the body. The estimation is based on the fact that muscles and other tissues conduct electricity better than fat.

The only way to get accurate numbers is on a machine called DXA Scan (formerly DEXA). Abbreviation for "Dual Energy X-Ray Absorptiometry." It is expensive and unnecessary for most people. Your BMI will tell you if you are overweight. Women tend to have more body fat than men. Men with more than 25% body fat are considered obese—30 % for women.

BLOOD TEST

They were fasting blood sugar. I decided to measure fasting blood sugar because it is a significant health indicator without risk of diabetes and a predictor of future health. Studies have shown that even moderate blood sugar levels are associated with an increased risk of heart disease, stroke, and long-term cognitive impairment. Ideally, we should have measured insulin sensitivity, but the test is complicated and expensive.

CHOLESTEROL
They measure two types of cholesterol: LDL (low-density lipoprotein) and HDL (high-density lipoprotein). Generally speaking, LDLs carry cholesterol to the walls of arteries, and HDLs have cholesterol away. Low LDL and high HDL are good. This can be expressed as a percentage: HDL to HDL + LDL. Anything over 20% is acceptable.

TRIGLYCERIDE
These are facts contained in the blood. They are one of the ways the body stores calories. High levels are associated with an increased risk of heart disease.

IGF-1
It is an expensive test and is not available on the NHS. It is a measure of cell regeneration and thus of cancer risk. It can also be a marker of biological aging. I wanted to know the impact of my 5: 2 fast on IGF-1. I found that IGF-1 levels dropped dramatically in response to a four-day fast, but after a month of the regular diet, they recovered from their previous condition. What is the best way to fast intermittently?

FASTING AND MOOD
One of the things Professor Valter Longo and his colleagues told me before starting the four-day fast was difficult at first, but after a while, I'm

happy to see what's going on. I was also surprised to find out how positive I was about intermittent fasting. I thought I would be tired and grumpy on a fasting day, but not at all. So is this a psychological effect that makes an intermittent fasting weight loss person feel better, or is it a mood-affecting. According to Professor Mark Mattson, one of the reasons why people think intermittent fasting is relatively easy is because of its effects on BDNF, Brain-derived neurotrophic factor. BDNF not only protects the brain from dementia and mental deterioration with age, but it can also improve mood.

At least in rodents, many studies date back several years to indicate that high levels of BDNF have antidepressant effects. In one study, BDNF was injected directly into the rat's brain and was found to be as effective as the repeated use of standard antidepressants. At least in part to stimulate the production of high levels of BDNF. Mark Mattson predicts that within a few weeks of starting the fasting plan, two days a day, BDNF levels will increase, control anxiety, and improve mood. He currently has no human data to support this claim entirely. Still, he did test volunteers to measure changes, including taking regular samples of cerebrospinal fluid (the fluid that bathes the brain). It occurs during intermittent fasting. This isn't a subtle cardiac test because it requires regular spine inflammation, but as Mark told me, many of his volunteers had early signs of cognitive changes.

You are very motivated. Marc is keen to explore and promote the benefits of intermittent fasting because he is seriously concerned about the possible effects of the current obesity epidemic on our brains and our society. He also thinks that if you are thinking of intermittent fasting, you should start early. Very early, perhaps decades before, subjects began to have learning and memory problems. For this reason, it is essential to start eating first so that young people and middle-aged people can delay the development of these processes in the brain and lives up to 90 years to function correctly.

Like Mark, I am convinced that the human brain enjoys a short period without food. This is an exciting and rapidly developing area of research that many people are pursuing with great interest. Intermittent fasting has a measurable beneficial effect on the brain and other parts of the body: the heart, blood profile, and the risk of cancer. And we are turning now.

FASTING AND THE HEART

One of the main reasons I chose to fast was because tests indicated that I had severe problems with my cardiovascular system. Nothing has happened yet, but the warning signals flashed orange. Tests have shown that my LDL levels in the blood (low-density lipoprotein, the "bad" cholesterol) are incredibly high, as well as my fasting glucose levels.

To measure fasting glucose, you need to fast overnight and then give a blood test. The standard and desirable range are 3.9 to 5.8 moles / l. and mine was 7.3 mole / l. Not yet diabetic, but dangerously high. There are many reasons why you should do everything you can to avoid diabetes, including the fact that it significantly increases your risk of heart attack or stroke.

Fasting blood sugar is an important measurement, as it is an indicator that your insulin level is not correct.

INSULIN:
THE FAT PRODUCING HORMONE

When we eat foods, especially carbohydrate foods, our blood sugar and pancreas, an organ under the ribs and near the left kidney, start to produce insulin. Glucose is the primary fuel that our cells use to generate energy, but the body does not like high blood levels. The hormone insulin has the function of regulating blood sugar and ensuring that it is neither too high nor too low. It is usually done with great precision. The problem occurs when the pancreas is overloaded. Insulin is a sugar controller. It supports the extraction of glucose from blood and stores it in a stable form called glycogen in places such as the liver and muscles. It can be used as needed. What is not well known is that insulin is also a fat regulator. It inhibits lipolysis and the release of stored body fat. At the same time, fat cells absorb and keep grease from your blood. Insulin makes you fat. Higher values increase fat accumulation; lower costs decrease fat.

As we do more and more, the problem with the constant consumption of high-sugar, carbohydrate-rich foods, and beverages is that we must release more and more insulin to cope with the spike in glucose. At some point, the pancreas can cope by simply excreting increasing amounts of insulin. This leads to increased fat deposits and an increased risk of cancer. Of course, this does not last forever. As you continue to produce more and more insulin, your cells eventually rebel and resist that effect. It is like yelling at your child. You can escalate further, but after a certain point, they just stop listening. Eventually, the cells stop responding to insulin. Today you can see that blood sugar stays high all the time, contributing to 285 million people worldwide with type 2 diabetes. This is a huge problem that is increasing worldwide. Over the past 20 years, that number has increased almost tenfold, and there is no clear indication that this trend has slowed.

Diabetes is associated with an increased risk of limb loss due to heart attack, stroke, impotence, blindness, and circulatory failure. It is also associated with brain contraction and dementia. It is not a beautiful image.

One way to prevent the worsening of diabetes is to cut down on carbohydrates and eat more vegetables and fats. Indeed, these foods do not lead to such an increase in blood sugar. They also have no dramatic effect on insulin levels. Another option is to try intermittent fasting.

FASTING AND CANCER

My father is adorable, but he wasn't incredibly healthy. Overweight for most of his life, by the time he was 60, he had not only diabetes but also prostate cancer. He had surgery to get rid of the tumor and left an embarrassing urine problem. Naturally, I do not try to walk this path.

My four day fast showed to me that under Professor Valter Longo's supervision, IGF-1 (insulin-like growth factor 1) levels could be significantly reduced. Prostate cancer risk. I later learned that intermittent fasting had a similar effect on my IGF-1 levels. The link between growth, fasting, and cancer is worth clarifying. The proliferation or replacement of dead, worn, or damaged tissue is fine as long as the development of the cells is controlled, but the cells can mutate, get out of control, and turn into cancer. Very high blood levels of cell stimulants like IGF-1 increase the likelihood that this will happen.

If cancer becomes epidemic, the standard options are surgery, chemotherapy, or radiation therapy. Surgery is performed to remove the tumor. Chemotherapy and radiation therapy are there to try and be addictive. The main problem with chemotherapy and radiation therapy is that they are not selective. Not only does it kill tumor cells, but it also kills and damages the surrounding healthy cells. Hair is usually shed after treatment, mainly because it is more likely to damage cells that divide faster, such as hair roots. As mentioned earlier, Valter Longo shows that if you are robbed of food for a short period, your body will react and slow things down, going into repair mode and survival mode until food becomes creamy again. This applies to normal cells. However, cancer cells follow their own rules. They are almost out of control in nature and grow selfishly under all circumstances. This "selfishness" creates opportunities. At least, in theory, fasting just before chemotherapy causes a situation in which normal cells become dormant, cancer cells become powerless and more sensitive.

In an article published in 2008, Valter and colleagues showed that fasting "protects cancer cells from high-dose chemotherapy.

If you do not have a fundamental health problem and you are not a fasting individual, you do not have this time. Ask yourself: When is it not now? It is advisable to wait for the advice of your doctor. You can choose to prepare, get rid of eating habits that are too long, empty the refrigerator, eat the last cookie in a jar, or scratch yourself. Or you may want to continue after a few weeks to see any visible progress. But let's start with the day when you feel healthy, decisive, calm, and committed. Tell your friends and family that you are about to start a fast diet. If you make a public promise, you are more likely to stick to it. Avoid busy days, holidays, days of three-course lunches that include bread baskets, cheeseboards, and four desserts. Also, busy days can help reduce flight times, while quilt days usually crawl like honey with a spoon. When you think about the beginning of the day and specify it, you'll be moved. Before you start, record your details such as weight, BMI, and goals, and record your progress in the journal. Dieters are more likely to lose pounds if they honestly record what they eat and drink. Keep them and take a deep breath and relax. Better shrug your shoulders. It does not matter as you lose nothing but weight. How tough will it be? If you've been hungry for a while and even with a few pointers, eating at least 500 or 600 calories a day, at least initially, can prove to be an easy challenge. Intermittent fasters report that the process becomes much easier over time. Mainly because the results are obtained with mirroring and scaling. The first early days are accelerating, supported by the novelty of the process. The early days of the third week of wet Wednesday may feel like a slogan. Your mission is to complete it. You say no to chocolate today, but tomorrow you will eat whatever you want. This is the joy of a fast diet and a big difference to other weight loss plans. How to win a hunger game!

There is no reason to be surprised by benignity, and occasionally, short-term hunger. If you are in good health, it will not be destroyed. They do not collapse in a heap and need to be saved by the cat. Your body is designed to be food-free for long periods, even if you lose your ability due to years of grazing, hunting, and snacking. Studies show that modern people tend to confuse different emotions with hunger. When I'm bored, thirsty, when I'm near food (when it is not), when they're together or when the clock tells us it is time to eat. Most of us also eat because we feel good. This is known as "hedonic hunger." You should try to resist the fasting days, but you can rely on your knowledge to lose the temptation the next day if necessary. You do not have to panic about it. Note that the human brain is good at persuading us to be hungry in almost any situation. You are faced with deprivation, withdrawal, or disappointment when you are angry, sad, happy, or neutral. The smell of freshly brewed coffee in a roadside cafe when influenced by advertising, social demands, sensory stimuli, rewards, and habits. Realize now that these are often learned reactions to external cues, and most of them are designed to let you get out of your money. If you are still preparing your last meal, it is unlikely that you will feel starving ("total transit time" if you are interested in things like sex, metabolism, and what you ate). Hunger can be as aggressive and uncomfortable as a sharp knife box, but it is more fluid and controllable than you might imagine. I'm not even hungry before the day of fasting begins. Also, the blow passes. Fasters report that the perception of hunger is riding the waves and not the walls of the ever-growing stomach bite. It is a symphony of differentiated movements, not a horrifying and endless crescendo. Treat the belly rumble as a good sign, a healthy messenger.

Also, do not always feel hungry, as you will not feel hungry for more than 24 hours. Wait a minute. You have the absolute power to overcome the feelings of hunger, just by turning your mind, riding the waves and doing other things-walking, calling friends, drinking tea, running, take a shower, take a shower and sing, get a friend from the rain and sing. It is commonly reported that after a few weeks of intermittent fasting, my hunger decreased. As we have seen, one of the most critical studies examining how obese people respond to intermittent fasting is the more sophisticated Alternative Day-Modified Fasting Method (ADMF) at the University of Chicago. Volunteers did it. In this study, "we found that hunger levels increased and corrected hunger every other day for the first week. However, after two weeks of ADMF, hunger levels decreased and remained low throughout the rest of the study." "This indicates that the subject is accustomed to the ADMF diet after about two weeks (that is, they are not very hungry on a fasting day)." "The ADMF diet was less satisfied in the first four weeks of the intervention, but gradually increased in the last four weeks of the study."

In short, researchers suggest that obese participants may be able to continue their diet over a more extended period as their feeling of hunger decreases significantly, and their satisfaction with their diet improves considerably in the short term. I decided it was high. The study was conducted with people who fasted every other day. In contrast, partial fasting two days a week - a fast diet plan - is discouraging. Take courage. Avoid, restrain, distract, fast. Before you know it, you are retraining your brain and starving from the menu. Tomorrow is another day: delayed strength, patience, and satisfaction.

Perhaps the safest and most innovative part of a fast diet is that it does not last forever. Unlike the lousy food that had failed before, this plan will always be different tomorrow. Simpler breakfast, including pancakes, lunch with friends, and wine, cream, and apple pies for dinner. This on / off switch is essential. So, on fasting days, you eat a quarter of your regular calorie intake, but tomorrow you can eat as much as you want. The fact that a fast is a short stay and a short break after a meal offers endless psychological comfort. Unlike a full-time fad diet, you still enjoy food, you will always have a snack, and you will attend regular and routine eating events in your everyday life. No special shakes, bars, rules, points, ailments, or singularities. However, do not always say "no." You ought to not feel like you've been robbed immediately. Like all those who have embarked on the tedious task of a long-term daily diet, the kind of persons who want to execute the Hara-kiri on the kitchen floor. Traditional meal plans fail when you open the refrigerator door. The key is to recognize that breakfast can be reached through the exercise of patience and willpower. The flavor sings—stab dance. If you have, without thinking, felt lazy disdain for the food you eat, then things are about to change. There is nothing like the satisfaction that has been postponed. A bit to make things better—compliance and sustainable: how to find smart meal models that work for you??

Most diets do not work. You already know it. Indeed, when a team of UCLA psychologists performed an analysis of 31 long-term diet trials in 2007, their analysis found that skinny people had lost pounds in the first few months, while the majority will return to their original weight in a year. Conclusively, the researchers agreed upon that most of the participants would have better been off not going for the diet plans at all. Losing the weight and gaining it back made their bodies to suffer wear and tear. Another massive study on a group of 19000 older people with two categories: people with diet history before the conduct of the study and people with no diet history. For four years, it was observed that people with no diet history were better off than the others in the group.

Therefore, to be effective, each method must be rational, sustainable, flexible, and long-term viable. What matters is not adherence to weight loss, but adherence itself. Therefore, the objectives must be realistic, and the program should be practical. It should fit into your life, not the life of your dreams but where you live. Any weight loss strategy must be tolerable, organic, and innate. It is not a fake supplement equivalent to a food resembling a good looking but an unpleasant shoe.

LONG TERM EXPERIENCE

The long-term experience of intermittent fasting is still being researched, but those who have tried it commented, how easily it fits into everyday life. They always get food variety (anyone who has tried to lose weight with the "only" grapefruit or cabbage soup knows how important it is). They always get rewards from food. They still have a life; there is no drama, no hopeless system, no masturbation. Do not sweat.

FLEXIBILITY: THE KEY TO SUCCESS

Your body is not my body. Mine is not yours. It is, therefore, worthwhile to adapt your plan to your needs, your day form, your family, your commitment, and your taste. None of us live a cookie-cutter, and a diet is not for everyone. Everyone has habits and modifiers. Therefore, there is no absolute command here, only suggestions. You can choose to fast in a certain way on a particular day and also first or last one or two times.

Some people want to know precisely what and when to eat. Others prefer a more informal approach. It is nice just to follow the primary method (500 calories or 600 calories twice a day, long without meals) twice a week, and you will reap the many benefits of the plan. Ultimately, you rarely need to do a dedicated calorie count. You know what a fast day means and how you can adapt it to your needs.

MAINTENANCE MODEL

You can consider a maintenance model as soon as you reach your target weight or shadow below it (providing range and abundant birthday cakes). It adjusts to fasting only once a week to maintain a maintenance pattern at the desired weight, but still utilizes fasting occasionally. Of course, if you wish, one day a week will give you fewer health benefits than two days in the long run. But it fits perfectly in life, especially if you are not going to achieve further weight loss.

What to expect: the first thing you can expect when dieting fast is to lose weight. In some weeks, you will find yourself stuck in a disappointing plateau, and in others, you will progress more quickly. As an essential guide, you could expect to lose around a pound per day of fasting. Of course, it is not all bold. However, you will need to lose about 10 pounds of fat in 10 weeks compared to an everyday low-calorie diet. The key is to maintain weight loss over time.

HOW YOUR ANATOMY CHANGES?

BMI, body fat levels, and waist size are expected to decrease gradually over the next few weeks. It should also improve your cholesterol and triglyceride levels. It is the path to better health and longer life. You are already dodging your unwritten future. But for now, as your body becomes thinner and lighter, noticeable changes begin to appear in the mirror.

For several weeks, you can see that intermittent fasting also has significant side effects. In addition to noticeable weight loss and preserved health benefits for the future, more subtle results, benefits and bonuses, may work. Changes in appetite expect your eating preferences to adjust. From now on, we opt for healthy food as standard and not for design. They start to understand, negotiate, and deal with hunger, and to know what it feels like to be hungry. Instead of moaning like an immobile sofa, you can also see a feeling of comfort and fullness. I am full and not a filling. What is the result? "Food hangover," improved digestion, no crack.

Interesting eating habits appear six months after a temporary fast. You may be eating half of the meat you eat once, not as a conscious movement, but as a natural movement that comes from what you want, rather than making a decision or believing. You can consume more vegetables. Many intermittent fasters instinctively withdraw from bread (and in some cases, butter), strange "comfort" foods are less attractive, and refined sugar is less attractive than before.

Hairdo's bag in the glove compartment of the car? Take it or leave it. Of course, you do not have to be proactive. It happens anyway. If you are a person like me, you'll someday arrive at a place you hate cheesecake. Not because I hate it, but because I refuse to treat myself. This is the raw power of intermittent fasting: it encourages you to check your diet. And this is your long-distance health ticket how your attitude changes.

So yes, you will start losing the bad eating habits. However, if you continue to notice and continue to fast and treat, all other types of changes should occur.

For example, you may suffer from "partial distortion" for years because you think the dishes on the plate are needed and needed. Over time, you will find that you are overdoing it. The muffin sits under the glass dome of the coffee shop, and when it is thick and moist, it looks big. The potato chips maxi bag makes an expansive view. To get from Venti to Grande, you only need half a cup, no sugar, no cream. You will soon become aware of what you have eaten and what unspoken wording you have been saying for years. The progression of doing so is more than anything else as part of the readjustment process.

I've changed my mind. Occasionally, fasting trains you in the art of "restricted nutrition." In the last example, this is the goal. It is all part of a long-acting game, which means that the fast diet ultimately does not become a fast diet, but a way of life.

After a while, you will develop a new approach to dietary, rational, and responsible eating, even if you do not even know you are. Intermittent fasting also reports increased energy and increased emotional well-being. Some people talk about "shine." Perhaps the result of winning a struggle for self-control or something that happens in smaller clothes, compliments, or at the metabolic level that determines our mood. I still do not know the exact reason, but I feel good. Much better than a cake.

Online fans say: "Overall, fasting seems right. It is like a reset button for your whole body." Even more subtly, I feel reassured as many fasts are no longer eating on their fasting days. Accept it. If you allow it, you have some freedom here. You may find that we look forward to fasting as we do.

FEMALE SPEED: MIMI'S EXPERIENCE

Most men I know respond well to numbers and goals (preferably using related gadgets), but I have found that women tend to take a more comprehensive approach to fast. Knowing that our body is unique and responds to stimuli given in its way, like many things in life, we want to find out what it does. Respond to shared stories and support from friends. And sometimes a snack is needed.

263

Personally, for example, I burn fasting calories in two batches, one fast and one late, to spare a day to limit and maximize profit prospects. Aim for a longer gap between the two: Health and weight loss. But in the meantime, I need a little something to keep me. A simple breakfast is usually low sugar muesli, probably containing strawberries, fresh almonds, and semi-skimmed milk. Then dinner: lots of leaves and lean protein-probably smoked salmon, tuna, or hummus-when a child goes into bed, a substantial and exciting salad. All-day long, I drink San Pellegrino mineral water with a splash of lime, lots of herbal tea, and lots of black coffee. They just help the day go by. In the four months since the fast diet started, I have lost 6 kg, and my BMI has changed from 21.4 to 19.4. If you are struggling with larger numbers, take advantage of the fact that more obese subjects respond wonderfully to intermittent fasting. The positive effects can be seen in a relatively short time. Nowadays, weekly fasting (Monday) is enough and seems to hold a stable and happy weight.

Many of the women I meet are familiar with diet techniques (longstanding practice), and I have found a few tips to help on a short day. For example, we recommend eating with a small bite, chewing slowly, and concentrating while eating. Why do you read magazines, and why do you mumble while eating? If you only get 500 calories, it makes sense to notice this while taking it.

Hunger turned out to be more than just a problem like many occasionally accelerated cases. For some reason - and we're wondering if it is suitable for the food industry - we've been plagued by fear of hunger, hypoglycemia, and more. On the whole, days with less food are more liberal than limiting me. It means that there are ups and downs: for a few days, it will fly like stones on water. On other days, I feel like I'm sinking and not swimming. Probably because emotions, hormones, or the tricky business of life has started. See how you feel and always give grace when this is special.

6 WAYS TO MAKE A FAST DIET EFFECTIVE

1. KNOW YOUR WEIGHT, BMI AND WAIST SIZE FROM THE START

As mentioned earlier, the waist measurement is an essential and straightforward measure of internal fat and a strong predictor of future health. People with intermittent fasting quickly lose those dangerous and unattractive centimeters. The BMI is the square of the weight (in kilograms) divided by the height (in meters). It looks ugly and may sound abstract, but it is a widely used tool to find a way to healthy weight loss. The BMI values do not take into account your body type, age, or ethnicity. You should, therefore, greet them informed. However, this is useful when you need a number.

Weigh yourself regularly. After the first phases, once a week is sufficient. If you want the numbers to drop, the morning after fasting is your best bet. Researchers at the University of Illinois noted: "Weighing can vary significantly from food to fasting days. This weight deviation is probably due to the extra weight of food in the digestive tract.

It is not a daily change in fat mass. Future solutions may require solutions that try averaging the weight measurements on consecutive feeding and fasting days to determine weight more accurately. There are 28 tasks. If you are a person who likes structure and clarity, you may want to track your progress. Think about your goals. When and where do you want to go? Be realistic: rapid weight loss is not recommended. Please take your time. Make a plan. Write it down.

Many people recommend keeping a diet journal. Add your experience next to the number. Note the three good things that happen every day. It is a message of happiness that can be referenced over time.

2. FIND A QUICK FRIEND

You need very few accessories to be successful, but a supportive friend can be one of them. Once you are on the fast diet, tell people about it; You may find that they join you, and you will build a network of shared experiences. As the plan appeals to both men and women, couples report that doing it together is more comfortable. This way, you get mutual support, camaraderie, shared engagement, and shared anecdotes. Also, mealtimes are infinitely more comfortable if you eat with someone who understands the basics of the plot.

There are also many discussions in online discussion forums. Mums net are an excellent source of support and information. It is remarkable how reassuring it is to know that you are not alone.

3. QUICK MEAL PREPARATION

Prepare your quick meal in advance, so you do not have to search for food and come across a sausage that irresistibly hides in the fridge. Keep it simple and effortlessly strive for the taste of the day. Buy and cook on non-fast days to avoid laughing at inappropriate temptations. Clean the house of junk food before embarking. It will only sing and coo in the closets, making your fasting day more difficult than it should be.

4. CHECK THE PARTIAL SIZE OF THE CALORIE LABEL

If the serial box says "30 g", weigh it. Continue. Be surprised. Then be honest. Your calorie count is necessarily fixed and limited on an empty stomach, so it is important not to worry about how much is flowing. Here, you'll find our recommended fast food calorie counters. More importantly, do not count calories on the late days.

You have better things. Wait before you eat. Resist at least 10 minutes, and preferably 15 minutes, to see if your hunger subsides (which is usually the case). If you need a snack, choose one that does not raise your insulin levels. Try carrot carrots, a handful of popcorn, apple slices, or strawberries. But do not pinch like chicken all day. Calories are stacked up quickly, and your fasting is fast. Eat consciously on a fasting day and fully absorb the fact that you are eating (especially if you have ever been in a massive traffic jam). Also, be careful with your vacation. Do not eat until you are satisfied (of course, this happens after a few weeks of practice). Find out what the concept of "satisfaction" means to you. We are all different, and it changes over time.

5. STAY BUSY

"We humans are always looking for activities between meals," Leonard Cohen said. Yes, see where it takes us. So, fill your day, not your face. "No one is hungry during the first few seconds of skydiving," said Brad Pilon, the advocate of fasting. Distraction is the best defense against the dark art of the food industry, with doughnuts and nachos on every corner. If you need this doughnut, keep in mind that it will remain tomorrow.

6. TRY 2 TO 2

Fast from 2:00 p.m. to 2:00 p.m., not from bedtime to bedtime. After lunch on the first day, eat modestly until late lunch on the next day.

This way, you will lose weight during sleep and will not feel uncomfortable for a day without food. This is a smart trick, but it requires a bit more focus than the all-day option. Alternatively, you can go from dinner to dinner quickly. In short, no day is fast and fun. The point is that this plan is "adapted to adjustment." Just like your waistband in 3 weeks.

A TERRIBLE FAST FOR WOMEN?

Women's bodies are designed to carry babies physiologically, making them more susceptible to starvation than men. When a woman's body detects impending famine, it responds by increasing the hormones leptin and ghrelin that work together to control appetite. This hormonal response is the means the female body uses to protect the developing fetus, even if the woman is not currently pregnant.

It is possible to ignore the hunger signals of ghrelin and lepton, but this becomes increasingly difficult, mainly as the body repels and begins to produce more of these hormones. If a woman becomes hungry in an unhealthy way-eating too much or eating unhealthy food-this can cause a chain of other hormonal problems related to insulin.

This process can also shut down the reproductive system. If the body believes that there is not enough food to survive, it can affect the ability to conceive to protect the chances of pregnancy. For this reason, fasting is not recommended for women who are pregnant or trying to conceive.

The hypothalamic-pituitary-gonadal axis (HPG) controls the endocrine glands involved in ovulation. The first part of the evaluation process is the release of gonadotropin-releasing hormone (GnRH) from the hypothalamus. The release of GnRH then triggers the pituitary gland and releases both the follicle-stimulating hormone (FSH) and the luteinizing hormone (LH). In women, the release of FSH and LH causes the ovaries and the production of estrogenic and progesterone. Increased estrogenic and progesterone cause the release of mature eggs (ovulation). This hormonal cascade usually occurs in regular cycles. However, GnRH is extremely sensitive and can be discarded by fasting.

This does not mean that intermittent fasting is not appropriate for women. That means you should be a little more careful about it. If you are the first fasting woman and you are trying to see if that's right for you, then you should start a fasting crescendo.

Crescendo fasting only fasts for 12-16 hours a few days a week, not every day. These short days should not be consecutive (e.g., Tuesday, Thursday, Saturday). On fast days, you should only do light exercises such as yoga or walking. Intense activities such as strength training should be booked for a few days without fasting when eating a regular meal. Drinking plenty of water is also essential. A general recommendation is ounces and half weight. Therefore, if you weigh 140 pounds, you should drink at least 70 ounces of water each day. Of course, the amount of water you need depends on many factors, such as your age, weight, activity level, and amount of coffee you drink. However, you should use this equation as a basis.

If you feel good after a few weeks of crescendo fasting, you can add another day fasting and see how your body responds. If you still feel good, you can add more days until you reach your fasting goal. The main point of Crescendo's fasting is to relax slowly and, at the same time, not to over-impact the body. The smaller the plate, the better.

It may be a trick in the head, but the small plates help control the parts. If you have a dish, you tend to fill it up. This means that you usually serve more meals on a large plate than on a small scale. Instead of a dinner plate, choose a salad or starter plate. If you are still hungry, you can always go back a few seconds, but take some time for the food to calm down. In many cases, it is recommended to wait 5-10 minutes between eating and returning to your next help. It gives your body the ability to decide if you are starving.

FASTING AND FUSSING

There is a general belief that if you eat too long, you end up eating unhealthy foods and eventually gain weight. Not so black and white. There are many factors to consider.

Fasting studies every other day show that fasting people tend to eat more calories the day after a 24-hour fast. However, the increase is less than 500 calories. Even if you include the calorie loss on an empty stomach in a minimal rise in next day intake, you are running out of calories.

Often, the desire for bulimia is also caused by a dramatic drop in blood sugar that occurs after a high-carbohydrate meal, or by carbohydrate addiction. As soon as the blood sugar level drops after a period of intermittent fasting, the feeling of hunger stabilizes, and the tendency to overeat decreases.

For people suffering from bulimia and eating disorders, fasting can lead to seizures. If you have had an eating disorder in the past, be sure to consult your doctor before beginning an intermittent fast.

CHOOSE THE RIGHT MEAL

The term "nutrition" is often associated with specific food restrictions. Still, the primary definition of nutrition is "the type of food that a person normally eats," so it is necessary to interpret the term here. Please note that there are no special diets you must follow for intermittent fasting, but choosing a diet with nutritious, unprocessed foods will, of course, be the most effective. Some different diets are popular for intermittent fasting but are not involved in the doctrine. You do not have to follow your diet plan exactly as described. For example, if you choose an old template, but find that your body responds well to brown rice, you can add it. It is not necessary to permanently exclude food just because it does not fall under the title of diet. Use intuitive food to find the best approach.

INGREDIENTS FOR HEALTHY FASTING-FOOD

Intermittent fasting is not just about eating. It will also let you know what you eat. Just as there are different ways to fast, there are other diets you can follow, including old foods, low carbs, and pagans. You need to find one that works for you and achieve what you want. Also, you need to make the right decisions when buying foods to find foods and beverages that promote maximum health.

If you already have a reasonable and happy weight, you can still fast effectively, but you should consider adjusting your intake on non-fast days to get more caloric foods. The leading researchers we spoke to in this area are all skinny and always fast. With practice, you will discover a nice balance between fasting and eating that will keep your weight within the prescribed range. Fast once a week, not twice a week. There are no specific studies to shed light on the effects, but use your common sense and look at the scales.

Do not slide as mentioned above, the fasting of any kind is not recommended if you are already skinny or have an eating disorder. If in doubt, contact your family doctor. How long do you need to continue?

Interestingly, the fast diet on/off diet is very similar to the approach of many naturally lean people. One day they will choose the other day they will treat themselves to a treat. In the long run, this is how fast diet works. Once in the routine, it will naturally adjust its caloric intake on fasting and eating days until the process is natural. Once you reach your target weight, you can change the frequency of fasting. Play with it, but do not drift. Be careful. Your goal is a permanent life change, not a moment, not a trend, not a cat for dinner. It is a long-distance road to sustainable weight loss. Accept to do it in a way that suits you indefinitely as long as you are alive.

FASTING FUTURE: WHERE TO GO FROM HERE?

As I mentioned at the beginning of the book, fasting has been practiced for thousands of years, but science has just caught up. The first evidence of the long-term benefits of calorie reduction was found about 80 years ago. A nutritionist who worked with rats at Cornell University in the US found that they could live longer if their diet was severely restricted.

Since then, there has been growing evidence that animals are calorie-restricted, not only when they live longer and healthier, but also when they starve at times. In recent years, rodent research has shifted to humans, and we see the same pattern of improvement.

So where are you going from here? Professor Valter Longo, who has done many pioneering studies with IGF-1, is working with colleagues at the University of Southern California on several human studies that examine the effects of fasting on cancer. You have already shown that fasting lowers the risk of cancer. Now they want to see whether fasting also improves the effectiveness of chemotherapy and radiation therapy. Dr. Krista Varady of the University of Illinois at Chicago is planning several projects. Research is currently underway to investigate how long-term people can withstand ADF. This is a critical study because the success or failure of a diet depends entirely on compliance.

Are people still looking forward to it? The last time we talked to each other, she also found out why people with ADF lose fat but not big muscles, and people with ADF do not completely burn the calories you have. He was again talking about future ideas, including research on why they didn't make up for them missed eating more on their feeding day. She has many theories but needs colder and harder facts.

Professor Mark Mattson of the National Institutes of Aging, Baltimore, is continually adding to dozens of previously published studies on the effects of fasting and intermittent fasting on the brain. In particular, I'm particularly keen to see the results of some of his recent studies, including further research into what happens to the minds of volunteers when they undergo intermittent fasting. Also, his team is considering drug therapy. Despite its benefits, it is used, for example, in the treatment of diabetes because it knows that many may not want to fast, but it activates the production of BDNF (the neurotrophic factor from the brain). This seems to protect the brain from aging damage, as we've seen. Even if Vietta or a related drug does not prevent dementia, it at least slows down its progression considerably. Intermittent fasting is one of the best-kept secrets of science.

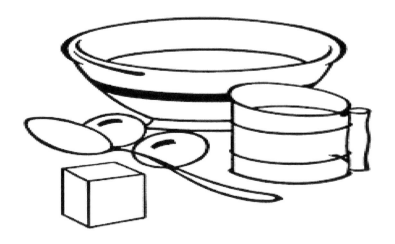

TIPS FOR A FAST DAY COOKING

1. Increase the amount of low-calorie, low-GI leafy vegetables listed here. Green vegetables are difficult to eat and should be purchased a bit earlier if large quantities are needed. Stir-fried vegetables are delicious. It is best to steam lightly. Invest in a tiered bamboo steamer to promote health and cook protein and vegetables at various stages that are environmentally friendly.

2. Some vegetables will benefit from cooking, but other vegetables should be eaten raw. Cooking certain vegetables, such as carrots, spinach, mushrooms, asparagus, cabbage, and peppers, destroys cell structure without destroying vitamins, allowing them to absorb more food.

Mandolin makes the preparation of raw vegetables quick and easy.

3. Fasting days should be low in fat and not fat-free. A teaspoon of olive oil can be used for cooking or sprinkled on vegetables to add flavor. Or use an edible oil spray to get a thin film. The plan includes fatty meats like nuts and pork. Add a light oil dressing to the salad. This means that you are more likely to ingest fat-soluble vitamins.

4. Lemon or orange dressing acids are said to absorb more iron from lush greens such as spinach and kale. Watercress and orange are a great combination with a small number of sesame seeds and sunflower seeds or blanching almonds interspersed with a small amount of protein and crunch.

5. Cook in a pan to reduce high-calorie fats. If the food sticks, splash the water.

6. Weigh the food after cooking for an accurate calorie count.

7. Dairy products are also included. Choose low-fat cheese and skim milk, avoid high-fat yogurt, and choose a low-fat alternative. Drop the latte and throw the butter on a simple day. These are calorie traps.

8. Similarly, avoid starchy white carbohydrates (bread, potatoes, pasta) and instead choose low GI carbohydrates such as vegetables, legumes, and slow-burning cereals. Choose brown rice and quinoa. Use oatmeal for breakfast longer than regular grains.

9. Make sure your fast contains fiber. Eat apples and pears, eat oats for breakfast, and add leafy vegetables.

10. Similarly, avoid starchy white carbohydrates (bread, potatoes, pasta) and instead choose low GI carbohydrates like vegetables, legumes, and slow-burning cereals. Choose brown rice and quinoa. Breakfast porridge stays full longer than standard grain.

11. Be sure to include fiber in your fasting. Eat apples and pears, prepare oats for breakfast, and add leafy greens.

12. If possible, add flavors. Chili flakes kick a delicious dish. Balsamic vinegar gave acidity. We also add fresh herbs - they are practically calorie-free but give the plate its personality.

13. If you eat protein, you stay longer. Stick to low-fat proteins, including some nuts and legumes. Remove meat skins and fats before cooking.

14. Soup on a hungry day can be a savior, especially if you choose a light soup with leafy greens (Vietnamese Pho is ideal, but keep the noodles low). Soup is a great way to consume the ingredients that you are fed up with and that you struggle within the fridge.

15. If desired, use agave as a sweetener. Lower GI.

IMPROVED APPETITE

When you were pregnant, you probably were suddenly hungry for some of the weirdest things you could think of. These cravings are a mix of psychology and physiology.

When you become pregnant, your body connects you to a new life. This new life requires all original parts and gets building blocks from my host mother. Sometimes the host does not have what it needs and sends the brain a sense of interpretation. The brain interprets this demand as a desire, and the body begins to look for a source of this nutrient.

However, that is just one step. The second step is for the brain to interpret what the body needs. To do this, look at the memory of past foods and search for foods that contain what you need. Knowing where its ingredients are can make your brain feel like eating this food.

This process of identifying the body's needs on different days is confusing, especially when processed foods are added to the mix or a lot of waste is added to the body. The best place for good nutrition is when your child is in the womb and when it is born. What the mother eats goes straight to the child, and this is a great way to get the child on the best possible diet.

If we eat for pleasure and if we eat processed foods, we cannot find a type of food that contains a healthy amount of the nutrients that we need. Therefore, you need to recognize your body with the right diet, without the massive amounts of sugar that are common in modern processed foods. When the body is reintroduced to a better source of dense nutrients, it builds a new library of nutrient information and a library that is available to the body when certain nutrients are needed.

TASTE AND INTERMITTENT FASTING

This is a delicate issue for most people, but a week's preparation should solve it. That's how we are affected by taste and need to protect our taste buds.

Initially, the taste is not just fun. Preference can choose the food you need, which is said to provide nutrition with your body needs.

Taste means appetite, and appetite determines what you eat. When your body needs a particular nutrient, it gives you a desire to look for and consume foods that contain that nutrient. It does not matter if you are a vegan of a lifetime, but if you are new to veganism, you have an appetite for something that's not on the menu.

The mechanism is as follows.

When you are a child, your parents will introduce you to foods that are part of your culture and upbringing. If you are in English, you get Bangers and Mash for breakfast. Mexicans get tortillas and quesadillas, and Americans call muesli and toast. It is what you grew up on (I know it is much more than that - it is just an example).

When you consume a particular set of foods, your body records and links different foods with different experiences, for example, if you had sunflower seeds with cereals in the morning, your body will record all of the nutrition you got from sunflower seeds by taking this vitamin E recipe.

From then on, when your body lacks vitamin E, your body unwittingly has an appetite for sunflower seeds. It gives you a desire for the taste of sunflower seeds and the relationship it has in your brain between the need for vitamin E and the preference of sunflower seeds.

Taste is essential to our ability to keep ourselves healthy and replenish what we need when we need it. It is necessary to protect the foods we eat and not be satisfied with aromatic foods. Starting an intermittent fasting lifestyle increases your sense of taste and your desire for what you need, not what you are addicted to. It enables you to let them know that the food they usually crave is no longer available. In this way, we prepared the mind and body of the first week to rely on taste as a guide for choosing the foods as needed.

What does that mean for you? Well, it saves you from eating unnecessary calories and gaining excessive weight. It works this way. When you want vitamin E from sunflower seeds, instead of picking natural sunflower seeds, you'll want to choose processed and salted ones. Salt appeals to my taste, and it creates habits, but the processed grains are low in vitamin E, and to get the vitamin E, I take more seeds to make up for the deficiency. This leads to higher calorie intake and gives me unnecessary extra weight.

So, apart from seasoning and taste, if you can choose the exact food source of the nutrients you need is the taste. You can find the most natural one you can see in this week of preparation and until the week of the Housewarming. Choosing foods will be clean, and your appetite will accurately reflect what your body needs to replenish.

Remember that intermittent fasting is a lifestyle change that we have to be used to. So, do not consider this a diet, and a week cannot bring you back to your old lifestyle. This is a change in the primary way of looking at you and understanding the senses. It is the direct way to use your natural fat-burning cycle. It is the natural way in which the human body grows.

FOOD TO RETHINK

There are no food groups that needed to be thought over, but the ones that catch the eyes out are the tasty side dishes. Stay away from them at all costs. Taste affects the taste, and its effects affect your food choice and frequency of consumption.

Eating a healthy diet will not only make you hungry in a few hours but will also allow you to work for 1-2 days without refueling. If you find that you cannot get away from the taste, you need to do more.

Therefore, the foods that will be reconsidered are foods that offer flavors such as packaged potato chips and dips, spices, and flavorful side dishes and snacks. An easy way to classify them is to find all pre-packaged and processed foods. After caring for and cleaning your palate, enjoy all the fruits, nuts, vegetables, and seeds available. I do not consume fake meat or fake milk-I know what's made from soy and other non-animal ingredients, but I'm trying to mimic the taste of dairy and meat. That's what you do.

The key to a successful intermittent fasting lifestyle is to change two things in your food efforts. The first is to remove the familiar elements from the food. In this case, we are talking about foods we eat for taste, not nutrition. The second is to change the way with which the taste buds are used to. Using taste buds to select the foods your body needs will increase your health and vitality.

In a week of preparation, there are some things you need to accomplish. First of all, you need to think about the food you eat and why you eat it.

There is nothing wrong with eating food for pleasure, as long as you can prevent it enough to distract you from choosing the right food based on taste. As a vegan, we have minimized most of the problems, but by adopting this new lifestyle, we can get rid of the confusion that the taste has to face. There is something like a healthy snack. If not, it is a matter of mindset. Junk food is not nutritious. That's not real Fruit and vegetables with the right mix of herbs and spices in the right amount are pleasant and healthy. Eating what your body needs is happier than eating junk food. This is one of the advantages of intermittent fasting. You can start to hear your body's needs more clearly, and if you give what you need, you will enjoy eating more than chemically flavored junk food.

This is a thing most epicureans do not recognize. Eating can be a fun experience if you eat temporarily and give the body what it is looking for. Eating only out of habit lacks the essential element of nutrition: the need for it.

After all additional flavors and addictive substances have been avoided and the preparation week is over, the palate is cleaned, and you are almost ready to start the start week from day zero (do not worry. Will be explained later). Ideally, it would be great to be able to leave for that. If you can spend a weekend, go to the mountains, go to the beach, work with someone who supports you, or go alone, your Zero Day will be more effective.

HOW TO CHOOSE ZERO-DAY?

There are three things to consider when choosing Zero Day. Remember that Zero Day is the day that begins the first full period of fasting. So, I want to pick it on days when you do not work or when you go to the snack bar or for lunch. You want to get away from this routine, so find a day when you can get away from work and everyday life.

If you can turn off the weekend, you can usually start on a Friday night and spend a Saturday in the wild or in a new place you've never visited before. Some students go to ranches in western California and to mountain monasteries in northern California to escape everyday life and experience not only a zero-day but also a fast. It will give you a whole new meaning. The second thing you have to consider is whether you want to try and do the challenge of dealing with your current routine, or do you want all the help you can get. If you are going to challenge, stay exactly where you are and head for the cold turkey. But if you need all the help you can get, go on a trip somewhere.

Finally, the third thing to consider (which depends on gender) is whether you are at a particular time in your menstrual cycle. If you are ovulating or menstruating, this is not the best time to start a zero-day.

Intermittent fasting lifestyle that you have seen so far is a week of periodic fasting induction designed to transform your body and act as a buffer between your old and your new lifestyle. You cannot help but do what you do every day for the past ten years, 20 years, 30 years or more. Also, expect your body to do well. This is the goal of the introductory week. It introduces your body to intermittent fasting.

But that concludes our introductory week - what's the next step? Well, now, you start your typical day. On regular days, you have two options to choose from. One does intense training, and the others do light exercise. Which one you choose depends on your goals. It depends on whether you plan to sculpt your body or whether you are concentrating heavily on a lot of energy. Overview after induction

The best way to fast intermittently is to go through fast cycles of celebration and fasting. While the Induction Week has allowed you to explore and use your resting metabolic pathway, this section will increase the switching speed between your regular metabolism and your fat-burning metabolism.

If you are a marathon runner, you know what it is like to move from normal metabolism (where you burn calories from foods you eat) to lean metabolism (where you burn stored fat for energy). This is what marathon runners call hitting the wall. When you have calories in your stomach and start the marathon, you come to a point where you exhaust them, and you come to the end of exhaustion. It takes a while for the body to rock and burn fat, and you know the body is rocking because, at that point, you feel like you cannot go on and want to stop. Then you see the athletes slow down, and you can see the immense pain on their faces. Then they get their second wind, and the energy comes back, and they pick up speed again. Why the second wind? Because his body just changed fuel. Most athletes train long hours not only to increase their speed and efficiency but also to deduce the time they spend when they are off when the body goes on to burn fat. What we did during the initial week was the opportunity to go online. With the 36-hour initial week and the 12-hour preceding week, you have trained your body to move faster. As you enter the real week and increase the pace and frequency to eighteen on and six off, you will find that your body will reach the increased rate, and your switching rate will improve soon. When this happens, you will find that once you eat, the body obediently gets its energy from the food you have just eaten and quickly goes on to burn fat during the 18 hours of fasting. It is an effective system that allows you to shed weight, keep it off, and have an abundance of energy - and what's best is that you will develop a habit for it very soon. This allows you to more easily switch to a lifestyle instead of an unmotivated forced train.

DAILY SWITCHING

During the day-to-day transition, we change our entire routine, so we spend a little of our time focusing on food and the rest of our time on other productive activities.

This is a daily breakdown of 16-8, which means fasting 16 hours a day, then 8 hours. You can reduce your dietary balance and reflect your lifestyle during these 8 hours. This will increase the return on your lifestyle change investment.

When you get into the habit of doing that, your body will spend 12 hours a day on the fat you eat, even 12 hours a day. It is as ideal as possible. The only difference between the different diets is whether you want intensive training or light training. It depends on the degree of your diet.

DAILY STRATEGY

Your daily strategy begins shortly after the admission week. The starting week ended after 3 hours, so there are 8-hour windows instead of 12-hour windows. It is not that bad a difference. In this window, you have to consider how many meals you need. You can adjust this over time. I know that many people have different metabolic profiles, so I do not want to force this onto a preferred number of meals. Some optimize for only three large meals. Whatever you choose, you have to follow it.

1. The intensity of the meals should be a descending profile - that is, the second meal in the window should be the largest, then the slightly lower, then the lower and finally the last meal in the window the smallest from all.

2. Fast after a light workout with an appetizer, protein shake, or BCAA.

3. Do heavy exercises before eating heavily.

4. Eat your most massive meal after your workout.

5. Eat a light meal before closing the meal window.

 If you do this:

1. You convert fat to muscle, and I'm not talking about fleas and cuts. I speak of slim tones.

2. When you have more muscle, it takes more energy to support you - it allows you to eat more and burn fatter.

3. The more overweight you burn, the more fuel you can let through, and the leaner energy you send to your brain. Remember that energy from fats helps your mind work better. It is sharper and more agile with faster response times and more acute observations.

4. When I start the day with a boost in metabolism, I burn energy all day. That's why I put myself in an automatic path to consistent fuel conversion in 3 weeks.

WHAT TO EAT?

1. DO NOT BE AFRAID TO THINK ABOUT YOUR FAVOURITE FOOD.

The psychological mechanism called "getting used" - the more people have something, the less it is tied to it - doing the opposite and trying to suppress food thinking is a faulty strategy. Does that mean? Treat food as friends, not as enemies. Eating is not magical, supernatural, or dangerous. Do not make it the hell Normalize it. Just eat.

2. ADD WATER

Find a non-calorie drink that you like, and then swallow it in bulk. Some people swear by herbal tea. Others prefer foamy mineral water to dance on their tongues, but also tap water. Much of our hydration comes from the foods we eat. Therefore, we may need to add additional drinks beyond our usual intake (check your urine; your urine is pale enough). Should be). There is no scientific basis for drinking the recommended eight glasses of water a day, but there are good reasons to continue drinking. A dry mouth is the last, but not the first sign of dehydration. So, act and recognition before your body are dissatisfied. A glass of water is a quick way to stop hunger, at least temporarily. Also, you will no longer confuse your thirst with hunger.

3. DO NOT EXPECT WEIGHT LOSS ON ANY PARTICULAR DAY

If you have a week where your scale does not seem to shift, even if you do not see the numbers falling, consider the health benefits you will get instead. Remember why you are doing this: not only smaller jeans but also the long-term benefits, the generally accepted advantage of intermittent fasting, destroy disease, and strengthen the brain. Extend life. Think of it as your body's pension fund.

4. BE WISE, BE CAREFUL, AND STOP IF YOU FEEL WRONG

This strategy must be implemented flexibly and tolerantly. You can break the rules if you need to. It is not a race to the finish. So be kind to you and be entertaining. Who wants to live longer when life is miserable? You do not want to growl or sweat in a tired life. You want to go dancing, Right?

5. CONGRATULATIONS

A complete fasting day implies potential weight loss and quantifiable health gains. You have already won. Is breakfast important?

The diet tradition has long indicated that breakfast is the most important meal of the day. Missing it in the morning is like leaving your house without a coat. But not always. According to a recent survey, the more breakfast you have, the bigger your lunch (and dinner). This is not surprising, but it does increase the total number of calories for the day. Wait for a quick later. It is up to you, and the pattern you choose may change over time. What can I drink?

Plenty-unless it has actual calorie content. In fact, as with most decisions on a fast diet, the choice is entirely up to you. Drink plenty of water-it calorie-free, actually free, fuller than you think, and avoids upset your thirst because of hunger. In summer, add a round of cucumber or a pinch of lime. Freeze it and smoke the cube. If you want warmth, miso soup is protein-rich, feels like food, and consumes only 84 calories per cup. Vegetable soup does the same trick. If you are having trouble sleeping, one low-calorie hot chocolate can contain less than 40 calories and can calm you down. Calorie-free drinks are best during the day. It is recommended to pour hot water with lemon to get faster. However, it is recommended to add a pinch of mint leaves or cloves, ginger root slices, or lemongrass. If you like herbal teas, try the unusual flavors (licorice and cinnamon, lemongrass and ginger, lavender, rose, and chamomile). Green tea can have good antioxidant properties. Yes, there is no jury. Please drink if you like it.

Black sugar-free tea and coffee on fasting days can be taken. It is okay if you like milk and artificial sweeteners. But remember that milk calories are added. You are trying to extend the time when you are not burning calories.

Fruit juices look healthy, but are generally surprisingly sugary, contain less fiber than whole fruits, and can increase stealth calories without leaving leaves. Commercial smoothies can have a sugar content similar to that of cola, and because they are acidic, they erode the teeth. They are also loaded with calories. If you want a taste, replace the juice and smoothie with very lean liquor. Probably a dash of elderflower with gushing water and lots of ice.

HOW ABOUT ALCOHOL?

Alcoholic drinks are comfortable, but they only offer "empty" calories. A glass of white wine contains about 120, while a can of 550 ml of beer contains 250. If you cannot say no, skip these on fasting days. This is a unique opportunity to reduce your weekly consumption without continuously feeling disadvantaged. Think of it as an alcoholic two days a week.

AND CAFFEINE?

There is growing evidence that drinking coffee far away from guilty pleasure is useful for preventing mental decline, improving heart health, and reducing the risk of liver cancer and stroke. So, if it moves you and keeps you moving every day, keep drinking coffee. It is a useful weapon against boredom in your arsenal, and coffee breaks can comfortably interrupt your day. There is no metabolic reason to avoid caffeine during the fast. However, if you have problems sleeping, limit your intake later in the day. Of course, please drink black. Chocolates not allowed.

Did you know that chocolate bars are hardly organic food, but did you know what a sweet mocha or apple bar can be? Although processed foods tend to have hidden sugars, which are practical, they do not have the nutritional benefits of useful old plants and proteins. Try carrots, celery sticks, hummus, or a few nuts. Always count them in your daily calories (do not cheat).

Even low-calorie, nutritious foods, and habitual snacks are not recommended. Do not overstimulate as this is part of the motivation to exercise your appetite. If your mouth desperately needs attention, give it a drink. Is it possible to get past the early days using a meal exchange?

SHAKE/JUICE?

Many people say that over-the-counter dietary supplement shakes helped them through the first, usually the hardest, week of intermittent fasting. Shaking is probably easier than counting calories, and on a hungry day, you can take a sip when the hungry waves hit. We aren't big fans because we think real food is better. But if you find it useful, definitely try it. It is best to choose a brand with low sugar content. What are the consequences of fraud and some chips or cookies?

For clarity, this is a book about fasting and voluntary abstention from eating. The reason why this is good for you goes far beyond the fact that you simply eat fewer calories. It occurs because our body is designed for intermittent fasting. Adversity only makes you stronger. While hunger is terrible, a little short, sharp, shocking food restrictions are reasonable.

Your goal is, therefore, to open a food-free breathing space for your body. It does not hurt to reach 510 calories (615 calories for men). Fasting never goes away. The idea of reducing calories by a quarter of your daily intake on a day of fasting has only been clinically proven to have a systemic effect on metabolism. There is no particular "magic" at 500 or 600 calories, but you should stick to these numbers. Specific parameters are required to make a strategy effective in the medium term.

An "extra cookie" on a fasting day is precisely the opposite of your goal (which will likely increase your blood sugar and consume most of your tolerated amount in a butter byte). Needless to say, if you are fasting, you need to think wisely and consistently about your food choices according to the plan outlined here. I will be motivated to exercise, and I will remember that tomorrow is approaching.

WHO ELSE SHOULD NOT FAST?

There are certain groups where fasting is not recommended. People with type 1 diabetes and people with eating disorders are included in this list. If you are already very slim, do not fast. Children should never fast. They are still growing and should not be exposed to any nutritional stress. If you have an underlying disorder, talk to your doctor about how to do it before starting to lose weight.

DO YOU HAVE A HEADACHE?

Doing so may be due to dehydration rather than a lack of calories. A slight withdrawal symptom may appear with sugar (or caffeine if you drop it), but the short fasting is not a particular concern. Continue drinking water. Treat the headache as usual. If you feel a particularly unpleasant fast today, stop it. You are responsible.

DO YOU HAVE TO WORRY ABOUT HYPOGLYCEMIA?

When you are in good health, your body is a very efficient and functioning machine that is used to regulate your blood sugar level effectively. A quick fast is unlikely to cause a hypoglycemic reaction. The recent widespread idea that pasture is necessary to prevent "blood sugar crashes" is a myth. If you eat low GI foods on a fasting day according to the guidelines here, your blood sugar will remain stable. But do not overdo it.

Fasting longer than the recommended biweekly, 24-hour nutritional program here may result in a drop in blood pressure, glucose levels, and dizziness. So be quick and smart. If you have diabetes, consult your doctor before you start changing your diet.

I'M TIRED!!!

Researchers in Illinois hypothesized that on a hungry day, subjects would feel "less and less physically active." Like everyday life, you have a few days up and down, good days and bad days. As an example, many of the intermittent fasting we encountered reports a surge in energy rather than exhaustion. How's it going? Early days may end earlier than usual-not drinking alcohol, and getting enough sleep is an excellent way to have breakfast first.

HOWEVER, DO I SLEEP HUNGRY?

Probably not, but it depends on your particular metabolism and how you measure your calorie consumption in the early morning. If you are hungry, please be careful. Bubble bath, a good book, stretching, and herbal tea adds psychology. Congratulations on the end of the next day of fasting. Surprisingly, the fasting people may report that even if the alarm sounds, they won't run into the fridge without waking up violently. Hunger is a subtle animal, and your appetite will soon find its rhythm.

WILL, MY BODY GO INTO HUNGER MODE AND CONTINUES TO GET FAT?

You do not limit your calories every day, so your body never goes into the legendary hunger mode. Your fasting is never intense. Your body burns energy from fat stores but does not consume muscle tissue because it is always conservative and short-lived. Studies have shown that occasional fasting does not suppress metabolism.

Intermittent fasting also does not increase the level of the hunger-stimulating hormone ghrelin. Researchers at the Pennington Centre for Biomedical Research in Louisiana found that "ghrelin remained unchanged after 36 hours of fasting in both men and women". A licensed path to health and well-being.

WHAT IF EVERYONE AROUND ME EATS ONE OF MY FASTING DAYS?

Get involved, but with a calm conscience. While support from family and friends is beneficial, you will only feel confident when you compose a song and dance on your fast. Diet becomes an obstacle that should integrate happily and calmly into your life. Think of your asset: you will generally eat again tomorrow. Of course, some days are more difficult than others. According to Varady among his subjects, hunger increased by the eighth week: "We think it may have happened because this week of study corresponded to Memorial Day weekend and the issues may have had hungry when they participated in culinary festivities."

If you know you have a social event - or food celebration - in the newspaper, fast the night before or the next day. The flexibility of the plan explicitly means - in fact, it requires - that you always go to this wedding, anniversary, birthday dinner, baptism, bar mitzvah, dinner, chic restaurant. Take a break for Christmas, Easter, Thanksgiving, and Diwali. Yes, you could gain some weight, but it is a life, not a life sentence. You can get around at any time, eat fries and dips and stuff on sticks, and then return to a more difficult fast after the party ends.

WHAT IF I AM CURRENTLY OBESE?

Clinical studies have shown that intermittent fasting is a lasting - if not one of the most effective - way for overweight people to lose weight and keep it off. The bigger you are, the more critical your initial weight loss will be. If you are overweight, traditional restrictive diets have likely failed for some reason. The fast diet is distinguished from the "stimulants" on non-fast days by its flexibility, guilt war, and expresses approval.

Illinois studies have shown that overweight people can adapt quickly to ADF. They were able to remain physically active despite the fast. In summary, "overweight and obese patients experience significant improvements in regimens." As with any underlying disease, we recommend that you fast under supervision. Should I add a third day if I want to see accelerated results? There is no reason not to do it; after all, this is what Dr. Krista Varady's Alternate Day Fasters (ADF) do. However, pay attention to rapid fatigue.

One of the keys to success is that fast nutrition only requires short-term engagement. Ask your body to do more than that, and it can sit up and refuse to behave, making the recommended fasting program more difficult. Experience has shown us that two days are enough. But if you have a date and little party pants on standby, one occasional sneaky day shouldn't hurt. However, do not try an intensive long-term diet. It is not worth it unless you are obese and under medical supervision.

Fasting is suitable for most healthy people, but some groups should not fast, and others should speak to their health care team before starting fasting.

Do not fast if:
- If you are pregnant or breastfeeding
- Severe weight loss or malnutrition
- Under 18 years

Talk to your doctor before fasting if you have:
- To take medicine
- History of eating disorders
- Cortisol deregulation or severe stress
- Diabetes (type 1 or 2)
- GERD (Gastroesophageal Reflux Disease)

LISTEN TO YOUR BODY
Listen carefully to your body to see if fasting is right for you. If you experience low energy or

dizziness while standing, you may need to adjust your fasting time or consult a doctor to make sure your body can regulate your blood sugar properly. Remember that it takes a long time for your body to get used to your new lifestyle. There is usually a transition period of 3-6 weeks during which your body and brain adapt to hunger. During this time, appetite, irritability, weakness, and even loss of libido occurs. This is a normal response.

However, if your symptoms are severe, call your doctor at these early stages. If you feel good after the conditioning phase, this is a good sign that your body likes your behavior. If, after this, you feel dizzy, lightheaded, or low in energy, stop fasting, and consult a doctor.

FASTING AND DIABETES

Fasting can be a challenge for people with diabetes, as the body has more difficulty controlling their blood sugar and insulin levels than people without diabetes. However, studies have shown that intermittent fasting can help restore normal glucose levels. The main concern with fasting and diabetes is hypoglycemia or hypoglycemia.

GET DOCTOR APPROVAL

If you have diabetes, make sure you have your doctor's approval and supervision before you start your fast. If your doctor has approved intermittent fasting, you should be familiar with the symptoms of hypoglycemia and plan for treatment if your blood sugar becomes too low. If your blood sugar exceeds 300 milligrams per deciliter or falls below 70 milligrams per deciliter, stop hunger immediately, and give appropriate treatment.

MANAGE CHRONIC ILLNESSES
The stress that fasting has on the body can be classified as stress for most people. It offers health benefits that will help you achieve your ultimate goals. However, if you are already experiencing chronic pain, you need to control it before you include intermittent fasting in your routine. With chronic stress, your body continuously excretes cortisol. If cortisol levels remain elevated for an extended time, they can cause:
• Anxiety
• Depression
• Sleepiness
• Digestive problems
• A headache
• Heart disease
• Memory and concentration problems
• Weight gain
Over time, chronic stress can also affect adrenal function, making it challenging to regulate hormones properly. If you are already experiencing chronic stress, it is essential to control cortisol levels and make the adrenal gland function properly before fasting.
Meditation can help lower cortisol levels. Avoid coffee, sleep well, and eat clean and healthy for a while before fasting. Avoid excessive exercise.

A yoga-like, low-impact meditation exercise can help.

PREPARE FOR FASTING

Except for spontaneous fasting, most types of intermittent fasting require some preparation. One of the most important things you can do to prepare for your fast is to develop a plan. What kind of intermittent fasting will you do? What days and times will you fast? What is your official start date? It helps to create a schedule for yourself and keep it where you can see it at all times. You can even set your phone's timers to run out when it is time to start fasting and when it is time to start eating again. But you do not have to go straight to a defined fasting plan. You can slowly relax to understand.

STARTING YOGA

In a study by the Yoga Research Society and Sidney Kimmel Medical College at Thomas Jefferson University, the researchers found that after a fifty-minute yoga class, the cortisol levels were decreased. Yoga poses like tree-laying, low-laying, and grasshopper-laying became popular. The researchers believe that this decrease in cortisol is due in part to the activation of the relaxation response by holding poses and breathing deeply. This relaxation reaction reduces the stress cascade, and therefore stress hormones are naturally reduced. High cortisol levels are also expected in people with depression. A study published in the Indian

Journal of Psychiatry found that yoga can help 'stop' the stress response in the hypothalamus area of the brain, which can help people with depression. The study found that yoga was more popular than antidepressants.

MAKE FASTING EASY

If you are not accustomed to intermittent fasting, or if you are accustomed to small meals or grazing 5-6 times a day, a straight transition to fasting can be a big transition. You do not have to make a complete change overnight. You'll be more successful if you get used to it slowly.

Start by moving from 5 or 6 small meals to 3 regular size meals throughout the day.

You do not have to eat in a certain amount of time. You will only get used to the habits and structure of the three-meal schedule.

You also need to get rid of snacks all day long. Snacks are not prohibited if you are occasionally fasting, but you can adjust by eliminating early snacks. Once you get used to fasting, you can eat snacks during the day if you eat during the feeding hours. **Yes, you are going to be hungry.**

It is impossible to say precisely how your body feels during the early stages of intermittent fasting. However, certain things commonly happen to most people when they start intermittent fasting. If you are used to eating 5 to 6 times a day, these effects may be more significant than if you were already eating three meals a day with minimal snacking.

As your body adjusts to intermittent fasting, you will usually feel hungry and hungry.

It is often mental or emotional hunger rather than physical hunger. You may also experience headaches, low energy, and irritability. You may feel a little dizzy, weak, or dizzy while standing.

The severity of these symptoms can change depending on several factors, including your previous diet, but it shouldn't be too dull and should decrease in about a week. **Your body will stabilize.**

After the initial adjustment period, your blood sugar and insulin levels begin to stabilize, and you will start to enjoy the benefits of intermittent fasting. One of the first things you will likely notice is the increase in energy.

You can feel sustained energy throughout the day; instead of feeling awake and productive in the morning, but after being struck by this dreaded afternoon collapse around 2 or 3 p.m., you will feel constant energy. Your blood sugar does not increase or decrease as you do when you eat several meals during the day.

How we do what our mind, body, and spirit are and how food is consumed by our watches, not when it is currently needed or when our body needs it. I saw how it evolved. Strangely, the ancestors of the cave decided to go out and look for lunch when they saw the sun hanging over the zenith. It didn't work that way.

Our body has grown accustomed to the planned meal. As food became part of our itinerary, so did our habits. Their eating habits were particularly useful in making room for organized work schedules. But they made no sense for our health or our lives.

The evidence-based diet review shows that the bottom line is trying to adjust intake but still keeps the frame in the context of a three-meal day. We are looking at the opportunity to cut fat, the chance to cut carbohydrates, and even talk about cutting the candy. But the problem is that it is all based on the dietary conditions that we know.

Food is no longer the natural source of energy that we have developed. Food has been processed for taste and convenience, stored for packaging, and colored for appeal. Food is no longer food. It is a set of marketing principles. Therefore, we know that our bodies adapt and that the long-term effects include illness and a regular diet. We are entering this cycle of unhealthy outcomes.

Doing these two things can increase the power of intermittent fasting.

1. Remove all highly processed foods from your diet and replace them with organic and natural foods.

2. Turn most of your diet into nutritious and should be part of your weekly diet. In the lights of food items like kale, garlic, ginger, Nora + fermented product, all types of berries and leafy vegetables can turn the course of effects in the diet.

Intermittent fasting is a powerful tool. Changing biology and psychology. For most people, the fasting process is mentally more challenging than physically limiting. By accepting intermittent fasting, they suddenly remove the restraint of their indoctrination and see the value of life in its original sense.

Welcome to a happy fast and a new you.

INTERMITTENT FASTING BIBLE & KETO DIET FOR BEGINNERS

The Simplified Guide to Lose Weight Safely, Burn Fat, Slow Aging with a Fasting-Diet, Autophagy & Metabolic Reset. Easy Guide to Detoxify your Body

BY

Karen Loss

TABLE OF CONTENTS

COPYRIGHTS   318

CHAPTER 1: INTRODUCTION   320

CHAPTER 2: FASTING   324

CHAPTER 3: FASTING & ITS BENEFITS 330

DONT SKIP BREAKFAST 339

CONSUME THE RIGHT FATS   339

CUT BACK ON CARBS   339

PLAN DISHES BEFOREHAND   340

CHAPTER 4: RECURRING FASTING   342

RECURRING FASTING, ISN'T THAT HUNGER?
343

RECURRING FASTING TECHNIQUES 345

HOW IT IMPACTS YOUR CELLS AS WELL AS
HORMONAL AGENTS?   346

A VERY EFFECTIVE FAT BURNING PROCEDURE
348

CHAPTER 5: BEST INTERMITTENT FASTING
TECHNIQUES   351

WHAT DO YOU REQUIRE TO LEARN ABOUT
OMAD?   359

THE 5:2 DIET PLAN   359

ALTERNATE DAY FASTING (ADF)   359

DANGERS AND DIFFICULTIES OF FASTING
OVER A DAY   360

42-HOUR FASTS AND ALSO ABOVE   360

CHAPTER 6: BENEFITS FROM INTERMITTENT FASTING   363

  PERIODIC FASTING FOR WEIGHT MANAGEMENT   365

CHAPTER 7: LIVE LONGER, DECREASE CANCER CELLS RISK, & ENHANCE COGNITIVE FEATURE   369

  IT MAKES YOUR DAY SIMPLER 370

  PERIODIC FASTING IS MUCH EASIER THAN DIET PROGRAMS 370

  ADVANTAGES OF PERIODIC FASTING FOR WEIGHT REDUCTION   372

  WEIGHT LOSS   373

  ILLNESS PREVENTION   374

  PROLONGED LIFE EXPECTANCY   375

  THERE ARE 3 KEY APPROACHES TO INTERMITTENT FASTING   376

  YOU MIGHT INTEND TO START EATING ON THE VERY EARLY SIDE 376

  IT'LL TAKE A COUPLE OF WEEKS TO SEE CHANGES 377

  RECURRING FASTING BENEFITS   378

  MORE ON INTERMITTENT FASTING BENEFITS   379

CHAPTER 8: A KETOGENIC DIET PLAN FOR NOVICE   386

  WHAT IS A KETOGENIC DIET PLAN? 387

  VARIOUS KINDS OF KETOGENIC DIETS PLANS   387

ADVANTAGES OF KETO 388

CHAPTER 9: EASY KETO DIET PLAN FOR BEGINNERS 391

FOODS TO ABSTAIN FROM   391

FOODS TO TAKE 393

A SAMPLE KETO DISH PREPARATION FOR 1 WEEK   395

HEALTHY AND BALANCED KETO SNACKS   397

TEST DISH STRATEGY 398

VEGETARIAN KETO SNACKS   399

POINTS TO NOTE400

KETO DIET REGIMEN FOR FAT LOSS 400

MAY DECREASE HUNGER   401

CAN PROMOTE LOSS OF WATER WEIGHT   402

CALORIE BALANCE   402

KETOGENIC ADDITIVES403

YOUR SPECIFIC CARBOHYDRATE INTAKE   404

WHETHER YOU'RE GETTING ENOUGH SLEEP   404

WHETHER YOU'RE LITERALLY ACTIVE   405

SUSTAINABILITY OF THE DIET   405

POINTS TO NOTE   406

BURN FAT QUICKLY   406

WHAT IS THE KETO DIET PLAN?   407

WHAT CAN YOU EAT?   409

HEALTHY PROTEIN   412

10 WEIGHT MANAGEMENT IDEAS   415

HOW QUICK WILL YOU LOSE WEIGHT?   417

POINTS TO NOTE417

ONE MEAL A DAY (OMAD)   424

DISADVANTAGES OF OMAD   428

TWO MEALS A DAY (TMAD)   430

PROS OF TMAD, TWO MEALS A DAY 430

DISADVANTAGES OF TMAD   432

DRY FAST, SOFT DRY FAST VS HARD DRY FAST   435

HARD, DRY FASTING   435

WHICH ONE IS THE BEST?   437

DIETS TO EASY INTERMITTENT FASTING   439

MORNING MEAL: ECO-FRIENDLY SMOOTHIE AT 8 A.M. 440

LUNCH: GRASS-FED BURGERS AT 12 PM   441

TREAT CINNAMON ROLL FAT BOMBS AT 2:30 P.M.442

CONCLUSION   449

COPYRIGHT 451

The information provided here is correct and reliable, as any lack of attention or other means resulting from the misuse or use of the procedures, procedures, or instructions contained therein is the total, and absolute obligation of the user addressed.

The author is not obliged, directly or indirectly, to assume civil or civil liability for any restoration, damage, or loss resulting from the data collected here. The respective authors retain all copyrights not kept by the publisher.

The information contained herein is solely and universally available for information purposes. The data is presented without a warranty or promise of any kind.

The trademarks used are without approval, and the patent is issued without the trademark owner's permission or protection.

The logos and labels in this book are the property of the owners themselves and are not associated with this text.

It takes you through the whole process of fasting, its benefits, how intermittent fasting should be done, and so much more. It represents the different fasting methods being adopted by humans, that details about the exact science and techniques of fasting that can variably be selected by humans, whichever suits them to be adaptable and workable. The book provides in-depth detail that is targeted from a layman perspective but can serve any expert as well. The term intermittent fasting has been variably used jointly with the words "Recurrent fasting" and termed "Periodic fasting" in this book. Make sure to read till the end. Although it seems like you've heard a lot about it lately, intermittent fasting is not a new concept. Fasting has been an essential part of history and religion for centuries. Many people are beginning to understand the health benefits of fasting, from increasing energy to losing weight and increasing mental clarity. Intermittent fasting is not a specific diet plan. It is a general term that describes the style of eating in which you alternate between eating and fasting. When you fast or once your body fasts, or later enters an absorbed state. When you fast, about four hours after a meal, your body relies on stored glycogen for energy. Blood glucose levels up as soon as cells start using sugar, and insulin levels fall in response to this lack of glucose. Because your body wants to maintain a blood glucose level of 70 to 99 milligrams, this drop of blood glucose stimulates the pancreatic alpha cells to release a hormone called glucagon. Glucagon goes to the liver, where it breaks down glycogen into glucose. Once glucose is made, it is released through the liver and travels to your brain and tissues.

Not every food is suitable for everyone because everyone is physically and genetically different and has a different lifestyle and taste preferences. However, Kato can work wonders for people who are overweight and obese, which is a significant cause of severe health problems. The Keto Diet has grown in popularity in recent years. Everyone is talking about it, and the Keto Diet is now known as the "Miracle Diet." Celebrities, professional athletes, and dieticians talk publicly about the benefits of the Keto diet. Its effects and incredible benefits, incredibly rapid weight loss, are enough to prove that Keto's diet works! Ketogenic diets are nothing new. It's been almost a century, and people are treating epilepsy which doesn't respond well to anti-epileptic drugs. In the 1920s, researchers found that a high-fat, low-carb diet significantly reduced epileptic seizures. Then, over time, his popularity grew, and now, everyone is a fan. Everything you need to know about diet, how it works, and why it is the right solution to your weight loss problem.

When it comes to Intermittent Fasting, there are probably not even more popular methods than the keto diet with periodic fasting routine and fasting.

Both approaches have wellness benefits consisting of improved metabolic process, weight-loss, and also much better cognitive function. Research studies have shown benefits for each and personal capacities that act as some lovely profound stories. When talking about Keto dieting, it is pertinent that numerous individuals adopt a keto diet with periodic fasting. It makes good sense that keto and frequent or recurring fasting have a great deal look-alike. Keto works in several patterns, similar to the way recurring fasting works. Adhering to a low-carb and high fat or ketogenic diet may make it a lot much more comfortable to practice than periodic fasting. The normality of keto with intermittent fasting can bring about some quite excellent benefits for your body. Keto diet includes the planning of food intake frequently in the day's routine. In contrast, intermittent has a particular pattern that comprises strategies of fasting on alternate days or twice a week or 24-hour fasting, or period restricted food strategy basis. Intermittent Fasting "IF," is a relatively brand-new term in its approach. It is used as an addition to your diet strategies. And it circles the timing of your food intake. As well as it benefits over time. Many individuals are misled on fasting, so we'll clear that up and also describe just how recurring or continuous fasting can be useful. On your ketogenic trip, it is essential to know that your success is determined by eating enough fat as well as healthy protein and limiting carbohydrates. When you eat, it how frequently you eat that shows the quality of food intake and also just how much you consume that shows the quantity of food intake has a significant effect on your health.

It is the nature of the human soul to get slow and bored and tired to strive. There is much happiness in trying, especially in the face of life's dilemmas or problems. The fasting person may face some difficulties during the first few days, such as headaches, weakness, irritability, and mood swings. It is because of the body getting rid of the rest of the precipitates in the tissues that result in its dissolution that has released toxic blood flow in the blood. As these substances pass on before leaving the bloodstream in the body, they have already gone through the body and all its organs such as heart, brain, and nerves, etc. While in the first days, it disturbs in the beginning, but these symptoms end within a few days of fasting.

Fasting also helps to excrete the waste in the intestines. If these substances remain in the body for a long time, they can turn into harmful toxins. Fasting is an effective way to get rid of body toxins. Fasting is the activity where the urinary and excretory system gets regular, and their performance gets improved. Which also plays an essential role in cleansing and regulating blood and body fluids?

The person who fasts on an empty stomach; it helps the body to reduce fat. Fasting is a means of reviving cells and tissues of the body. Fasting guarantees the restoration of physical energy and is distributed according to the needs of the body. Fasting improves the digestion process, facilitates absorption, and balances the body weight. Fasting opens the mind and strengthens the impression and looks of the human appearance.

Fasting is a cure for many ailments; this reduces the load on the circulatory system. Preserves the levels of fat and uric acid in the blood and thus protects the body from atherosclerotic, gout, and other diseases. Fasting is very beneficial for many heart patients. While fasting, the amount of blood that the heart pumps through the body is circulated better. Also, it helps the digestive system and digestion. In the meantime, the amount of toxins reduces during fasting because there is no intake, and the body has to do digestion during the day. That means less effort and more relaxation for the heart muscle to work smoothly and efficiently.

Fasting does not mean to drop weight using the ketogenic diet plan. If it doesn't benefit you, then do not force yourself. Limiting yourself unrealistically and without benefit to this approach is meaningless and not worth it dissatisfies you. There are two fundamental terms we need to explain right here initially:

feeding and fasting. Your body gets fed when eating your food, and you remain in a fasting state when you are between your meals (i.e., the time between one meal to another lunch and dinner). There are a couple of techniques when it comes to intermittent fasting.

Avoided dishes: This is when you miss over a meal to induce added time of fasting. Typically, individuals select a morning meal, yet others like to skip lunch. It could be any food or dish that can be avoided for some time, and also it can be any meal that can be skipped.

Eating windows: In this option, you set up fast and feeding windows. For example, you fast 16 hours a day and eat only eight hours a day. Since most people fast before bedtime, this method is popular. It is convenient because you skip breakfast at night and increase the speed of not eating until lunch.

There are some widespread approaches:

Method 16/8: Lunch only from 11 a.m. to 7 p.m. or noon and 8 p.m.

14/10 Method: Eating from 10 a.m. to 8 p.m.

If this is your personal preference - you can repeat it once or twice a week if you wish. It can take days to find the right food and fasting window, especially if you are very active or if you are hungry for breakfast.

The approach of 24-48 hrs Fasting (or eat: wait: eat).

This procedure includes a full 24-48 hours fast. Most of the time, this is done only once or twice a week. Most people fast from breakfast to breakfast or lunch.

It is where you enter into prolonged fasting periods and do not eat for 1-2 days.

Usually, individuals limit themselves to the hours of 5 pm-11 pm: People typically describe their fasting home windows by numbers: 19/5 or 21/3, as an example, means 19 hours of fasting then 5 hours eating or 21 hours not eating and also 3 hrs.

When you have the hang of eating on a routine, you can try short durations of 18-24 hours of fast. Then you can judge if the periodic fast is right for you. Whether you determine to do it daily, once a week, or twice a week is up to you do what makes you feel best and listen to your body. If with this version, side effects can be severe, such as fatigue, headaches, irritability, loss of appetite, and low energy content. If you follow this procedure, you should return to a regular, healthy diet during the fasting days.

By understanding their usages, you might assume that the Keto diet routine plus these fasting procedures certainly be well taxing on the body when made use of with each other.

However, based on the research study, it is found that the perfect method to assemble them into a solitary system as well as with the right implementation, one can incorporate the results of being in ketosis with that of fasting. Ketogenic diet plan addresses this by enhancing the body's insulin level of sensitivity, glucose guidelines, and also developing hormonal agent production. Not eating can likewise help your body achieve ketosis much faster. As soon as you remain in ketosis, it certainly is much easier to stay with your schedule, considering that you will, without doubt, experience fewer hunger pains.

Bear in mind that it keeps your metabolism high, which helps you adjust rapidly to your reduced carbohydrate consumption. Furthermore, being in ketosis, while in fast, enables your body to begin utilizing your body fat as a fuel source. It results in reducing body fat and making it a leaner body. Individuals commit to lots of diet routines as well as physical fitness routines for different reasons. Some do it to get over physical concerns, while others simply want to improve their health.

We are all taking more calories and consuming them less. The food we eat has much energy, and we eat it more often. We were eating more than 500 calories every day comparatively the last few years ago. Pair it with our growing lifestyle, as if we have a prescription for weight gain, and that leads to health problems. Fasting is not something many of us think about, food is everywhere, and most likely you be at a distance from the emergency bed and taking muffin at that time. Now I like to eat just like the next person, so I like fasting as much as eating delicious things like abstaining from it. And there are no side effects that you get from following a crazy diet or popping pills because fasting provides a natural high, internal stimulus that works with your body, not against it.

Fasting was in the context of an invitation to engage in deep meditation treat. Many things have been amazed by you, like yoga. Fasting has been going on for different times and periods during the year. Many major religions around the world incorporate some form of fasting into their religious practices. So, while fasting may surprise those who are inspired by the mantras of breakfast, lunch, and dinner. It was a way of life for our ancestors, and it is still the status of yogis and Muslims. Mormons and millions of Jews have done so. Indeed, fasting often brings clarity to mind, but, as I hope you finds yourself, the body does what is truly extraordinary requires. Fasting connects your life and your life to your years of living. It is the best way to help change pounds and change your shape. However, as you find, it also helps your body to function better internally. One of the extraordinary impacts of fasting is that it effects at the cellular level, the only place that counts. This anterior approach can help to create a radiant beauty. It is because fasting gives your body a break and allows you to create a "to-do list." By allowing your body to maximize what it needs and minimize what it doesn't need, you put less pressure on your body's resources and give it more time to handle.

Fasting is very easy, and you can't fail. Breakfast is breaking down for about 12 hours. And let's not forget any of the best things to do - if you "do" the fasting the right way. There is an endless hamster cycle of weight loss and benefits that you see more successful people adopt for their sober personality. Fasting implies that you aren't eating for a prolonged period. If you think of it, not eating isn't all that is unnatural. Your ancestors lived and have adopted to eat less when they were in situations of food scarcity. Recurring/Intermittent fasting is a cycle of the in and out periods of fasting and also eating in a straightforward eating plan that takes care of your body's fat-burning systems. Research studies have shown that periodical fasting is tried and tested to help individuals reduce their body weight and fats to shape up their body posture. The routine is the hardest part of intermittent fasting; however, after six to eight weeks, one does not feel the same food cravings. "For women who have 20 extra pounds of body weight, if they understand it, they can reduce their body fat and weight. It could be a little bit more effort than you believed it was going to be. Also, know that it gets much easier with time, and you can preserve as you progress in your fasting. It truly isn't that poor once you start it, but know that it's extremely effective."

Periodical fasting also provides enormous advantages for your body and mind. You can get rid of chronic illness, and aid your body with better and improved mood. Intermittent fasting sets off an ideal storm of metabolic modifications to deal with weight-loss and fat reduction.

HOW DOES IT WORK?

Intermittent fasting can be helpful for those who want to lose weight without following traditional diets, or the need to learn the difference between physical appetite and mental appetite. It is a helpful tool, and you can continue to use it regularly. But that's not the end of it all, and it's all about nutrition or fitness. Instead of fasting intermittently for decades, people are coming in large numbers - and living in excellent condition. Successful nutrition plans, whether small, eat more frequently or use less frequent meals. When calories are controlled, progress is made. Whether you make them with regular meals with small meals or large meals, it is up to you.

Pay attention to food quality. It should be fresh, un-processed, ample nutrient-based foods that are important, regardless of your eating habits and regularly. Exercise regularly. Exercise is an important part. When our food is full of carbohydrates, our body releases insulin due to the level of glucose in the blood. Now the job of insulin is to signal to the cells how much energy they can handle. Energy is first stored in the form of glycogen and then converted into fat. A ketogenic diet eliminates carbohydrates from your diet, which prevents the body from releasing too much insulin. When the body's insulin levels are low, it begins to burn fat very quickly, resulting in significant weight loss. Now, this may mean that you continue to burn body fat while sleeping. That way, the fat burning process can take place 24/7. Remember what kind of fat you use when eating a ketogenic diet. Eat foods that are high in fatty acids but help you burn fat.

The following are some recommended foods that you can eat during a Ketogenic diet. Grass-Fed

Meat, Seafood & Wild Caught Fish, Pastured Poultry, Gelatine Ghee and Butter, Olive Oil and Avocados, Spinach, Broccoli, Kale, Chives, Chard, Bok Choy. In beverages, such as black coffee and tea, Fats like mayonnaise, mustard sauce, pickles and snacks, Spices and herbs. Mushrooms and all fruits, Macadamia Nuts, Almonds, Walnuts, Pecans, Pumpkin Seeds, Flaxseed, Chia Seeds.

The ketogenic diet helps treat Alzheimer's disease in humans. The ketogenic diet contains about 70% of healthy fats, which are essential for a healthy brain. And to treat Alzheimer's, you need to help your brain, and it's the nervous system. It is where the Ketogenic diet helps treat Alzheimer's disease.

Because you need to use high fats for this diet, it is only recommended for people with type 2 diabetes. If you have diabetics and use insulin, then we recommend that you should contact your doctor before taking a ketogenic dose. Others, who are not on insulin, can benefit greatly from this diet, as it helps to balance your blood sugar levels. If you're a snack lover or have a tendency always to grab food on the move, you may be eating even more calories than your body needs, and that indeed appears on the scale. As a whole, you often tend to eat much less when you limit the amount of time you can eat throughout the day.

Periodic fasting is a pathway to the fat-burning state of ketosis. During the fasting, your body burns fats with its glucose gets carbohydrates for energy. After that, you begin shedding fats from your body. To optimize weight-loss, take a ketogenic diet plan in between periods of fasting.

Recurring fasting influences insulin in the way to decrease insulin levels. First, your body ends up being more sensitive to insulin, which can help to stop weight gain and lower your danger of diabetes mellitus. Second, not eating decreases your insulin levels in the body, which can allow your body to start burning stock up fat.

Improves metabolic process: Recent studies have shown that recurring or continuous fasting reprograms metabolic passages to get even more energy out of food. Fasting additionally raises your degrees of adrenaline as well as non-adrenaline hormones that assist your body in releasing more strength. Improving your relaxing metabolic rate helps your body burn more calories throughout the day, even while you rest.

Numerous research studies have shown that intermittent fasting accelerates weight loss. In a review, a pool of 40 in various research studies, individuals dropped 10 pounds in 10 weeks on average. One smaller study of 16 overweight adults adhering to an "alternating day" periodic fasting routine (eating 25 percent of their daily calories, and also eating generally within the day) led them to shedding as much as 13 pounds over eight weeks.

Recurring or ketogenic fasting also is successful where lots of weight-loss regimes fall short: by targeting as well as minimizing natural fat.

Visceral fat is the persistent, inner fat packed deep around your abdominal body organs. Throughout six months, individuals on such fasting and diet plan can reduce 4 to 7 percent of their natural fat. Intermittent fasting isn't just about attaining a healthy weight. Right here are some additional benefits you'll experience in the process:

Boosts cardio wellness: Periodic fasting diet plans have been introduced to improve cholesterol levels in the body. It reduces high blood pressure and also minimizes cardio risk.

Lowers inflammation: According to early research studies, the decreasing fat in the body may be the secret to keeping a healthy and balanced weight, increasing durability and significantly decreasing the dangers of visible health problems, that is why anti-inflammatory foods those are at the core of the ketogenic diet routine Keto / Recurring fasting reduces oxidative stress and also inflammation across the board, including inflammatory markers such as adiponectin, leptin and also a brain-derived neurotrophic factor (BDNF).

Helps in Self Eating or Autophagy: Autophagy is the process of cleansing damaged body cells to regenerate new and healthy cells. "Auto" means self, and "pugi" means food. Therefore, autophagy means "self-eating." It is also known as "self-destruction." While this may sound like something you never want to keep with your body, it is beneficial for your overall health. It is because autophagy is an evolutionary self-defence system through which the body can remove dysfunctional cells and recycle parts of them in the direction of cellular repair and cleansing.

The purpose of autophagy is to remove dead cells and organize itself for regular smooth operation. It not only presses the reset button on your body but also recycles and cleanses. Besides, it promotes survival and adaptation to the various pressures and toxins that accumulate in our cells. Gradually, the body collects damaged cells that can disrupt body function. In short, it detoxifies the system.

Supports healthy aging: Research studies have revealed that periodic fasting can help to safeguard your cardio system. And handle your blood sugar levels to support healthy and balanced aging. It also assists present sensations of peace as well as awareness. In rodent researches, periodic fasting has been shown to increase life expectancy and also safeguards one against illnesses. There is better than one way to begin intermittent fasting, which is terrific because every human is different from the other. The trick is to experiment and pay attention to your body to see what works best for you. Below are a few of the techniques to start:

16/08 Hours Technique: You eat everything, by taking your daily calories to consume within a reduced duration (commonly 6-8 hours) and also restrain from food the rest of the time.

Recurring Fasting: Comparable to 16/08 hours, however, with one vital difference, so you don't get hungry: You should drink a cup of coffee in the early morning. The quality fats keep you full till lunch, and you stay in a fasted state, so you reap all the benefits of recurring fasting. And don't get stressed because the coffee does not break your fast.

One meal a day (OMAD): It is the process of eating once a day. You eat all of your daily calories in only one meal each day and then extend it to fast for the rest of the day.

5:2 days in a Week: You'll eat for five days a week. On the various other two days, you "fast" with eating before-hand in between 500-600 calories. Alternative Day Fasting: Normal eating on an alternative day within that day, by eating 25 percent of your regular daily calories. A research study located that overweight or obese adults were complying with an "alternative day fasting" using period fasting timetable shed their weight within 13 pounds over eight weeks.

If intermittent fasting triggers tiredness or various other adverse signs and symptoms for you, try fasting just one or two times a week, and also develop your routine from there. Similar to any type of diet routine or workout strategy, consult your doctor to establish what's ideal for you. It's not easy to withstand the food cravings, yet there are some easy ways to stay clear of feeling starving appetite that can likewise aid you to get back at more results out of your fast.

DONT SKIP BREAKFAST

Breakfast is the most important meal of the day after 10 to 14 hours of night fasting. After waking up, you break the fast (Whole Night). Now why it's the most important meal of the day, because all nutrients, fats that are required by your body to go through a healthy day depend upon how healthy and ketogenic your breakfast is. We understand that going without your breakfast can be challenging. So, as opposed to avoiding morning meal, delight in a creamy cup of satisfying black coffee. This easy method keeps you in a fasted state as well as maintains the "hunger" away while nourishing your body with excellent fats.

CONSUME THE RIGHT FATS

The most fantastic hack for your intermittent fast: Your body transforms into ketones, which assist to melt fat, and also power your brain with even more energy, better mental efficiency, and also fewer cravings.

CUT BACK ON CARBS

Comply with the ketogenic diet plan throughout your eating periods to supercharge the effect of recurring fasting. Restricting carbohydrates reduce your hunger and also makes it much easier for your body to shift into fat-burning ketosis.

PLAN DISHES BEFOREHAND

When it's time to eat, those desserts, as well as snacks, tempt magnificently. To stay out of carbohydrates or junk food, prepare healthy alternatives food recipes with the ideal fats, including top-level meats as well as vegetables.

Periodic fasting, just stating, is a cycle between durations of fasting and eating. It's presently a modern approach to drop weight and improve health and wellness. But there is absolutely nothing "new" regarding fasting. Periodic fasting could be an old key to health and wellness. It is old since it has been practiced throughout every age of human history. It's a secret because possibly has effective behavior which in lots of ways has been neglected specifically regarding our health.

Nevertheless, many people are currently re-discovering this nutritional treatment. The variety of online searches for "Ketogenic fasting" has boosted by around 10,000 Percent. Recurring fasting can provide significant wellness advantages if it is done right, including loss of excess weight, treatment of diabetic issues, and many other health defects. Also, it can save you money and time.

RECURRING FASTING, ISN'T THAT HUNGER?

Fasting isn't starvation in a defined way: hunger, which we all know is the involuntary lack of food for a long time. It can bring about severe suffering or even fatality. It is neither intended nor regulated. Fasting, on the other hand, is the volunteer stop of taking food for spiritual, health and wellness, or other reasons. It's done by someone who is not undernourished hence has sufficient energy levels kept in the body fat to live off. Periodic fasting, if done right, must not trigger suffering and certainly never lead to fatality. Food is easily offered: Food is easily offered even if you pick not to eat it. It can lead to any amount of time, from a couple of hours to a couple of days intermittently or with doctor's guidance taken for a week or more. You might start fast at any time of your liking, and also, you might finish a fast on your will too. You can start or quit a voluntary fast for any reason or no reason whatsoever.

Fasting has no typical period, as it is just the abstaining from eating. Whenever you are not eating, you are intermittently fasting. For example, you might fast between your supper and the breakfast to the next day, a period of about 12-14 hours, because recurring fasting is a part of daily life whether we perceive it or not. Consider the term "breakfast." It describes the dish that breaks your fast, which is done daily. Rather than being some sort of extreme and uncommon penalty, the English language unconditionally recognizes that not eating ought to be executed daily, even if just for a brief duration. Periodic fasting is not something unusual and also curious; however, it is a part of the daily, everyday life. It is probably the earliest and also the most effective dietary treatment possible. Yet in some way, we have missed its power as well as overlooked its restoring potential.

Periodic fasting is currently among the globe's most popular health and fitness trends. People are utilizing it to reduce weight, boost their wellness, and also simplify their way of life. Many studies show that it can have significant impacts on your body and also brain as well as may even aid you to live much longer, as mentioned earlier. Recurring fasting is an eating pattern those cycles in between durations of fasting and also eating. It does not define which foods you should consume; however, what it does instead when you must and must not consume them.

In this regard, it's not a diet in the conventional feeling but more precisely described as an eating pattern. Standard periodic fasting techniques entail daily 16-hour fasts or fasting for one day, two times a week. Fasting has been a technique throughout human progress. Old hunters or gatherers didn't have grocery stores, fridges, or food readily available for the whole year. Sometimes they could not get anything to eat. As a result, people developed a habit or appetite to be able to proceed with such things as living without food many times. Fasting once in a while is all-natural than continually eating 3-4 (or more) dishes each day. Fasting is frequently done for religious or spiritual purposes, especially in Islam, Christianity, Judaism, and Buddhism. It is a way to cleanse oneself from sins, get closer to the creator, and shed body mass. It is one of the beliefs Muslims hold as per fasting.

RECURRING FASTING TECHNIQUES
There are several various means of doing such fasting in all of which entails splitting the day or week right into eating and fasting periods. Throughout the fasting periods, you consume either extremely little or absolutely nothing. These are some of the most popular techniques: The 16/8 technique: It is called the Lean gains method; it involves skipping breakfast and restricting your day-to-day eating duration to 8 hours, such as 1-9 p.m. Than increasing it to sixteen hours.

Eat-Stop-Eat: This involves fasting for 24 hours, one or two times a week. For instance, not eating dinner until the next dinner of the day.

The 5:2 diets Routine: With these methods, you take in only 500-600 calories on two non-consecutive days of the week, but consuming the food, usually the rest of the other five days.

By minimizing your calorie intake, all of these techniques must cause weight loss as long as you don't compensate by eating much more throughout the eating periods. Many people find the 16:08 hour's routine method to be the most comfortable, most sustainable, and most straightforward to work. It's also the most preferred way of ketosis as well.

HOW IT IMPACTS YOUR CELLS AS WELL AS HORMONAL AGENTS?

When you fast, numerous happenings occur in your body on the molecular level. For example, your body changes hormonal agent to some degrees to save body fat more usable. Your cells likewise launch necessary repair procedures as well as bring change in the genes. Here are some adjustments that take place in your body when you get on periodic fast:

Human Growth Hormone (HGH): Human growth hormone (HGH) is an important hormone produced by your pituitary glands. Also known as Growth Hormone (GH), it plays a crucial role in growth, anatomically cell repair, and metabolism. HGH promotes muscle growth, strength, and exercise performance while helping you to recover from injury and illness. Low HGH levels can lower your quality of life, increase the risk of getting caught up by disease, and make you fat. The degrees of growth hormonal change rapidly, rising for as much as five times. It has advantages for fat loss as well as muscle mass gain, among others.

Insulin: Insulin is hormones made by the pancreas that can make your body consume carbohydrates from sugar (glucose) that you eat or store glucose use. Insulin helps your blood sugar levels from getting too high hyperglycemia or too low (hypoglycemia). Your body's cell needs sugar for energy. However, sugar cannot go directly into most of your cells. When you eat food, and your blood sugar level rises, the cells in your pancreas (known as beta cells) signal the release of insulin into your bloodstream. Insulin then binds to the cells and signals the absorption of sugar from the bloodstream. Insulin is often called a "key" that unlocks sugar to the cell to enter into the cells and is used for energy.

If you have too much sugar in your body, insulin helps to store sugar in your liver and releases it when your blood sugar level is low or when you need more sugar, such as between meals or during physical activity. Therefore, a pancreas that produces insulin helps to balance blood sugar levels and keep them within normal limits. When blood sugar levels rise, more insulin is secreted than enzymes. If your body does not make enough insulin or your cells are resistant to the effects of insulin, you may develop hyperglycemia (high blood sugar), which can lead to long-term complications if blood sugar levels rise. If it lasts long, stays cautious for it. Insulin considerably increases, and also, levels of insulin drop dramatically. Lower insulin levels get stored as body fat a lot more usable. Cellular repair work: When on fasting, your cells start repair service processes. It includes autophagy, where cells absorb and eliminate old and useless proteins that accumulate inside cells.

Gene expression: Genes carry proteins and cell proteins directly into cell function. Therefore, thousands of genes are expressed in a particular cell that determines what this cell can do. Furthermore, each step in the flow of information from DNA to RNA to proteins provides the cell with possible control points to regulate its functions by adjusting the amount and type of protein produced.

At any given time, the amount of a particular protein in a cell represents the balance between the synthetic and mitigating biochemical pathways of that protein. From the artificial side of this balance, remember that protein production begins with replication (from DNA to RNA) and continues with translation (from RNA to protein). Therefore, the control of these processes plays a vital role in determining what protein is present in a cell and in what quantity. Besides, the way a cell processes its RNA transcripts and newly formed proteins significantly affect protein levels. There are adjustments in the feature of genetics connected to durability as well as protection against harmful conditions. These adjustments in hormonal agent degrees, cell features and gene expression are responsible for the health and wellness advantages of periodic fasting.

A VERY EFFECTIVE FAT BURNING PROCEDURE

Weight reduction or fat burning is one of the most common factors which people try recurring fasting, by making you consume dishes, intermittent fasting can lead to an automated reduction in calorie consumption. Furthermore, periodic fasting makes adjustments to hormonal agent degrees to assist in fat burning. In addition to reducing insulin and increasing growth hormone levels, it sparks the launch of neither fat loss hormonal agent called nor-epinephrine (nor-adrenaline).

Because of these modifications in hormones, temporary fasting may enhance your metabolic rate by 3.6-14%. By assisting you to eat fewer (in quantity and periods) and shed more calories. Recurring fasting techniques triggers fat burning by changing both sides of the calorie formula. Researches reveal that periodic fasting can be a very effective weight reduction tool. A testimonial study found that this eating pattern can trigger 3-8% weight management over 3-24 weeks, which is a substantial amount, contrasted to the majority of weight loss studies. According to the very same research study, individuals additionally shed 4-7% of their waist circumference, showing a considerable loss of harmful belly fat that develops around your body organs, which, without doubt, triggers the disease.

One more research showed that periodic fasting causes much less muscle mass loss than the common method of constant calorie restriction. However, remember that the primary factor for its success is that periodic fasting assists you eat fewer calories in the long run. If you consume enormous quantities throughout your eating periods, you may not shed any bit of weight in all.

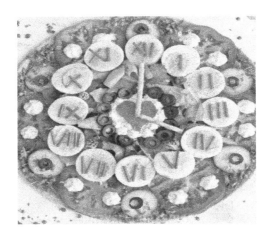

Every method can be efficient, yet identifying which one functions ideally depends on the person. Some methods listed below may have been mentioned above, but it was explained.

HERE ARE POPULAR WAYS TO PERFORM PERIODIC FASTING:

CONSUME QUIT EAT

Eat Quit Consume involves a 24-hour quick pattern or routine once or twice per week. This method was promoted by fitness expert Brad Pilon and also has been rather prominent for a couple of years. By not eating from dinner

351

someday to supper the next day, this totals up to a full 24-hour fast. For example, if you finish supper at 7 p.m. Monday, then do not eat till dinner at 7 p.m. the next day, that is Tuesday. You've completed a full 24-hour fast. You can additionally fast from morning meal to morning meal or lunch to lunch as long as completion result coincides.

Water, coffee, as well as various other zero-calorie beverages are cool throughout the fast, yet no healthy foods are allowed. If you always do this to lose weight, it's vital that you eat generously during the eating periods. To put it simply, you need to eat the very same quantity of the food as if you hadn't been eating whatsoever. The possible disadvantage of this approach is that a complete 24-hour quickly may be relatively tough for lots of people. Nevertheless, you don't need to go straight in today. It's great to start with 14-16 hours then move upward from there.

This period of fasting has numerous crucial benefits. First, as a longer period fast, it tends to be a lot more efficient. Because you still consume daily, medications that need to be taken with food can still be taken. As an example, Metformin, or iron supplements or aspirin, must all be taken with food that can be taken with the one dish on the fasting day. The significant benefit of 24-hour fasting is that it is easily included right into day-to-day life. Many people, for example, eat supper with their family every day. As you still eat supper on a daily basis, it is possible to regularly fast for 24-hour without anybody understanding any sort of changes, given that it only implies missing breakfast and lunch on that day. It is specifically easy throughout a workday. You simply drink your early morning cup but miss breakfast. You overcome lunch and reach home in time for supper again. It saves both money (yeah) and time (time for preparing food). There is no cleaning or food preparation for breakfast. You save an hour at lunch break where you can work, then get home for dinner without anyone also realizing you had fasted for 24 hours.

For weight loss, in our Intensive Dietary Administration program, we'll recommend this timetable of 24-hour fasting to be done three times each week. Many individuals locate it so easily that they often increase it to five times per week, as well as often on a daily basis. We likewise advise this timetable regularly for those people that are older or taking medications. One of the major worries of fasting is the loss of flesh or resulting lean body mass, or muscle mass. Several research studies have been done on this, and also these anxieties are mostly lost, particularly for obese or fat people. In one study, not eating every other day did not generate any type of losing body-mass over 22 days, even as bodyweight progressively lowers. An additional name for this fast procedure is OMAD, meaning One Meal a Day.

ALTERNATE-DAY FASTING

In alternate-day fasting, you need to fast every other day. There are several variant versions of this technique. Some of them enable 500 calories throughout the fasting days. Many of the researches introducing health and wellness advantages of periodic fasting used some variations of this approach. A full fast every other day can appear instead extreme, so it's not suggested for beginners. With this approach, you might go to bed really hungry numerous times weekly, which is not pleasurable and most likely unsustainable in the long term.

THE WARRIOR DIET

The Warrior Diet routine was popularized by health and fitness specialist Ori Hofmekler. It entails eating percentages of raw fruits and vegetables during the day and also eating one important meal at night. Generally, you fast through the day and make your feast during the night within a four-hour eating home window. The Warrior Diet plan was among the very first popular diet plans to consist of a kind of intermittent fasting. This diet's food selections are relatively similar to that of the Paleo diet plan, which is mostly whole, unrefined food.

SPONTANEOUS DISH ABSTINENCE

You do not require sticking up to an organized periodic fasting strategy to gain several of its advantages. Another alternative is to simply skip meals periodically, such as when you don't feel hungry, or you don't feel like cooking or even eating, or there's just no appetite. It's a myth that individuals need to take food every few hours lest they enter the hunger mode or lose muscle. Your body is well geared up to take care of long periods of famine (so to say), let alone missing one or two dishes every so often. Thus, if you're actually not hungry one day, skip breakfast and just take a healthy and balanced lunch then dinner. Avoiding a couple of dishes when you feel likely it is generally a spontaneous intermittent fast, as it has no specific start or end period. Just ensure to eat healthy foods during the other dishes.

FASTING FOR 12 HOURS A DAY

The rules for this diet are straightforward. A person needs to choose as well as stick to a 12-hour fasting home window each day. According to some scientists, not eating for 10-16 hours can cause the body to burn its fat stocks right into energy substances, which releases ketones right into the bloodstream. This aids weight-loss. This sort of periodic fasting strategy may be an excellent choice for novices. It is as a result of the fact that the fasting home window is not long, much of the fasting takes place during rest, and the person can eat the same variety of calories daily.

The simplest means to do the 12-hour fast is to include the period of sleep in the fasting window.

As an example, a person might choose to fast between 7 p.m. and also 7 a.m. They would for sure need to finish their supper before 7 p.m. then wait up until 7 a.m. to take breakfast but would be asleep for much of the time in between.

LONG TERM FASTING

Extended fasting and fasting-seeming diets, while they still employ fasting protocols, are not specifically the same as intermittent fasting. According to longevity specialist Valter Longo, Ph.D. "long term fasting, as well as fasting-mimicking diets, are extremely variant considering that they last two or even more days, and have not attached any periodic significance that can be done when required. Also, they don't have particular intervals." Attia, as an example, does a 7-day fast four times each year. What's the point? While any type of fasting is most likely to promote healthy aging. These longer fasts might be particularly beneficial for targeting long life and also for autophagy.

Can't discard food that long? The Prolonged 5-Day Fasting-seeming Diet, created by Longo at the USC Long life Institute, basically states the effects of fasting without completely discarding food. On the plan, you reduce calories to around 1,100 on the initial day and after that to around 800 the following four days (while eating certain, lower-carb, and nutrition filled whole foods). The factor of this program is to permit the body to get in a full ketogenic proportion. Indicating it breaks down and also [reuse] harmed cells and also cellular components, turn on stem cells, and then preferentially decrease visceral and also stomach fat."

Much more research is needed on extended fasts, as well as they're most likely not ideal for all. Long term fasts that pass up all food needs to be done under the assistance of a medical practitioner, most especially if you have any type of health and wellness problems (e.g., stomach ulcer).

36-HOUR FASTS

A 36-hour fast is a way that you fast one whole day. You take dinner on day one at 7 pm, for example, then skip on meals on the second day and not eat once again until breakfast on day three by 7 am. To make sure that is an overall of 36 hrs of fasting. We frequently recommend 36-hours fasts 2-3 times weekly for patients with Type 2 diabetes. From experience, this longer fasting duration generates quicker results and also still has good conformity. Because type 2 diabetic has more insulin needs, the much longer fasting duration is the extra efficient than shorter fasting durations, although we have had good results with that too.

We covered fasting programs utilizing durations less than one day formerly. The longer routines are typically done less frequently. The significant determinant of which fasting routine is right for you is an individual choice. Some people find longer fasting plans which are less complicated and but also some find them a little harder.

Lots of people find that appetite increases into day 2. At that point, hunger peaks, and after that, slowly declines. It is necessary expertise if you are attempting a longer fast (3-7 days). It is easier to proceed, knowing that hunger gradually gets better. Please note: While many periodic fasting methods have been tried and tested for achieving benefits, it's still controversial. A possible risk is known with drugs, particularly for diabetes mellitus, where dosages usually are required to be adjusted. People that must NOT make fasting attempts include those that are undernourished or have eating disorders like anorexia, women who are pregnant or breastfeeding, and also under-aged people (kids).

Around one day long, not eating durations as for the 24-hour fasts, this is very comparable to the 'Warrior Dieting' procedure of fasting, although that permits a 4-hour eating window, so it is practically for a 20-hour fasting duration. This period of fasting has numerous essential advantages. Initially, as a longer duration fast, it has a tendency to be a little bit more effective. Because you still consume daily, drugs, or medicines that need to be taken with food can still be taken.

WHAT DO YOU REQUIRE TO LEARN ABOUT OMAD?

THE 5:2 DIET PLAN

Untitled-7A associated strategy is the 5:2 technique promoted by Dr. Michael Mosley, a TV producer and doctor best understood for popularizing this approach. He showed up on a BBC program called Horizon entitled "Eat, Quick, and Live Longer." The fundamental diet routine was not quite a 24-hour fasting period. Instead, the 5:2 diet routine entailed five days of a normal diet. On the other two days, you could consume an overall of 500 calories. If, as an example, this is taken as dinner, it would correspond a 24-hour fast. Nevertheless, you can spread out those 500 calories out into multiple meals rather. These two strategies are reasonably comparable, and the difference from a physical standpoint is most likely relatively marginal.

ALTERNATE DAY FASTING (ADF)

It is the dietary method that has the most research behind it. It was majorly done by Dr. Krista Varady, an assistant professor of nourishment with the College of Illinois--Chicago. She authored a book concerning her approach in The Alternate-Day Diet plan, although it isn't the immense success of the 5:2 diets. Although it seems like you just eat every other day. That is not factual because there's more to it. You can consume up to 500 calories on fasting days, similar to in the 5:2 diet routine. Nevertheless, fasting days are done on alternate days instead of 2 days each week, so it is an extra intensive routine. The significant advantage of this routine is that even more study is offered on this program than any other.

DANGERS AND DIFFICULTIES OF FASTING OVER A DAY

As you go longer in fasting progressively, the advantages build up much faster, but there are also more threats and difficulties. Given that I typically talk about people with type 2 diabetes and strongly advise to treat excessive weight situations, I have a tendency to be attracted towards longer fasting durations. Still, you need to recognize that I always keep track and extremely careful with regards to high blood pressure. I cannot take stress enough, that if you do not really feel well at any type of point, you should stop. You can be starving, but you ought not to feel unwell.

Another major factor to consider is that medication must be very carefully checked by a doctor. The significant trouble is that a diabetic person won't respond to medications well enough because if you take the very same dose of medicine without eating, you come to be hypoglycaemic, and that is harmful.

42-HOUR FASTS AND ALSO ABOVE

We always ensure to advise our clients to make a regular pattern not to miss the morning meal and also end their fast around midday hour. It makes it simple to comply with a 16:08 fasting duration on normal routine days. After a couple of days, lots of people begin to really feel rather typical, just starting their day with a glass of water as well as their common cup of coffee. When you combine that with 36-hour fasting, you obtain a 42-hour fasting duration. For example, you would eat supper at 6 pm on day 1. You avoid all meals on day two and also consume your regular 'breakfast' dish at 12:00 PM. It is a total amount of 42 hours. For more extended period fasts, we usually try NOT to restrict high-calorie foods throughout that eating period. Frequently, as people get accustomed to fasting, we hear extremely typical, that their appetite begins to go down enormously. They must eat to their appetite on their eating day.

There's an excellent factor for this decline in cravings. As you begin to break the insulin resistance cycle, insulin levels begin to reduce. In response, hunger is suppressed, and also total energy expense is preserved. So, hunger goes down, and also TEE remains very same or increases. Bear in mind that chronic daily caloric constraint approaches generate the opposite. Appetite rises, and also TEE decreases, most likely resulting in inferior results. You can expand fasts much longer. The highest record was 382 days fast (yeah, don't try even a quarter of that), yet many individuals can fast 7-14 days without difficulty. Without a doubt, the Master cleanse utilized by Beyoncé is simply a variant of the 7-day fast, which enables some mixture.

Stimulating autophagy has some theoretical benefits, a cellular cleaning process which usually calls for two days of fast or more. A state of ketosis may require not less than 36 hours of not eating getting in. There are lots of theoretical advantages, including appetite reductions and also better psychological clarity. For cancer cells prevention, some suggest a 7-day fast. A number of these advantages are academic and also unproven, however. Nevertheless, many have discovered the 7-day fast to be a lot less challenging.

Intermittent fasting's most noticeable advantage is weight loss. However, there are lots of possible benefits beyond this, several of which have been recognized since ancient times. The fasting periods were commonly called 'cleanses,' 'detoxifying,' or 'filtrations. Still, the idea is similar, e.g., to avoid eating food for a certain amount of time, frequently for health and wellness factors. People always imagine that this period of abstinence from food would certainly remove their bodies' systems of contaminants and revitalize them. They may have been more on point than they recognized.

Some of the known health advantages of recurring fasting include:

- Weight and also body weight loss.
- They rose fat burning.
- It reduces blood insulin and also sugar degrees.

- It is the probable turnaround of type 2 diabetes mellitus.
- Potentially boosted psychological quality and focus.
- Possibly boosts power.
- Possibly increases growth hormone.
- It possibly enhances blood cholesterol profile.
- Potentially longer life.
- Possibly activation of boosting autophagy.
- Possibly decrease of swelling.

Furthermore, not eating brings about several critical unique benefits that are not available in regular diet plans. Where diet routines can make one's life a complicated life, intermittent fasting would streamline things. Where diets can be costly, periodic fasting can be complimentary. Where diets can require time, fasting conserves time. Where diet plans might be limited in their availability, fasting is offered anywhere. And also, as discussed previously, fasting is a powerful method for lowering insulin levels & decreasing body weight.

PERIODIC FASTING FOR WEIGHT MANAGEMENT

At its very core, intermittent fasting merely allows the body to utilize its kept power. As an example, by burning excess body fat. It is necessary to recognize that this is typical, and people have actually developed to fast for shorter periods of hours or days without harmful wellness consequences. Body fat is simply food energy that has been stored away. If you do not eat, your body will just "consume" its very own fat for energy.

Life is about balance. The affluent and the poor ones, the yin and also the yang, the same applies to eat as well as not eating. Fasting, nevertheless, is simply the reciprocal of eating. If you do not engage in eating, you are fasting. Below is just how it functions:

When we consume, much more food energy is ingested than can promptly be used. A few of this power must be kept away for later usage. Insulin is the crucial hormonal agent associated with the storage of food power. Insulin rises when we eat, aiding in keeping the excess energy in two different means. Carbs are broken down into individual sugar systems, which can be linked into long chains to develop glycogen, which is after that saved in the liver or muscular tissue.

There is, nonetheless, really minimal storage room for carbohydrates, and as soon as that is reached, the liver begins to turn the excess sugar into fat. This procedure is called de-novo lipogenesis (definition actually "making brand-new fat"). Some of these newly produced fats is stored in the liver, yet most of it is exported to other fat down in the body. While this is a much more complicated procedure, there is nearly no limit for fat that can be produced.

So, two food power storage systems exist in our bodies. One is conveniently obtainable but with restricted storage space (glycogen), and the second is harder to gain access to but has a nearly endless storage area (body fat).

The process enters a reverse mode when we do not eat (recurring fasting). Insulin levels fall, signalling the body to begin melting stored energy as no more is coming through food. Blood sugar falls, so the body has to pull glucose out of storage to melt for energy currently. Glycogen is the most conveniently available power source. It is broken down into sugar molecules to provide power for the body's other cells. It can give sufficient power to power much of the body's requirements for 24-36 hours. After that, the body will mostly be breaking down fat for energy.

So, the body only truly exists in double states the fed (insulin high) state and also the fast (insulin low) state. Either we are saving food energy (raising stores), or we are burning saved power (reducing stores). It's one or the other. If eating and also not eating are balanced, then there ought to be net weight adjustment. If we begin eating the minute we go out of bed and then do not stop up until we go to sleep, we spend nearly all our time in the fed state. With time, we may put on weight, because we have not enabled our body any time to shed kept food power.

In other to restore your balance or to lose weight, we may simply require to raise the quantity of time invested, shedding food power. That's intermittent fasting. Periodic fasting permits the body to utilize its stored power. Besides, that's what it is there. The vital point to recognize is that there is absolutely nothing wrong keeping that. That is how our bodies are designed.

If you are eating after every 3rd hour, as is frequently suggested by some practitioners, then your body continuously adds to the inbound food power. It may not necessarily burn much body fat, that's if any is burned during the few hour's intervals. You might simply be saving fat. Your body would then be waiting for a time when there is nothing to consume. Clearly, weight loss is one of the benefits of recurring fasting. However, it's verified that recurring fasting does more than simply weight loss to our body.

Researchers uncovered long ago that calorie restriction is a way to promote durability in lifespan. A large section of information sustains the concept that limiting food intake reduces the danger of illness, usually in old age, as well as lengthens the period of life when invested healthily. Yet in the last few years, scientists have focused on this method recurring fasting as an encouraging option to calorie limitation. Which means you do not require starving yourself to live longer always? The initial cross research between calorie limitation and periodic fasting was done way back in 1945 when it was found that recurring fasting extends the life expectancy of mice. Besides, there is research asserting that recurring fasting likewise decreases the danger of cancer, while at the same time: enhances our cognitive feature. The theory behind this is that recurring fasting acts partially as a kind of mild tension that constantly revs up mobile defenses against molecular damage.

IT MAKES YOUR DAY SIMPLER

In my individual experience, this is the component I enjoy the most (because I haven't lived enough time to experience what it suggests to live longer). It makes your day easier. I'm a huge fan of minimalism and also simplicity, and I choose to place my focus on many essential things in life. I delight in eating and don't mind not cooking; however, at the same time, I prefer to read, compose, make coffee, plan for my service, spend time with family, and also take some vacations. Obviously, I'm not the one who prepares seven meals a day for seven days a week, and I simply don't have time for that.

PERIODIC FASTING IS MUCH EASIER THAN DIET PROGRAMS

The factor most diet routines stop working isn't because we switch to the wrong foods; it's because we do not, in fact, follow the diet plan over the long term. It's not nourishment trouble and its action-change trouble. It is where recurring fasting beams since it's incredibly easy to execute once you get over the thinking that you require to consume all the time. For example, this study discovered that periodic fasting was an efficient technique for fat burning in overweight adults.

"Diet routines are very easy in the reflection, tough in the execution." Recurring fasting is just the opposite; it's hard in the reflection but very easy in the execution. A lot of us have considered going on a diet. When we locate a diet plan that appeals to us, it appears as if it will be as easy as a breeze. Yet when we get involved in the nitty-gritty of it, it becomes challenging. As an example, I remain on a reduced carbohydrate diet routine mostly all the time. However, if I think of taking a low-fat diet routine, it looks simply. I think about bagels, whole wheat bread, and jelly, mashed potatoes, corn, bananas by the dozen. Every one of which sounds appealing.

Recurring fasting is challenging in the consideration, of that there is no question. "You went without food for 24 hours?" people would ask, incredulously when we described what we were doing. "I might never do that." Once began, it's a breeze. No issues with what and also where to consume a couple of or all out of the three dishes daily. It's a great liberation. Your food expenditures plummet. And also, you're not particularly starving. Although it's tough to get rid of the suggestion of being without food, when you begin the routine, nothing could be much more comfortable." In my viewpoint, the convenience of recurring fasting is the best factor to give it a try. It provides a variety of health advantages without calling for a huge way of life modification.

ADVANTAGES OF PERIODIC FASTING FOR WEIGHT REDUCTION

The primary factor with which intermittent fasting benefits weight-loss is that it helps you eat low calories. All of the various methods entail avoiding dishes during the fasting periods. Unless you compensate by eating a lot more during the eating durations, after that, you will certainly be absorbing low calories. These outcomes are very impressive, and they do reveal that whereby periodic fasting can be a helpful weight reduction help.

All that being claimed, the benefits of intermittent fasting go past simply weight loss. It additionally has many advantages for metabolic health and wellness, and may also help prevent chronic disease as well as expand life expectancy. Although calorie checking is generally not called for when doing recurring fasting, the weight reduction is primarily moderated by an overall decrease in calorie intake.

Studies comparing periodic fasting and constant calorie constraint show no difference in fat burning if calories are matched between teams. Intermittent Fast might help you hold on to muscle when weight loss sets in. One of the awful side effects of diet programs is that the body tends to shrink muscle along with fat. Surprisingly, some researches are revealing that recurring fasting might be beneficial for holding on to muscle while shedding body fat. In one testimonial study, periodic calorie restriction triggered a comparable quantity of weight loss as continuous calorie limitation, but with a much smaller sized decrease in muscle mass. In the calorie restriction research studies, 25% of the weight shed was muscle mass, contrasted to only 10% in the periodic calorie restriction researches. Scientists have been researching periodic fasting for years. Research searching for is often inconsistent and inconclusive. However, the study on periodic fasting, consisting of 16:8 fasting, indicates that it might offer the following benefits:

WEIGHT LOSS

Eating throughout a set period can aid individuals to reduce the number of calories that they take. It may additionally assist in boosting metabolism. A 2017 research study suggests that periodic fasting brings about more effective weight management and weight loss in men with excessive weight than routine calorie restriction. A research study from 2016 records that men who adhered to a 16:8 approach for eight weeks while resistance training showed a reduction in fat mass the participants preserved their muscle mass throughout, in contrast, a research study found very little difference in fat burning between participants that exercised periodic fasting in the form of alternate-day fasting rather than 16:8 fast with those that lowered their total calorie consumption. The failure level was totally high amongst those in the intermittent fasting team.

ILLNESS PREVENTION

Advocates of intermittent fasting recommend that it can stop some problems and also diseases, including:

- type 2 diabetes mellitus
- heart conditions
- some cancers
- neurodegenerative conditions

Nevertheless, the research in this area remains minimal.

A 2014 testimonial reports that intermittent fasting reveals guarantee as an alternative to conventional calorie limitation for type 2 diabetic issues, aids fat burning in individuals that have overweight or weight problems. The researchers warn, nonetheless, that even more research study is necessary before they can get to reputable verdicts. A research study indicates that along with fat burning, an 8-hour eating window may help reduce blood pressure in grownups with weight problems.

Various other research studies report that intermittent fasting reduces glucose by 3 to 6% in those with pre-diabetes, although it has no effect on healthy and balanced individuals. It may additionally lower fasting insulin by 11-57% after 3 to 24 weeks of recurring fasting. Time-restricted fasting, such as the 16:8 techniques, might also aid grasping things and memory and decrease conditions that affect the brain. An annual evaluation notes that animal research has actually indicated that this kind of fasting reduces the danger of non-alcoholic fatty liver disease as well as cancer.

PROLONGED LIFE EXPECTANCY

Research studies recommend that periodic fasting might help animals live longer. As an example, one study located that short-term repeated fasting raised the life-span of female mice. The National Institute on Aging mentions that, even after decades of research study, scientists still cannot discuss why fasting may extend the life span. Therefore, they cannot confirm the long-term safety of this method. Human studies in the area are restricted, as well as the prospective advantages of periodic fasting for human longevity is not yet understood. The length of time prior to you seeing benefits of recurring fasting.

When it pertains to becoming healthier and toning up your body, one of the most preferred of the numerous choices out there right now is periodic fasting. Intermittent fasting includes numerous various approaches to select. Still, most involve eating for a short period of time during the day and restricting the quantity of calories you take in. The results appear to those who've tried the approach; however, according to the experts, you need a minimum of 10 weeks of complying with a few basic policies to see any modifications.

THERE ARE 3 KEY APPROACHES TO INTERMITTENT FASTING

Two of the widely known plans are the 5:2 diet and the alternate-days strategy, under the 5:2 diet, individuals usually consume, however healthfully for 5 days of the week. Also, they eat just 500 to 800 calories on 2 non-consecutive days. On the restricted-calorie days, some may choose to divide their calories into two or 3 mini dishes. Under the alternate-days strategy, you would certainly consume generally eventually, after that quick for part of the day and consume less than 600 calories the following day. A third, though less popular, the approach is an everyday technique, in which individuals restrict their eating to six to eight hours just, every single day, without modifying their calorie intake. A popular choice is the 16/8 plan, in which you fast for 16 hrs and also consume for the remaining eight.

YOU MIGHT INTEND TO START EATING ON THE VERY EARLY SIDE

Have you ever before listened to the phrase "morning meal is the essential meal of the day"? By Dr. Sriram Machineni, supervisor of the Medical Weight Clinic at the College of North Carolina at Chapel Hillside and also an assistant teacher at the UNC College of Medication. A current research study might have verified just that when it revealed that individuals who ate closer to the moment when their bodies launched melatonin "at the onset of the day" said, Machine had more significant weight and also higher body fat percentages than those who ate later. What this suggests is that if you start your calorie consumption right when you get up, you could have better luck with weight loss.

IT'LL TAKE A COUPLE OF WEEKS TO SEE CHANGES

Outcomes of fasting are usually apparent around the 10-week mark, including that is seen a typical fat-burning of 7 to 10 extra pounds over that duration through any one of the three approaches to Intermittent Fasting pointed out previously. It could take longer than that, considering that everyone's metabolic rate functions in different ways. I tell individuals who make any type of diet routine modification to give themselves within one and two months. On the other hand, "if you're quickly slimming down as well, you're doing it incorrectly." In such a situation, you should re-evaluate your calorie intake.

Our specialists say research studies are undetermined until now. Still, because you're eating healthier with low calories, the approach can have an impact past the range and also on your total health, including your cholesterol, triglycerides, and blood sugar level.

The response to how long before you see goods to intermittent fasting really depends upon the persons fasting and their goals. Let's take, for example, if your goal is to shed off 10 pounds, and it will take less time than a person aiming to lose 50 pounds. How promptly you attain your goal is about what your objective actually is. But that does not imply you won't begin seeing and feeling the various other outcomes quicker! AEN peeps have reported zero bloating after just 1 day of the Program. After only 2-3 days, they have also reported dramatically enhanced sleep and enhanced power degrees. Weight loss results likewise differ, but peeps have reported a variety of 1-5 extra pounds of weight reduction within only the initial week of the 21 Day Recurring Fasting Program. Slow-moving aging with a fasting diet routine Periodic fasting might help slow down aging and also illness like cancer and diabetes even if you don't reduce weight.

RECURRING FASTING BENEFITS
THERE ARE SEVERAL DESIGNS OF INTERMITTENT FASTING:

Intermittent fasting, or limiting mealtimes to a specific, limited period, has swiftly come to be preferred thanks to its numerous purported wellness benefits like weight loss, enhanced focus, and also far better cardio health. An expanding body of evidence supports the insurance claim that periodic fasting can reduce the threat of lots of illnesses, including cancer, diabetes mellitus, and also cardiovascular disease, to aid you in living a long, healthy, and balanced life. While there are challenges, the researchers think the eating pattern can someday be a necessary part of any type of healthy and balanced way of living.

Recurring fasting or intermittent fasting has turned into one of the fastest-growing nutrition routines of the year, topping checklists ranging from celebrity-endorsed eating strategies to Google searches by interested dieters. There is likewise a boosting number of researches that back up the hype with clinical proof, suggesting intermittent fasting can ward off disease, assist in controlling blood glucose, and bring about weight management even without reducing body calories. Researchers discovered that intermittent fasting of all kinds could assist reduce aging as well as age-related health problems like cancer, heart disease, and also diabetic issues. It can likewise assist with weight and also fat loss.

MORE ON INTERMITTENT FASTING BENEFITS
THERE ARE NUMEROUS STYLES OF RECURRING/INTERMITTENT FASTING:

Periodic fasting or limiting nourishments to a particular restricted period has rapidly come to be preferred due to its many purported health benefits like weight-loss, enhanced focus, and also better cardiovascular health and wellness. A growing body of evidence sustains the case that recurring fasting can minimize the threat of several diseases, consisting of cancer cells, diabetic issues, and heart problems. It helps to give you a long life, a healthy and balanced life.

While there are barriers to arriving, the research writers think the eating pattern might someday be a fundamental part of any kind of healthy lifestyle. There's likewise a boosting number of researches that support the news with scientific evidence, recommending intermittent fasting can ward off illness, aid regulates blood glucose, and also bring about fat burning also without cutting calories. Researchers assessed more significant than 70 released studies regarding the most common sorts of intermittent fasting the 5:2 approach (usually eating for 5 days a week as well as fasting the various other 2 days), not eating every other day (alternate fasting), or restricting meals each day to a smaller sized amount of time (usually 06 to 08 hrs as well as not eating the other 16 to 18 hours of the day).

It was discovered that Intermittent fasting of all types could aid reduce aging and also age-related diseases, which include; cancer, heart disease, and diabetes. Much more appealing, the benefits of intermittent fasting aren't only seen in people who reduce weight. The scientists think an extra procedure, called metabolic changing, is the root cause of most, if not all, of intermittent fasting's advantages, according to the study.

"Metabolic changing" can bring about benefits even after you've eaten once again. Commonly, a sort of simple element called Insulin is human's major energy resource. We get sugar from food, most especially from carbohydrates, which our digestive system converts to glucose, following the Harvard T.H. Chan Institution of Public Health. Throughout fasting, though, the body has to turn to another power source so the liver breaks down fatty acids right into ketones, which can be utilized as body fuel instead. Intermittent fasting nonetheless enables the body to switch over in between the two resources of power, glucose as well as ketones, in a process called "metabolic changing," as the study found.

Alternating body fuel sources are thought to be responsible for a lot of the benefits of intermittent fasting, according to the researchers, given that it stimulates a lasting cellular reaction to shield the body from health issues. It includes decreasing fat, enhancing metabolism, and also shielding against oxidative anxiety, which is linked to health problems connected with aging, from cancer to Alzheimer's.

Experts are still finding out just how ideal for applying fasting to optimize its advantages. Earlier studies have located that Intermittent Fasting can assist with athletes eating habits. Including one of the young men discovering that those that haven't eaten for 16 hours a day were able to lower body fat while maintaining muscle mass throughout two months of resistance training A different study found that lab mice that did not eat every other day had better running endurance than those that really did eat every day. The pattern may also assist secure brain health and wellness and also stop cognitive thinking decrease in older individuals, according to several scientific trials that linked recurring fasting to improvements in memory. Regardless of the evidence of intermittent fasting benefits, however, there are a couple of barriers in making it wide as a health remedy for the public. Initially, according to the researchers, it hasn't yet come to be extensively approved to eat less than three dishes a day, although that might be changing. The availability of cheap, high-calorie snacks, as well as various other foods, may make it tough for individuals to adhere to a fasting way of life.

What's even more, the clinic does not yet have an established protocol for "suggesting" not eating in the same way that it now motivates individuals to eat a well-balanced diet and also workout. It's additionally crucial to keep in mind that fasting might not be for everyone. The procedure can bring about impatience, tiredness, and anxiety and can be dangerous for people at risk for medical conditions (e.g., ulcer patients).

More research requires to be done on the lasting impacts of periodic fasting. Yet, research author Mattson has examined the health and wellness impacts of recurring fasting for 25 years. Then embraced it himself for twenty years ago thinks the robust evidence until now recommends the eating pattern can one day be a conventional part of any healthy lifestyle. Fasting to stop you from aging could sound strange, never heard of, but the idea is backed up by some significant scientific studies. A research study from Japan showed that not just does fasting quicken up the metabolic process, it additionally would reverse the aging process.

A researcher from the Okinawa Institute of Science and Modern Technology Grad University (OIST) & Kyoto College studied what happens when the body goes without food. Though their research study was so little, with just four persons, the outcomes were intriguing: They located 44 compounds that increase in the body throughout fasting, as well as much of them, are connected to wellness advantages. The 04 persons did not eat for 34 to 58 hrs. The substances they measured are called metabolites, the molecules that give micro-organisms energy as well as allow them to grow, according to the scientists. The 44 they located, 30 of which were formerly unknown, boosted between 1.5 to 60-fold over the total fasting period.

Three of the metabolite's leucine, isoleucine & ophthalmic acid have been shown to lower individual aging effects. In those who fasted, it was noticed that it could boost molecules that aid people live longer. These are essential metabolites for maintenance of muscle and antioxidant task respectively, this result suggests the possibility of an invigorating impact by fasting, which was not known until now.

The human body normally depends on carbohydrates, which it converts to glucose, for body energy. But when it's tossed right into a malnourishment state, it starts to search for different energy resources and also leaves certain components in its wake. A few of those, like purine and also pyrimidine, increase anti-oxidants in the body, which researchers discovered as evidence of the 4-fasting people that were trailed. Anti-oxidants protect the body from essential elements generated in the process of converting food to energy. Fasting enlightened the researchers to make efforts to enhance those aspects of older individuals.

"Recent aging research studies have shown that caloric restriction and fasting have an extending result on life-span in animals, but the detailed mechanism has continued to be a mystery," said Teruya. It could be possible to verify the anti-aging result from different viewpoints by establishing workout programs or drugs (medicines) with the ability to cause the metabolic response comparable to fasting. Fasting appears to be beneficial for metabolic rate and even for the human lifespan, yet is it good for our brains, which are made active by components, one of which is sugar. Valter Longo, the director of USC's Longevity Institute, informed that experts in the field are beginning to see fasting as a "real reset."

"Firstly, it compels the body to move far from making use of sugar as an energy source and start making use of the results of fat," said Longo. "It triggers these genetics as well as pathways that have possibly been shut off for the majority of a person's life. And also, the mind starts depending 50-50 on ketone bodies and also glucose."

Throughout that process, autophagy happens an all-natural method our bodies clean up scrap on a healthy degree, removing harmed cells. While fasting can do a great deal of excellent in the body, it remains in the refuelling process after not eating that a lot of the benefits show up. Fasting can be considered as a great and also a poor thing. Given that the research study was small, researchers want to continue to research the effects of not eating on a large no of individuals to figure out the benefits.

People have an interest in whether human beings can take pleasure in the results of the prevention of metabolic diseases and extending life span by fasting or caloric limitation, just like tested animals. Recognizing the metabolic modifications triggered by fasting is anticipated to offer us wisdom for keeping wellness.

A keto (ketogenic diet) routine is a low-carb, modest protein, higher-fat diet routine that can assist you to burn fat more effectively. It has lots of advantages for fat burning, health, as well as performance, as received over 50 research studies. That's why it's suggested by so many physicians.

The ketogenic diet routine (or keto diet routine, for brief) is a low-carb, high-fat diet plan that provides health and wellness benefits. Over 20 research studies reveal that this sort of diet routine will help you to lose weight and improve your wellness.

WHAT IS A KETOGENIC DIET PLAN?

The ketogenic diet is a low-carb, high-fat diet that shares lots of similarities with the Atkins and also low-carb diet routines. It involves dramatically minimizing carbohydrate consumption as well as changing it with fat content. It, in turn, decrease in carbs puts your body right into a metabolic state called ketosis. When this takes place, your body comes to being only left with melting fat for energy. It turns the fat into ketones in the liver, which could provide power for the brain. Ketogenic diet plans can create massive reductions in blood sugar levels and insulin levels. It adds to the boosted ketones, also has many wellness advantages.

VARIOUS KINDS OF KETOGENIC DIETS PLANS

There are many versions of the ketogenic diet routine, consisting of:

Criterion ketogenic diet routine (CKD):

It is a really low-carb, moderate-protein, and also high-fat diet routine. It usually has 75% fat, 20% protein, and just 5% carbohydrates.

Intermittent ketogenic diet routine (IKD): This diet plan involves percentages of higher-carb diets, such as five ketogenic days complied with by two high-carb days.

Targeted ketogenic diet routine (TKD): This diet plan enables you to include carbs around exercises.

High-protein ketogenic diet routine: This is similar to a typical ketogenic diet routine, yet includes much more protein. The ratio is typically 60% fat, 35% healthy protein, and also 5% carbohydrates. However, just the usual, as well as high-protein ketogenic diets, have been examined thoroughly. Targeted ketogenic (or Cyclical) diets are more advanced methods and also mainly made for bodybuilders or athletes.

The ketogenic diet plan (or keto diet plan, for brief) is a low-carb, high-fat diet plan that offers many health and wellness benefits. Over 20 researches reveal that this kind of diet plan can assist you to drop weight as well as boost your health. What's even more, the diet routine is so filling up that you can lose weight without counting calories or tracking your food consumption.

One study discovered that individuals on a ketogenic diet lost 2.2 times more weight than those on a calorie-restricted low-fat diet plan. Triglyceride and also, cholesterol levels enhanced. There are numerous reasons that a ketogenic diet plan is superior to a low-fat diet plan, including increased protein consumption, which gives countless benefits. The enhanced ketones, lower blood sugar levels as well as boosted insulin sensitivity may additionally play a key role.

ADVANTAGES OF KETO

The ketogenic diet, in fact, came from as a tool for treating neurological conditions such as epilepsy. Researchers have now revealed that the diet routine can have advantages for a wide variety of different health problems:

Heart problem: The ketogenic diet routine can boost risk aspects like body fat, HDL cholesterol levels, blood pressure, and also blood sugar level.

Cancer: The diet plan is presently being made use of to treat some sorts of cancer and also slows down tumor growth.

Alzheimer's condition: The keto diet might reduce signs of Alzheimer's condition and also reduce its development.

Epilepsy: Research study has revealed that the ketogenic diet routine can cause large reductions in seizures in epileptic kids.

Parkinson's condition: One research located that the diet routine helped enhance signs of Parkinson's disease.

Polycystic ovary Syndrome disorder: The ketogenic diet plan can help reduce insulin levels, which may play an essential role in polycystic ovary syndrome.

Brain injuries: One pet study found that the diet can minimize concussions as well as aid recovery after getting a brain injury.

Acne: Lower insulin levels and also eating much less sugar or processed foods may reduce acne effects.

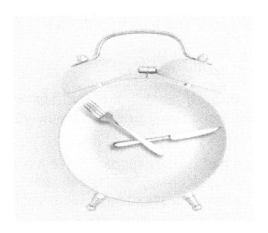

FOODS TO ABSTAIN FROM

Any food that is high in carbohydrates must be limited. Below is a checklist of food that needs to be reduced or gotten rid of on a ketogenic diet routine?

Sweetened foods: like carbonated soft drinks, juice, shakes, cake, gelato, candy, and so on.

Grains or starch: The Wheat-based items, rice, pasta, cereal.

Fruits: only small portions of berries like strawberries are exempted; basically, most fruits are included.

Legumes: This includes Peas, kidney beans, lentils, chickpeas.

Vegetables and also bulbs: Potatoes, pleasant potatoes, carrots, parsnips.

Low-fat or diet plan items: These are very refined and also often high in carbohydrates.

Some condiments or sauces: These commonly consist of sugar and also harmful fat.

Unhealthy fats: Restrict your intake of refined veggie oils, mayonnaise.

Alcohol: Due to their carbohydrate material, several alcoholic beverages can throw you out of ketosis.

Sugar-free diet routine foods: These are typically high in sugar alcohols, which can affect ketone degrees in many cases. These foods additionally tend to be extremely processed.

On a vegan keto diet, you must avoid all meat and also fish and shellfish. High-carb foods like grains, legumes, fruits, and also starchy vegetables are allowed just in small amounts, as long as they match your everyday carb allotment. You ought to get rid of the following foods:

Meat: beef, pork, lamb, goat, as well as veal.

Birds: Chicken, hen, turkey, duck, and also goose.

Fish and also shellfish: salmon, tuna, sardines, anchovies, as well as lobster.

The following are the foods that you need to limit the intake:

Starchy vegetables like potatoes, yams, beets, parsnips, carrots, and sweet potatoes.

Sugar-sweetened beverages: soft drink, excellent tea, sports beverages, juice, as well as energy beverages.

Grains like: bread, rice, quinoa, oats, millet, rye, barley, buckwheat, as well as pasta.

Legume like: beans, peas, lentils, and also chickpeas.

Fruits like: apples, bananas, oranges, berries, melon, apricots, plums, and peaches.

Spices like: BBQ sauce, honey mustard, ketchup, marinades, and also sweetened salad dressings.

Processed foods like morning meal grains, granola, chips, cookies, biscuits, as well as baked goods.

Sweeteners like: brownish sugar, white sugar, honey, syrup, and agave nectar.

Alcoholic beverages like beer, a glass of wine, as well as sweetened mixed drinks.

FOODS TO TAKE

You must base your meal around the following foods:

Meat: Red meat, steak, ham, sausage, bacon, and poultries.

Fat-fishes, like Mackerel, Salmon, Trout, and Tuna.

Eggs: Get pasteurized or omega-3 whole eggs.

Your diet should include nuts, seeds, Walnuts, Almonds, Flax-seeds, Pumpkin seeds, Chia seeds.

Your diet should include Healthy oils, extra virgin olive oil, coconut oil as well as avocado oil Avocados: Entire avocados.

Your diet should include Low-carb veggies: A lot of veggies, tomatoes, onions, peppers.

Dressings: You can use salt, pepper, as well as different healthy natural herbs and also spices.

A healthy vegetarian keto diet should consist of a variety of non-starchy vegetables, healthy and balanced fats, and also proteins sources, such as:

Vegetables (Non-starchy): spinach, broccoli, mushrooms, kale, cauliflower, zucchini, as well as bell peppers.

Healthy and balanced fats: olive oil, coconut oil, avocados, MCT oil, and also avocado oil extract.

Your diet should include Nuts: which includes: almonds, walnuts, cashews, macadamia nuts, pistachios, and Brazil Nuts?

Seeds: which includes: chia, Indian hemp, flax, and pumpkin seeds.

Nut butter: almond, peanut, pecan, and hazelnut butter.

Full-fat dairy products: milk, yoghurt, and also cheese.

Healthy protein: eggs, tofu, tempeh, spirulina, natto, and also dietary yeast.

Low-carb fruits (in moderation): berries, lemons, as well as limes.

Natural herbs and also seasonings: basil, paprika, pepper, turmeric extract, salt, oregano, rosemary, and also thyme.

A SAMPLE KETO DISH PREPARATION FOR 1 WEEK

To assist in starting, below is a sample ketogenic diet routine meal for a week:

On Mondays
For breakfast: Bacon, eggs with tomatoes.

For lunch: Chicken salad with olive oil as well as feta cheese.

For dinner: Salmon with asparagus prepared in butter.

On Tuesday
Morning meal: Egg, tomato, basil, and goat cheese omelet.

Lunch: Milk of Almond, peanut butter, chocolate powder, and also stevia milkshake.

Your diet at dinner should include Meatballs, cheddar cheese, and veggies.

On Wednesday
Morning meal: A ketogenic milkshake

Lunch: Shrimp salad, olive oil, Avocados.

Dinner: Beef chops garnished with Parmesan cheese, broccoli, and salad.

On Thursday
Morning meal: Omelette with avocado, salsa, peppers, onion, and also spices.

Lunch: Small number of nuts and maybe celery sticks to guacamole and salsa.

Your diet should include Dinner: Chicken packed with pesto and some lotion cheese, together with veggies.

On Friday
Breakfast: Sugar-free yogurt with peanut butter, cacao powder, and stevia(s).

Lunch: Beef stir-fried in coconut oil with vegetables.

Your diet should include Dinner: Bun-fewer hamburgers with bacon, egg, and cheese.

On Saturday
Breakfast: Meat and also cheese omelet with vegetables.

Lunch: Ham and cheese slices with nuts.

Supper: Whitefish, egg, and also spinach prepared in coconut oil.

On Sunday

Morning meal: Fried eggs with bacon and also mushrooms.

Lunch: Hamburger with salsa, cheese, and also guacamole.

Supper: Steak as well as eggs with a side salad.

Always try to turn the veggies and meat over the long-term, as each offers various nutrients and also wellness advantages.

HEALTHY AND BALANCED KETO SNACKS

In case you feel the hunger in between meals, right here are some healthy and balanced keto-approved treats:

Fatty meat or fish; not appropriate for sure populations.

Because the vegan keto diet plan is too restrictive, it may not be an excellent option for every person. In particular, youngsters and ladies who are expecting or breastfeeding ought to stay away from it, as it can limit the number of nutrients crucial for the proper development of the child as well as advancement. It might likewise not be appropriate for professional athletes, those with a background of eating disorders, or people with type 1 diabetic issues. If you have any type of underlying health and wellness conditions, or are taking any medications, talk to your healthcare expert before starting this diet routine.

TEST DISH STRATEGY

This five-day example dish strategy can aid kick start a vegan keto diet.

Monday
Morning meal: shake with full-fat milk, spinach, peanut butter, MCT oil, and chocolate wheat in powder.

Your diet should include Lunch: zucchini noodles with tempeh meatballs than a creamy avocado recipe.

Your diet should include Dinner: coconut curry prepared with olive oil, mixed veggies, as well as tofu.

Tuesday
Breakfast: omelet prepared with coconut's oil, garlic, cheese, tomatoes, and onions.

Lunch: cauliflower-crust pizza with cheese, mushrooms, diced tomatoes, olive oil, as well as spinach.

Supper: salad with mixed eco-friendlies, tofu, avocados, tomatoes, and bell peppers.

Wednesday
Morning meal: tofu shuffle with olive oil, mixed veggies, and cheese(s).

Lunch: cauliflower, cheese, and mac with avocado oil, broccoli.

Dinner: frittata and coconut oil, spinach, asparagus, tomatoes, and feta.

Thursday
Morning meal: Greek yoghurt topped with walnuts as well as chia seeds.

Lunch: taco lettuce covers with walnut-mushroom meat, avocados, tomatoes, cilantro, sour lotion, as well as cheese.

Dinner: zucchini pizza watercraft with olive oil, marinara, cheese, spinach, and garlic.

Friday
Morning meal: keto oatmeal with hemp seeds, flax seeds, whipping cream, cinnamon, and peanut butter.

Lunch: baked egg-avocado watercrafts covered with chives, coconut bacon, and paprika.

Dinner: cauliflower fried rice made with coconut oil, veggies, as well as tofu.

VEGETARIAN KETO SNACKS
Below are a couple of simple snacks that you can delight in between dishes:

- Zucchini chips
- Celery with peanut butter

- Roasted pumpkin seeds
- Flax biscuits with sliced up cheese
- Combined nuts
- Chia seed dessert covered with bitter coconut
- Carrots with guacamole
- Whipped lotion with blackberries
- Full-fat cottage cheese with black pepper
- Full-fat Greek yogurt with walnuts

POINTS TO NOTE

The vegetarian's keto diet is a high-fat, low-carb eating pattern that removes meat, fish, and shellfish. Independently, vegan and keto diets may claim blood sugar control, weight reduction, and several other advantages. Nonetheless, this diet plan may enhance your threat of dietary deficiencies though hasn't been examined, still as a hypothesis. Although, if you are vegan and also thinking about trying keto or currently the following keto and also interested concerning going meat-free, it's certainly possible to combine both.

KETO DIET REGIMEN FOR FAT LOSS

The ketogenic (or keto) diet is deficient in carbohydrate, a high-fat eating pattern that increased in the last few years. It has been shown to bring about several outstanding health advantages-- consisting of weight-loss. Therefore, many individuals rely on this manner of eating to reach their weight-reducing objectives.

While research study indicates that the diet can assist in dropping body fat, long-term researches sustaining its efficiency are lacking. When following the typical keto diet plan, your carbohydrate intake is restricted to less than 5-10% of your total daily calorie intake. It makes your body to get in ketosis, a state throughout which the body switches to utilizing fat rather than carbohydrates as its main energy source, and ketones are produced in the liver.

The minimized carb consumption is typically made up for by raising intake of fats to about 70-90% of Kcals, or 155-200 grams for a 2,000-calorie diet plan (1, 2). Healthy protein intake is modest, typically around 20% of calories, or 100 grams for a 2,000-calorie diet. There are some recommended weight management devices associated with the ketogenic diet plan.

MAY DECREASE HUNGER

One of the primary weight reduction treats connected to the keto diet plan is likely its capacity to lower after the ketogenic diet has been linked to decreased levels of ghrelin, one of your body's main hunger hormones. Education in gherkins levels and hunger can result in you eating fewer calories throughout the day, which is no doubt a treat for weight loss. Factually, a study of 20 people with obesity following the keto diet associated this way of eating with reduced food and alcohol cravings. Hence, the keto diet may be an effective means to regulate your hunger levels, though its long-term safety must be taken into consideration.

CAN PROMOTE LOSS OF WATER WEIGHT

One other potential weight loss mechanism of the keto diet is the loss of water weight that accompanies the significant reduction in carbohydrates intake. It is as a result of carbs, in their stored form in your body hold water. Hence, when you reduce your intake of carbs, in the initial stage, diet's stored carbs are released along with some other fluids, which bring about weight loss.

CALORIE BALANCE

To determine if the Kato diet can help with weight loss, it is essential to look at how traditional weight loss is achieved. To lose weight, you need to eat fewer calories than you burn, which is also called calorie loss.

One study made on 17 men with obesity or excess weight found that the keto diet was associated with a small increase in the number of calories burned. Although, this did not lead to increased body fat losses compared with a traditional baseline diet. These results show that the ketogenic diet is not better than the traditional diet type for weight loss when calorie consumed is gotten. The effects of keto diet's weight loss are much more likely to result in reduced calorie consumption as per the changes in safety signals associated with high fat and very low carb diets.

KETOGENIC ADDITIVES

Here are some of the top keto additives or supplements with their functions as follows:

Exogenous ketones are ketones from an outdoor resource, as opposed to normally produced endogenous ketones. They can increase blood ketone levels and also assist you to attain ketosis much more rapidly.

Keto protein powders: These healthy protein powders are developed to have low carb content.

Keto electrolytes Electrolyte deficiency is common when first starting a keto diet as a result of water fat burning Electrolyte supplements can assist by avoiding deficiency of typical electrolytes, such as salt, potassium, as well as magnesium.

Gastro-intestinal enzymes: As a result of the high-fat content of the keto diet, some individuals may experience digestive problems: digestive enzyme supplements, especially lipase which can assist in breaking down fat.

When it comes to the weight management results of ketogenic supplements, researches are restricted. It is discovered such that numerous exogenous ketones, along with MCT oil, may help weight-loss by decreasing cravings as well as causing you to eat fewer calories normally.

Still, human research study supporting these insurance claims is lacking. Although keto supplements are not required, they can still help keto dieters' change into this instead of restrictive means of eating and also raise the tolerability of the diet. That stated, these supplements ought to not be used entirely for weight-loss, as the data is insufficient, and their long-lasting adverse effects are unknown. Various other points that may impact weight loss. When complying with a keto diet for weight loss purposes, some other aspects likewise require to be born in mind to ensure development.

YOUR SPECIFIC CARBOHYDRATE INTAKE

When beginning a ketogenic diet plan, it may assist in tracking exactly how many carbs you are eating daily. This assist ensures that you get in ketosis relatively quick as well as avoid several signs and symptoms associated with the "keto influenza," which is an array of signs consisting of frustrations and brain haze, about starting a plan on the keto diet. If you eat way too many carbohydrates, you will certainly not stay in ketosis, and also the possible benefits of the diet routine consisting of weight reduction will totally have vanished. Consuming less than 50grams of carbohydrates per day must be sufficient to promote ketosis.

WHETHER YOU'RE GETTING ENOUGH SLEEP

Sleep is a commonly forgotten element of any diet routine. Researches show that a lack of sleep and persistent stress and anxiety can negatively affect weight management results. Lack of sleep can adversely impact cravings hormones, such as ghrelin and leptin. It can cause enhanced appetite, neutralizing the hunger-reducing effects of the keto diet. Making sure that you take time to unwind than getting a minimum of 7hours of rest per night can help support the benefits of a ketogenic diet routine.

WHETHER YOU'RE LITERALLY ACTIVE

While the keto diet routine alone might supply weight-loss, combining it with a correct exercise program can boost this result. When adjusted to the diet, your body can make use of fat as its primary fuel resource for the workout. Research studies recommend that this is most valuable in endurance-based sports. It is essential to know that you must be well understood to the keto diet plan before executing any type of reasonably extreme workout to stay clear of adverse side effects.

SUSTAINABILITY OF THE DIET

One of the significant drawbacks of the keto diet plan - particularly for weight-loss is its long-term sustainability. Keeping that in mind, the diet is relatively restrictive; some people may find it hard to stick. It basically develops difficulties when dining out or gathering with friends and family for the holidays, as a new means of eating must be adopted, potentially affecting social interactions. Moreover, research studies on the health effects of complying with the keto diet routine for extended periods are lacking. These aspects have to be thought about before starting it.

POINTS TO NOTE

The keto diet plan is an extremely low carb, the high-fat diet plan that has been shown to use various wellness advantages, including fat burning. While the specific weight management methods related by doing this of eating patterns are still under examination, it shows up that weight-loss is caused by a calorie shortage, a decrease in hunger degrees, as well as water fat burning. Keto supplements may reduce appetite and also aid you in getting involved in ketosis a lot more rapidly, though they ought not to be made use of to advertise fat burning. While the weight reduction advantages of the keto diet plan may appear promising, it's essential to consider its future side effects, downsides, and also the lack of long-lasting research on it.

BURN FAT QUICKLY

The Ketogenic diet is a preferred low carb plan which promises to help people lose weight fast. A professional reveal the key error you should avoid. Weight-loss gets on the minds of many people; however, this doesn't mean it is simple to achieve. There are several intend on the marketplace guaranteeing to help obese people to get into shape promptly. The low carbohydrate high fat keto diet plan can assist melt fat quickly, and an expert exposed how to get the very best results.

WHAT IS THE KETO DIET PLAN?

The keto or ketogenic diet routine plan requires people to consume roughly 25 grams of carbohydrates in a day. Instead, dieters can stay on foods high in fats and with modest healthy protein content by cutting carbohydrates out of the diet plan, and people can choose from healthy choices to stay completely satisfied. The concept of keto is to absorb such a low amount of carbs that your body switches over to a metabolic state called 'ketosis' where it uses fat and ketones for gas rather than glucose.

People that follow the keto diet routine will eat a high percentage of their calories from fat, some healthy protein as well as marginal or no consumption from carbohydrates. Common foods people consume on the keto diet routine tend to be anything with high fat and also low carbohydrate content, such as oils, cheese, and also milk products, eggs, nuts, and other protein food items.

As well as eating high-fat foods such as meats, fish and dairy, there are some dishes dieters ought to stay clear off. High-carb foods consisting of bread, pasta, rice, sweet deals with high sugar fruits must have stayed side. Although the diet routine plan can help gluttons drop weight, they should be wary of making inevitable mistakes. First of all, avoid believing that there is some inherent magic to the diet when it pertains to weight reduction or body shape-up.

There are some medical uses that the keto diet works for by relieving some medical issues. However, for stable populations searching for weight loss or body structure modification, so long as a calorie shortage remains in place, any kind of diet certainly function. It is claimed any diet plan which calls for people to consume less than they burn certainly give weight loss results.

It is why numerous specialists choose to suggest a keto-style diet. That consists of plenty of veggies and lean meats, which is higher in fat, higher in protein, and has lower carbohydrate, which is likely to be helpful and also a lot more sustainable. As opposed to purely adhering to the keto diet plan, someone who wants to get slim can see similar results by following a less restrictive version of this. It would involve eating foods high in fat and protein and reduced in carbs. When attempting to drop weight, people are likewise encouraged to exercise consistently to get the most effective outcomes.

Weight-Loss: It is hard to achieve yet adhering to a diet routine strategy that can assist speed up outcomes. A professional stated the very best diet routine to comply with to burn fat fast - what can you consume? Weight loss is is bothersome on the minds of numerous Britons, with many of them seeking the best means to shed fat quickly. A search online brings up different fat burning plans, all assuring to offer the very best outcomes. Nevertheless, the reduced carb and also high fat keto diet could be better than others when it comes to burning fat.

The keto diet is the high-fat, high protein as well as low carbohydrate diet plan. The body then gets into a state of ketosis, where it's melting fat as the primary power source, as opposed to carbs.

WHAT CAN YOU EAT?

The food that is reduced in carbohydrates, high in fat, and has moderate protein content Foods on the plan consists of meats, fish, veggies, eggs, avocados, and milk products. High carbohydrate treats such as bread, pasta, rice, and also high sugar fruits are off the table for slimmers.

Some dieters just shed fat when they eat foods reduced in carbohydrates and participate in ketosis. Eating fat only assists in burning fat if you remain in a state of ketosis. When you are on a reduced carbohydrate, high protein, and also fat diet, the body makes use of fat as its primary power resource; this procedure is called ketosis. Fat is an energy power resource and generally supplies our body with about 9.5 calories of energy per gram, which is double that of carbohydrates. When carbs are cut to exceptionally reduce levels and fats increase, in time, the body's metabolic process shifts and quicken to burn fat as its energy resource.

It implies that fat sources in the body are directly being used up as well as a shed for power. Following this plan quicken the metabolic process while dieters must still ensure they are not eating more calories than they are burning off. To refine and to obtain energy from fat, the metabolic rate is elevated, which suggests the body is naturally melting even more calories. Nonetheless, you will just shed fat as part of a calorie managed diet routine. If you remain in a state of ketosis but eating 1,000 even more calories than you are shedding every day, you will put on weight.

Dieters must see the kinds of fats they are eating when trying to move the excess weight. Eating meat with every meal, downing entirely with milk and also covering everything with oil or butter just because 'you can' or just because 'its high fat' is lousy diet technique to enter You are not required to remove all carbohydrates, it's various for everyone, yet the odd slice of bread, crackers or something carby does not prevent all your development. There are numerous ways to shed much weight quickly. Several diet plan strategies leave you feeling hungry or dissatisfied. These are significant reasons you may discover it tough to stay with a diet routine. Nevertheless, not all diets have this effect. Reduced carb diet routines work for weight loss and also might be easier to adhere to than other diet routines.

Here is an extra step to the weight-reduction plan that uses a low carbohydrate diet routine and aims to:

- considerably lower your hunger.
- trigger fast weight reduction.
- enhances your metabolic wellness at the same time.

1. REDUCE ON CARBOHYDRATES

One of the most vital parts is to cut down on sugars and also starches or carbs. On doing that, your hunger decrease, and also you usually wind up eating considerably fewer calories against the melting of carbohydrates for energy; your body now begins to burn stored fat for storage. One more advantage of cutting carbohydrates is that it reduces insulin degrees, causing the kidneys to drop excess salt and also water. This decrease bloating and unnecessary water weight.

According to some dietitians, it's not unusual to shed approximately ten extra pounds (4.5 kg) sometimes extra in the very first week of eating this way. This fat-burning consists of both body fat and also water weight. One study in healthy females with weight problems reported that a deficient carbohydrate diet was more reliable than a low-fat diet routine for temporary fat burning.

Research recommends that a low carbohydrate diet plan can lower hunger, which might lead you to eat fewer calories without thinking of it or feeling starving. In other words, reducing carbohydrates can cause quick, very easy fat burning.

Getting rid of sugars and also starches, or carbohydrates, from your diet, can reduce your hunger, lower your insulin levels, as well as make you drop weight without really feeling starving.

2. CONSUME PROTEIN, FAT, AND VEGETABLES

Each one of your dishes should consist of a healthy protein source, fat resource, as well as low carbohydrate vegetables. As a general policy, attempt to eat two to three meals a day. In a case whereby you are hungry in the afternoon, including a fourth dish.

Creating your dishes by doing this ought to bring your carb consumption down to around 20-50 grams per day.

HEALTHY PROTEIN

Eating lots of protein is an essential part of this strategy. Evidence recommends that eating lots of protein might boost calorie expense by 80-100 calories each day. High healthy protein diet routines can also minimize desires and obsessive thoughts concerning food by 60%, reducing the desire to eat late during the night, and make you feel full. In one study, individuals on a higher healthy protein diet routine consumed 441 fewer calories each day.

1. Healthy protein sources include Meat: beef, poultry, as well as lamb.
2. Fish and seafood: salmon, trout, as well as shrimp.
3. Eggs: entire eggs with the yolk.
4. Plant-based healthy proteins: beans, legumes, as well as soy.
5. It reduced carbohydrate vegetables.

Don't be afraid to pack your plate with reduced carbohydrate veggies. They are loaded with nutrients, and then you can consume massive amounts. A diet routine based primarily on lean protein resources as well as veggies has all the fiber, vitamins, and minerals you require to be healthy and balanced.

Numerous vegetables are low in carbs, consisting of:

- broccoli
- cauliflower
- spinach
- tomatoes
- kale

Brussels sprouts

- cabbage
- Swiss chard
- Lettuce
- cucumber

Healthy fats

Do not hesitate when it comes to eating healthy fat. Trying to do low carbohydrate as well as slim at the same time can make sticking to the diet routine hard. Resources of healthy fats consist of:

- olive oil
- coconut oil
- avocado oil
- butter

Put together each dish out of a protein source, fat source, and also reduced-carb vegetables. It will usually put you in a carbohydrate series of 20-50 grams as well as dramatically reduced your hunger levels.

3. **RAISE WEIGHTS 3 TIMES WEEKLY**

You do not require working out to lose weight on this plan. However, it undoubtedly has added advantages. By raising weights, you burn lots of calories and also avoid your metabolism from reducing, which is a common adverse effect of dropping weight.

Researches on reduced-carb diets reveal that you can gain a little muscle mass while losing considerable quantities of body fat. Attempt going to the gym 3 to 4 times a week to exercise If you're brand-new to the fitness center, ask an instructor for some guidance. Do some cardio workouts like walking, jogging, running, cycling, or swimming will certainly suffice? Both cardio, as well as weight training, can help with weight reduction.

Resistance training, such as weight lifting, might be the best choice. If that's not possible, cardio exercises are additionally useful. If you need to, you can take someday off weekly where you eat many more carbs. Many people select to do this on Saturday. It is essential to stay with healthy carb resources like oats, rice, quinoa, potatoes, excellent potatoes, and also fruit. If you should have a rip off the meal as well as consume something undesirable, do it on now.

414

Restriction of this one more significant carb per day for a week, if you aren't reducing carbohydrates enough, you could not experience weight-loss. You could obtain some water weight during your refeed day, and also you generally lose it once again in the following 1-2 days. Having one day weekly where you consume much more carbs is acceptable, although not necessary.

WHAT CONCERNING CALORIES AND SECTION CHECK?

It's not needed to count calories in as much as you take low carbohydrates and adhere to healthy protein, fat, as well as reduced carbohydrates and veggies. However, to count them, you can utilize a cost-free online. Enter your gender, weight, height, and also activity levels. The calculator will inform you how many calories to consume per day to preserve your weight, drop weight, or reduce weight fast. You can additionally download complementary, simple calorie counters from internet sites and also application shops. It's not essential to count calories to slim down on this strategy. It's essential to keep your carbohydrates in the 20-50gram variety purely.

10 WEIGHT MANAGEMENT IDEAS
Below are ten even more ideas to drop weight much faster and manage them:

- Eat a high healthy protein morning meal. Eating a high healthy protein morning meal could decrease food cravings and also calorie consumption throughout the day.
- Stay away from sweet drinks and also fruit juice. These are amongst the most fattening things you can take into your body.
- Drink water before meals. One research study revealed that drinking water a half hr before meals increased weight loss by 44% over three months.
- Pick weight-loss-friendly foods. Some foods are better for weight management than others.
- Consume soluble fiber. Researches show that soluble fibers might advertise weight-loss. Fiber supplements like glucomannan can likewise help.
- Drink coffee or tea. High levels of caffeine enhance your metabolic process by 3- 11%.
- Base your diet routine on whole foods. They are healthier, more filling, and slightly triggers overeating than processed foods.
- Do not rush food. Eating hasty can result in weight gain in time. While eating slowly makes you feel much fuller and also improve weight-reducing hormones.
Researches show that people who evaluate themselves each day are far more likely to slim down and also keep it off for an extended period.
- Get high-quality rest. Rest is essential for several reasons, and also lousy sleep is one of the most prominent danger elements for weight gain.

HOW QUICK WILL YOU LOSE WEIGHT?

You might shed 5-10 pounds (2.3-4.5 kg) of weight, in some cases a lot more in the first week of the diet strategy, and then lose weight regularly after that. If you're new to dieting, weight management may occur more quickly. The more weight you need to shed, the faster you will lose it. For the first few days, you may feel a little bit strange. Your body is utilized to escaping carbohydrates, and also it can take some time for it to get used to burning fat instead. Some individuals experience "keto flu" or "low carb flu." It usually over within a few days.

After the first few days, lots of people report feeling great, with much more power than in the past. Other than weight reduction, the low carbohydrate diet routine can improve your health and wellness in several methods.

Many people shed a considerable amount of weight on a reduced carbohydrate diet. However, the speed depends on the person. Reduced carb diet plans likewise enhance particular markers of health, such as blood sugar and also cholesterol degrees.

POINTS TO NOTE

By lowering carbohydrates as well as reducing insulin degrees, you'll likely experience lowered hunger and cravings. It gets rid of the major factors it's typically difficult to maintain a weight management plan. On this strategy, you can likely consume healthy food up until you're complete and also still lose a substantial quantity of fat. The preliminary decrease in water weight can bring about a drop in the scales within a few days. Weight loss takes longer. Researches contrasting reduced carb and low-fat diet routines suggest that a reduced carb diet routine could also make you shed as much as two to three times as much weight as a typical low fat, calorie-restricted diet plan.

If you have kind two diabetes speak to your doctor before making changes, as this strategy can minimize your demand for the drug. Speed keto incorporates periodic fasting and the keto diet plan. It improves weight reduction; however, specialists claim it's a flawed concept.

"Speed keto," a combination of periodical fast and keto diet do give faster weight management results without desires or issues. It holds that both ketos as well as periodic fasting have been found to have health and wellness advantages, including weight-loss, when done correctly.

Nevertheless, professionals do not recommend speed keto, particularly for those brand-new to keto. While it benefits temporary weight loss, it can be difficult to maintain and can be risky for people with clinical problems. As the high-fat, low-carb keto diet will always be a frequently used nutrition, variations of keto from Mediterranean keto to vegetarian, also trends together with an unpredictable market of keto products or services that promise quicker, easier results from the diet plan.

Go into fast keto, a combination of keto and periodic fasting. Although there's evidence to sustain both strategies, experts do not suggest integrating them, specifically if you're a beginner, since the unexpected severe change will likely be undesirable, as well as the short-term payback isn't worth the negative effects. Fasting can be challenging at times early in the keto process since dieters haven't permitted their body system to acclimatize to melting fat, resulting in appetite, fatigue. That added stress and anxiety is not just unhealthy, but can disrupt the metabolic rate, he added.

"Rate keto" is a trademarked diet routine strategy developed by Harlan Kilstein, an entrepreneur as well as a self-proclaimed "way of a life coach." Kilstein identifies himself as a physician as well as technically, he is, with a doctorate in education and learning, not nourishment or any other field of medication.

Individually, both the keto diet routine, as well as intermittent fasting, can assist weight loss, if done correctly. Keto, often called a way of life rather than a diet plan, has been deemed for weight loss, more power, and much better metabolic health. Recently, doctors have begun making use of keto as a therapy for diabetes, although nutritionists are commonly doubtful of the high fat in a keto diet plan, specifically hydrogenated fat.

There's also an expanding body of proof to support the benefits of periodic fasting, consisting of weight loss, but likewise avoidance of chronic illness and other ailments.

Nevertheless, not every option is right for everybody. People with a history of disordered eating, as an example, should not attempt limiting diet routines that removed food teams or need not eating for extended periods. Also, it's always best to collaborate with a doctor and nutrition specialist if you're attempting to reduce weight or significantly alter your diet plan. However, the mix of both right into "speed keto," with the goal of participants eating simply one low-carb, high-fat meal per day, has an even higher risk of becoming a fad diet, considering that the sudden, dramatic modification to eating habits likely leave people hungry, tired, and unlikely to adhere to the eating strategy, according to professionals.

Rating keto is particularly challenging for newbies, though people do often tend to eat much less after a while on the keto diet. As soon as adjusted to a keto diet, some individuals naturally eat much less typically throughout the day, because high-fat dishes are extra loading. "[Rate keto] is a memorable marketing method of describing what individuals already do."

However, the key is that those people have already adjusted to the ketogenic diet plan in time, an extensive procedure that varies depending on the person, yet can take 2 to 4 weeks after restricting carbohydrates. Fasting can indeed quicken the process by a lot more rapidly, minimizing the body's saved power, but it's most likely to be unpleasant, he included.

Trying to go on fasting before then, particularly a strenuous fasting style of simply one dish a day, can be difficult since the brain is made use of to relying upon glucose for energy- without a steady supply from food, Limansky said, The person will be weak, famished, and vulnerable to food cravings and hunger pains.

"I think it's a lot more difficult to start that way. I recommend getting adapted to initially, so you do not experience symptoms," Short-term, it's more effective, however long term, it's not lasting. One meal a day' isn't backed by proof and also can make it tougher to get daily nutrients. The particular kind of periodic fasting advertised in rate keto is "one meal a day" eating schedule, often abbreviated to OMAD. It can help with fat burning, according to Limansky, considering that eating less frequently likely creates you to consume fewer calories generally and also, keto or otherwise, slimming down always calls for a calorie deficiency.

But there's no proof that it's any much better than various other, much less severe designs of recurring fasting, according to Robin Foroutan, a signed up dietitian nutritionist said that "solitary dish needs to be premium as well as well balanced, or you'll be losing out on important nutritional elements like vitamins, minerals, and fiber".

"That suggests you might be adhering to a strategy that requires far more initiative without added pay-off in terms of health and wellness benefits. It is possibly not that easy to get all the nutrients you'll need for the day in one meal without overstuffing yourself, which isn't excellent for food digestion as well as absorption. Professionals recommend a milder technique to diet routine changes, preferably with the help of a medical professional.

For individuals that are still wanting to apply for the advantages of keto or periodic fasting, the specialists recommend a sluggish as well as steady technique in addition to consulting a nutritional expert or medical doctor. Any kind of diet routine, including keto or fasting, with the intention of quick weight loss.

I look at it as this is how I'm most likely to live for the rest of my life. As an effect, I'll observe a reduction in weight. You should concentrate on health and wellness from the start and not weight-loss. The takeaway right here is that like other extreme dieting strategies, like extremely low-calorie strategies, it likely benefits weight loss; however, it's not worth it lasting. Also, not every person needs to fast, or do keto, to feel excellent or lose weight if that's their goal. Straightforward concepts like avoiding processed food and also sugar-coated can make a big distinction for many people, without the added tension of difficult diet strategies or obsessive carbohydrate counting.

It's a choice not all individuals need to do this. If people are starving, they'll consume. If they drop weight and also muscle mass, they'll shut metabolic price down as well as get the weight back. However, if people do the essentials, it cares for many issues. Intermittent fasting, the one way of life to guide them all.

Two meals a day (TMAD) is good since you still attain similar outcomes as well as not have that unpleasant, full feeling contrasted to one dish a day. Water fasting is very good for the body as it helps the body to auto-fix itself. Dry water fasting is just one of the most effective recurring fasts because 3 days of water fasting coincides as 1 day of dry water fasting.

Not only are you going to save an excessive quantity of time and money, but your wellness and mood will improve considerably. You can anticipate seeing as low as 2 weeks. There are no adverse side effects or any wellness issues connected to OMAD (One meal a day), TMAD (Two meals a day).

This isn't trending, a fast-type weight management program like all those online, or transform my life. When you comply with the one meal a day, 2 dishes a day, and fasting way of life, it needs to be done regularly for a minimum of 3 months.

Remain to comply with the recurring fasting of OMAD or TMAD for the remainder of your life, as well as you be awarded health as well as joy. You will certainly reap all the benefits as long as you correspond. As soon as you quit complying with the OMAD/TMAD and fasting, you might never have the wish to re-follow it. Therefore, it is highly advised that you advance with this way of life for as long as you can, or else you go right back right into your undesirable lifestyle.

ONE MEAL A DAY (OMAD)
The one meal a day no doubt the best periodic fasting it is recommended as said earlier for those who are working long hours or simply lesser time for their family, buddies, and job. The benefits consist of conserving long periods from cooking and also preparing your meals vs. eating 3- 4 meals daily. Your bank account won't reduce so quickly because you will be eating less. You won't have the ability to fit 3 square meals right into one dish. Consequently, you eat less as well as save even more; nevertheless, OMAD is one of the most challenging out of the 3. Packing three full meals right into one can be unpleasant at first; however, your body adjusts to it after several days.

Follow these easy policies as well as you certainly get on the one meal a day (OMAD) in a snap:

Eat anytime you desire but only within a one-hour structure.

It is very suggested you eat after you exercise or five to 6 hrs before bed.

If you consume after exercising after that, you can consume extra because you will certainly be hungrier, and your body will call for more energy from the lost during the workout. See to it you consume 5-6 hours before bed so the food can be fully absorbed. If not, you can be stocking bed for a while until your food has been absorbed.

I have got some problems for you if you are just one of the few and uncommon that likes to hit the bed right after stuffing yourself. The stomach acid moves up into your esophagus and can cause esophagus cancer cells as well as melt your throat (not essentially turn it off). Anytime you consume right before bed, your body can not melt the carbohydrate and also sugar throughout the day, along with other gastrointestinal aches.

Rather sugar and carbohydrates are stored as fat, which is the complete opposite of what we want. Sumo wrestlers do this, as well as you can see the horrible results that it creates. Resting or taking a slow-moving walk after each dish is the most useful thing for your body after a square meal. Right here are the important things, carbohydrates and also sugar will, at some point, convert into fat if it is not burnt or utilized as energy. Possibly since one exercise and also the various other does not. So, sugar and carbs are cleared out when you utilize the bathroom? Yes, but not as high as you believe.

Throughout the day, with one meal a day, you are regularly shedding power, and also, after 16-20 hours, your HGH degrees would sky-rocket. Human development hormone is the elixir of life, the eternal youth. It has been within us all along. The human race has been looking for this potion for ages; however, they were searching in all the incorrect areas. HGH has been revealed to slow down aging, improve muscular tissue development, enhance mood and cognitive thinking, fix the body of illness and also disease, and so a lot more.

The advantages of HGH You get this free of cost, daily, all day, but the cost is just OMAD, and can you afford such an asset?

Periodic fasting of one meal a day permits you to consume much less. Therefore, you slim down, and its simply simple common sense that eating much less indicates you certainly slim down (unless it's pure sugar or fats).

Recurring fasting issues:

- Oxidative tension and swelling throughout the body.
- The chances to get cancer and tumor growth due to such activity.
- The chances to get blood pressure and blood glucose degrees.
- Triglycerides and also LDL cholesterol.
- The chances to have heart problems and neurodegenerative disease.
- Excess body fat because of enhanced fat oxidation.

- The chances to get diabetic problems and insulin resistance.

Intermittent fasting improves:

- Insulin sensitivity, and also, it makes you endure much more carbohydrates and permits you to regulate your blood sugar level levels better.

Human Development Hormone (HGH) after 18-23 hrs of fasting, it does so by an astonishing 1300-1500%.

Metabolic rate; Quicken your metabolic rate by 3-14%.

Nutrient dividing, you'll absorb your nutrients extra successfully as well as enhance protein synthesis because the body regards not eating as a malnourishment signal. Fat loss and oxidation, you'll use your body fat for fuel at the expenditure of preserving even more muscle. Cleansing the procedure called 'autophagy' gets rid of waste and also safeguards your cells against malignant lump factors. Psychological clearness and also emphasizes you boost your focus and brainpower because of increased BDNF levels. Neurogenesis and neuroplasticity, you develop a lot more mind cells that secure against neurodegenerative illness, such as Alzheimer's as well as Parkinson's. It is likewise very closely gotten in touch with increased psychological power. Mitochondrial thickness and also function enable you to generate even more energy and do it a lot more effectively. You will feel regularly invigorated without having consumed anything.

You're most likely questioning if I do not eat throughout the day how will I have sufficient energy to last? The human body works in several great means. When we eat sugar and also carbohydrates, our body uses it as energy and burns it throughout the day.

If you do not work out or are inactive a lot of the day, the sugar and also carbs can not be made use of or melt. It eventually is transformed and stored as fat. It takes a while, and most are used throughout the day. However, the others, well, they obtain kept. If you're overweight or huge, the one dish a day permits your body to utilize your saved fat and also shed it until you eat once more. That is why you require to eat 5-6 hours before you go to bed; if not, then your body won't have the proper amount of time to burn those carbs and sugar. The OMAD, one meal a day is a quick and efficient way to lose weight, assuming you eat a healthy and balanced diet.

DISADVANTAGES OF OMAD

You will need to incorporate raw fruits and vegetables. Eat easily digestible meat and carbs, take liquids and fruit first since they are the fastest to digest. After that, your veggies. You probably read from another article where OMAD can be taken with anything and still result in weight loss. That is correct because let's say you eat up to 2000 calories per day, but there is no way you can eat 2000 calories per meal if you do it in 3 servings. However, if you truly want to make the best from eating a meal in a day to four servings of fruits and veggies daily. You achieve your goals faster. Avoid taking food items like sandwiches, McDonald's, fatties, sugar, and more as some would wrongly say it, are allowed with one meal a day. They are trying to sweet talk and are not truly factual.

You want to feed your body with efficient nutrients because if you're going to do the one meal day. Of course, you can eat unhealthy things seldomly, but if you are going to do it every day because of hunger and the cravings for unhealthy food, then maybe one meal a day is not meant for you. Eat once a day. No snacking, drinking milk, or juices. When eating, you may drink milk or juice. You must eat all in one sitting within 1 hour to an hour and a half there about. It recommends starting with two meals a day, and then you can work your way up to one meal a day. Some things to keep in mind:

Se you get so hungry and might keep thinking about food all day, so that is why it is advisable you start-off with two (2) meals a day. The hunger pain does become annoying, and you may think about is food all day.

When eating, make sure you are only 90- 95% full—eating to total satisfaction results in abdominal pains (For the first couple of days only). Although after a few days, your body adapts to the 23 hours of hunger pain, and eventually, you will be able to observe OMAD consequently. Hence this will require you to change your lifestyle and get rid of the bad habits.

TWO MEALS A DAY (TMAD)

Two meals a day (TMAD) is my favorite out of the three and the most suitable for me. It fits my travel and busy schedule perfectly, and I have been on two recommend starting with two meals a day, and then you can work your way up to one meal a day. Here are some things to keep in mind:

Se meals a day, and I don't ever plan on stopping. I can notice an improvement in my body, although it's not easy.

My meals are so quick and cost-effective. I make fruit smoothies for the 1st meal and have raw vegetables. My second meal is always taken along with some fruits and probably with a bunch of raw veggies again.

PROS OF TMAD, TWO MEALS A DAY

The benefits of intermittent fasting of two meals a day allow you to eat two meals instead of one, which is much easier. Taking Two (2) meal servings in a day is not as well different from one dish a day. It will not give you the exact outcomes like one meal a day, however, near to it. You can say it has to do with 80-90% equally as efficient as OMAD.

Your first dish you must eat regarding 80% full and the 2nd meal you can eat till you are 100% full. You won't have belly discomforts or feel uneasy as if you were eating one big meal. Now the method is you need to consume within a 4, 5, or 6-hour amount of time; however, the much shorter the time framework, the better. When the body fasts for a longer amount of time, it, therefore, causes a greater production of HGH, although it does not make a significant difference.

When preparing my meals, I planned for both the very first dish as well as the second meal to ensure that method I am not in the cooking area regularly. TMAD (2 meals a day) did change my life as well as the timetable for the better. TMAD gave me 1-- 2 hrs of additional time daily and saved about $100 every month from the supermarket.

If we do the math over twenty years for food.

($100/month X 12 month= $1200 X 20yr = $24,000 conserved).

Currently for time saved.

(90min/day X 365 days = 32,850 min X 20yr = 10,950 human resources gained).

I didn't state the expense of gas as well as time going to the supermarket so you'll really save more money and also time.

DISADVANTAGES OF TMAD

Eating two dishes a day is so much easier than eating one substantial meal a day; however, your HGH manufacturing will certainly not be 1500% or MAX out for your age but close. You must eat within a 4-Hour amount of time to obtain near the optimum HGH manufacturing. Do not forget you still require eating your last meal 5 to 6 hrs before going to bed, so your tummy has fully digested everything. The very same guidelines use below for intermittent fasting of TMAD as well.

Eating two dishes a day permits you to consume all the healthy and balanced food that your body requires on your very first meal. Then you can take whatever you want for the second meal. OMAD will become uncomfortable and also intolerable as you attempt stuffing all that food in one resting and after that having to deal with the pain that comes afterward from a stomach that looks expecting. I can't even stroll properly or stand up correctly after OMAD. I prefer eating for half an hour two times a day, and it makes me appreciate my food a lot more without needing to deal with the belly pains from OMAD.

FASTING

These are one of the most common means to fast. Regular fasting is where you do not consume anything, yet you can consume liquids throughout the day. Soft completely dry fasting: is when you can shower as well as wash your face, but you can't consume water or consume anything. Hard, dry fasting: When no water or food is enabled to touch your body whatsoever form or type. (You can cleanse your hands with among those antibacterial papers).

They claim that a person's day of completely dry not eating amounts to 3 days of normal fasting. My very first dry fasting was for 36 hrs, felt revitalizing, and, however doesn't be surprised, and it wasn't like a powerful burst of modification or anything enchanting. The idea of food, as well as water, did not impact me in any way. Your body is constantly doing two things, fixing it or digesting food.

If our bodies can do both, after that, we could eat whatever and whenever we wished to, but life isn't that fantastic. That is why fasting is so effective because your body is repairing itself through.

If you're constantly eating, your body does not have time to fix itself, whether that be burning kept fat, creating even more HGH, renewing dead as well as old cells, and so on. Likewise, whenever you eat or drink anything over 50 calories, your body starts the digestion procedure, which after that, generates more insulin. (I encourage from snacking or eating numerous tiny dishes a day). Insulin is a hormone produced by your pancreas, which affects the amount of sugar in your blood.

The food you consume gets converted into sugar and also made use of as energy. Insulin plays a major role in this process.

REGULAR FASTING

It can be done every other day, as you please. As long as you are fasting, you're offering your body a chance to repair itself. Some people fast for 24 hr, 36 hrs, or 48 hours. It just depends how much you consume before each fast, and the more task you do during not eating, the less energy you have throughout the day. I like to fast when I am not working out or non-active the majority of the day. The method I can conserve my power, particularly if I am fasting for two days.

When fasting, you shed much fatter and your body repair work itself far better than the OMAD. Other benefits consist of reduced cholesterol, boost metabolic rate, aids heart health and wellness, reduce inflammation, as well as a great deal even more. You can take a look at even more benefits below. Obese individuals can last much longer than thin people because their body has more fat to make use of energy or gas. It is safe and healthy and balanced too quickly for a couple of days or even a couple of weeks.

CRUCIAL POINTERS

If you have been not eating for a couple of days or a week, as well as you, feel light-headed, less energy, lightheadedness, or something is wrong after that, you ought to stop fasting ASAP. Don't fast for more than a few weeks except you are obese and have already fasted for a couple of days before your initial substantial fasting. (Building up resistance for anything certainly protect against fewer troubles).

Begin eating food again but little by little after extensive fasting. If you stuff on your own after a pair week of fasting, you can essentially pass away. It is what took place during the Holocaust when the Americans provided the Jews food to consume. Water with lemon, alcohol, mineral water, as well as other healthy vitamins and also nutrients that your body requires throughout your fast is needed. You can consume some sugary drinks, beers, juices but try to keep the calories to a minimum. Water is constantly best.

DRY FAST, SOFT DRY FAST VS HARD DRY FAST

Soft dry fasting is when you can neither drink liquids nor can you eat anything; however, you can shower wash, your face also. Soft-like fasting and hard, dry fast are slightly comparable.

HARD, DRY FASTING

It happens in the case whereby you cannot have contact with any food or water. It should be done within two (2) full days. Most cells and organs in your body require water to function properly; it can be dangerous if you go over 48 hours without taking at least water. Dry fasting is advisable so far. It comes along with negligible side effects. It is not advised, though, especially for first-timers. Dry fasting is three times more beneficial than normal fast since your body does not consume anything, even water, and your body is purged of many toxins.

Benefits of dry fasting include:

- It improves gut health.
- It enhances brain functions.
- It eliminates toxin waste.
- It improves cholesterol levels.
- It removes inflammations.

Autophagy-The sickest cells are sacrificed for the other cell's survival. The healthiest and strongest cells being preserved.

DRAWBACKS OF DRY FASTING

Here is the list of don't-do conditions of dry fasting. But if you notice any of this, then your fast needs to be supervised, otherwise:

- Malignant tumours of any localization; haemophilia, leukaemia, lymphocytic leukaemia.
- We are getting active tuberculosis of the lungs and other organs.
- Irregular heart rhythm and conduction.
- A person might get the condition of coronary artery disease and myocardial infection.
- Chronic ischemic cerebrovascular disease.
- The chances for severe underweight.

- Thrombophlebitis and thrombosis.
- Pregnancy and lactation.

WHICH ONE IS THE BEST?

All three can be the most effective or none, whichever one fits your schedule, needs, and you know it is most suitable. Whether you plan on adhering to recurring fasting of one meal a day or more dishes a day and regularly, fast a minimum of once in a month and also completely dry fast at least every other month, it is important to listen to your body. If you're an overweight individual, you can observe the two meals a day with regular fasting once a week and dry fasting once every other month. There is no definite answer. Each individual has different needs and body structure. "The state of the science on an intermittent fast is a healthy food consumption and exercise, to improve and maintain health as a lifestyle approach," the senior author explained Health Day Reporter.

Mattson, who has studied and practiced the issue himself for over two decades in the Johns Hopkins Medicine Newsroom, said that intermittent fasting assumes two forms.

Mattson and his co-author Rafael de Cabo looked at studies and coined out its additional health benefits, they included:

Cognitive Abilities: A study has shown that it improves memory function. Obesity and Diabetes: Studies (100 overweight female) have shown that 5:2 intermittent fasting diet is, however, of the same benefits as simply taking of limited calories, but also healthier insulin sensitivity and lower tummy-fat than those on the lower-calorie diet.

The authors said more researches are needed to be carried out to see if the diet would extend to all types of people; they reported that; even till at present, studies have only focused on young or middle-aged adults who are overweight. People who are interested in the diet shouldn't embark on it without first seeking the consent of their doctors, as cautioned, by Newsweek, but Mattson said the diet would likely benefit from obese people.

It is legitimate to assume intermittent fasting as a trending diet," she said. "The reason for that is that it does not completely cut out any food groups. It's not telling you don't eat carbs, avoid fatty foods. And so on."

How do you get started after which you might have spoken to your doctor about you start intermittent fasting? Try starting intermittent fasting with a spouse, partner, or friends at work," Mattson told Newsweek. "Just as with starting an exercise routine, intermittent fasting is of greater ease when done with someone else than alone. You should also be sure to take plenty of water, healthy foods like veggies, fruits, nuts, fish, and meat, he exclaimed.

DIETS TO EASY INTERMITTENT FASTING

It takes about half-a-day to use the energy stored in the liver. Then what happens is that fats provide the body with energy. In the newly published paper, Mattson and colleagues summarized that intermittent fasting could:

Stabilize blood sugar levels, increase resistance to stress. The goal of it would be to achieve a 6-hours feeding period in seven days a week, the researchers wrote. Mattson and Kittrell warn that you'll likely be uncomfortable as your body gets to adapt to your new eating pattern. Intermittent fasting is a style of eating whereby you go without food for a certain amount of time each day. To help you navigate your day, here is a guide to how to schedule your meals in the process of intermittent fasting. And just remember: Although this eating plan is done when you are eating. Just ensure you concentrate on fats, clean protein, as well as carbohydrates from whole food sources.

How to schedule dishes when you are on intermittent fasting: While the concept of fasting can be frustrating, especially if you have not done it in the past, periodic fasting can be a lot easier than numerous various other kinds of eating plans. When you start your recurring fasting journey, you'll probably discover that you really feel fuller longer and also can keep the dishes you do eat extremely simple. There are a couple of various means you can quickly, so I separated each of the various strategies listed below into newbie, intermediate, as well as progressed together with a normal dish plan for daily.

The combination of nutrients offers you the energy you need to boost the benefits of your fasting journey. Simply ensure to take into consideration any kind of private food intolerances, and utilize this as an overview for your specific health and wellness situation, and also readjust from there.

Bear in mind, and recurring fasting does not necessarily indicate calorie-controlled, so make certain to consume according to your calorie requirements.

1. THE BASIC RECURRING FASTING MEAL PLAN FOR NOVICES

If you are a newbie, start by only eating in between the hrs of 8 a.m. as well as 6 p.m. is a terrific method to dip your toes into the fasting waters. This plan enables you to eat every meal plus some treats, however, still enter 14 hrs of fasting within 24 hours.

MORNING MEAL: ECO-FRIENDLY SMOOTHIE AT 8 A.M.

After fasting, I prefer to delve into my day of eating with a "shake," given that it is a little less complicated for my intestine to absorb. You'll intend to choose an eco-friendly smoothie mix as opposed to a high-sugar fruit smoothie to prevent aging your day on a blood-sugar roller coaster. Add in lots of healthy fats to maintain you going up until lunch!

ACTIVE INGREDIENTS

1   Avocado.

1   Cup coconut milk.

1   Small handful blueberries.

1   Cup spinach, kale, and orchard.

1   Tablespoon chia seed.

Method:

Include all components right into the blender, blend, and enjoy.

LUNCH: GRASS-FED BURGERS AT 12 PM

Grass-fed liver burgers are one of my favorite options for lunch during the week, and also, they are exceptionally very easy to prep to have throughout the whole week.

You can consume this in addition to a bed of dark leafy environment-friendlies with an easy homemade dressing for a dish loaded with B vitamins for healthy and balanced methylation as well as detox paths.

Ingredients:

1/2-pound ground grass-fed beef liver

1/2-pound ground grass-fed beef

1/2 teaspoon garlic powder

1/2 teaspoon cumin powder

Sea salt and pepper to preference

Preferred food preparation oil

Procedure:

Mix all ingredients in a dish as well as create with each other desired-size patties. Put cooking oil in frying pan and heat it on medium heat. Cook hamburgers in a frying pan till preferred doneness. Shop in a container in the fridge and also use it within four days.

TREAT CINNAMON ROLL FAT BOMBS AT 2:30 P.M.

Fat bombs suppress your sweet tooth as well as provide you with sufficient healthy fats to maintain you up until supper, and also, these are particularly satisfying because they taste like cinnamon rolls.

Ingredients:

1/2 cup coconut lotion

1 teaspoon cinnamon

1 tablespoon coconut oil

2 tablespoons almond butter

Approach:

Mix coconut lotion as well as 1/2 teaspoon cinnamon.

Line an 8-by-8-inch square pan taped with parchment paper and ground coconut as well as the cinnamon grate. Mix them 1/2 teaspoon of cinnamon with coconut oil and also almond butter. Spread, freeze and cut the lotion. For Dinner: Salmon as well as Veggies at 5:30 p.m.

Salmon fish or any wild fish to serve alongside a few of your preferred veggies roasted in coconut oil, and you have a fast and also very easy superfood meal.

Active ingredients:

1 extra pound salmon or other fish of choice

2 Tablespoon fresh lemon juice

2 tablespoon ghee

4 cloves garlic, carefully diced

Approach:

Preheat the oven to 400 ° F. Mix lemon juice, ghee, and garlic. Put salmon in foil and also pour lemon and also ghee mixture over the top. Wrap salmon with aluminium foil and place it on a flat pan. Bake for 15 minutes or up until salmon is prepared. If your stove dimension allows, you can roast your vegetables together with salmon on a separate baking sheet.

2. INTERMEDIATE NOT EATING MEAL STRATEGY

With this plan, you will be eating just in between the hrs of 12 PM and also 6 p.m. for a complete 18 hrs of fasting within 24 hours.

I exercise this strategy throughout the workweek. I'm not a morning meal individual, so

I just enjoy a couple of cups of organic tea to start my day. Even though you are missing the morning meal, it's still essential to stay hydrated. Make certain to drink sufficient water still. You can also have natural tea, (Most specialists agree coffee and tea do not damage your fast.) The catechins in tea have been shown to improve the benefits of fasting by helping to lower the cravings hormone ghrelin, so you can make it till lunch as well as not feel robbed.

Considering that you have raised your fasting duration an added four hours, you need to make certain your first dish (at noontime) has good healthy and balanced fats. The burger in the 8 to 6 window strategy, works well, and you can add even more fats in with your dressing or top with avocado.

Nuts, as well as seeds, make excellent treats that are high-fat and can be eaten around 2:30 p.m. Saturating these in advance can aid neutralize normally happening enzymes like phytates that can contribute to gastrointestinal problems. Eat dinner around 5:30 PM, and much like in the 8-to-6-window plan, a supper with some kind of wild-caught fish or another clean protein source with vegetables is a terrific choice.

First meal 12 PM: Grass-fed hamburger with avocado. Snack (at about 2:30 p.m.): Nuts and seeds. The second dish (at about 5:30 p.m.): Salmon as well as veggies.

3. ADVANCED: THE MODIFIED 2-DAY MEAL STRATEGY

Calorie limitation opens a number of the same advantages as fasting for an entire day. On your non-fasting days, you'll need to ensure you're entering healthy fats, tidy meats, vegetables, and also some fruits, and you can structure your meals nevertheless outstanding works for you.

On restricted days, you can have smaller sized meals or snacks throughout the day or have a moderate-size lunch as well as dinner and also fast in the morning as well as after dinner. Again, focus on healthy fats, clean meats, as well as generate. Applications can aid you to log your food and track your calorie consumption, so you do not review 700.

4. ADVANCED: THE 5-2 DISH PLAN

On this plan, you'll consume clean 5 days of the week but will not eat anything for two non-consecutive days of the week. As an example, you can fast on Monday and Thursday yet eat tidy meals recently. Food on these 5 days looks just like the rest of the fasting strategies-- healthy and balanced fats, clean meat sources, vegetables, and some fruit. Keep in mind that this strategy is not for novices, and you must always speak to your physician before starting any fasting program, particularly if you get on medicine or have a medical problem.

Monday: Take a fast.

Tuesday: Consume healthy and balanced fats, tidy meat resources, veggies, and some fruit.

Wednesday: Consume healthy fats, clean meat resources, veggies, and also some fruit.

Thursday: Fast.

Friday: Consume healthy and balanced fats, clean meat sources, vegetables, and also some fruit.

Saturday: Consume healthy fats, tidy meat resources, veggies, and also some fruit.

5. Advanced: Every-other-day strategy or alternate-day fasting.

Even though this plan is progressed, it's very straightforward. Don't consume anything every other day. Every other day, eat healthy fats, clean meats, veggies, and also some fruit, and afterward, on your fasting days, you can heat water, natural tea, and modest amounts of black coffee or tea.

Monday: Consume healthy and balanced fats, clean meat resources, vegetables, and some fruit.

Tuesday: Fast

Wednesday: Consume healthy fats, tidy meat sources, vegetables, and also some fruit.

Thursday: Fast

Friday: Eat healthy and balanced fats, tidy meat resources, vegetables, and some fruit.

Saturday: Fast

Sunday: Eat healthy fats, tidy meat resources, veggies, as well as some fruit.

With this info in hand, you should understand exactly just how to schedule dishes when beginning the recurring fasting strategy. As well as while it could appear made complex in the beginning, when you get into the routine of fasting, it certainly feels like acquired behavior and also fit rather effortlessly right into your days. But constantly begin sluggishly and progressively work up to more advanced strategies. "Off" days are permitted when intermittent fasting doesn't help you. Listen to your body. If you need to eat beyond your regular window, it is okay simply to reboot when you're feeling better.

A ketogenic diet routine is a diet routine that is high in fat and very low in carbs, which forces you to release fats that are stored for power due to the absence of glucose in the bloodstream. Before the periodic fasting, A popular form of intermittent fasting the 16/8 technique which requires not eating for 16 hrs every day with an 8-hour eating home window Typical, throughout the fast, you only take in water. Nonetheless, some have been known to consume alcohol black coffee as there is some argument as to its effects on autophagy and weight loss.

With intermittent fasting, insulin levels go down significantly; therefore, accelerating the fat-burning system of the body. It is also shown to decrease free radicals as well as increase the mobile fixing procedures in the body. Combining the Keto Diet with Intermittent Fasting. By understanding their specific usages, you might assume that the Keto diet and IF be too tiring on the body when made use of with each other.

For instance, while obtaining muscle mass is much harder with a ketogenic diet plan, intermittent fasting addresses this by enhancing the body's insulin sensitivity, blood glucose policy, as well as growth hormonal agent production. Not eating can also aid your body in achieving ketosis much faster. Remember that intermittent fasting keeps your metabolic rate high, which aids you to adapt promptly to your lowered carb intake. Finally, being in ketosis while fasting permits your body to start using your body fat as a gas source, which results in reduce BF% and a leaner body overall. If all these are proven to be real, then the Keto and also IF mix would certainly be an advancement.

This book

"INTERMITTENT FASTING BIBLE & KETO DIET FOR BEGINNERS: The Simplified Guide to Lose Weight Safely, Burn Fat, Slow Aging with a Fasting-Diet, Autophagy & Metabolic Reset. Easy Guide to Detoxify your Body"

Written By

Karen Loss

This Document aims to provide precise and reliable details on this subject and the problem under discussion.

Lightning Source UK Ltd.
Milton Keynes UK
UKHW020248221120
373825UK00010B/632